GRANT

as Military Commander

Other volumes in the
Military Commanders Series

———

NAPOLEON

James Marshall-Cornwall

STONEWALL JACKSON

John Selby

WELLINGTON

Michael Glover

ROMMEL

Ronald Lewin

SLIM

Geoffrey Evans

MACARTHUR

Gavin Long

1 Major-General U. S. Grant in 1862

GRANT

as Military Commander

General Sir James Marshall-Cornwall

KCB CBE DSO MC

You just tell me the brand of whisky Grant drinks;
I would like to send a barrel of it to my other generals

*Abraham Lincoln, in November 1863, to an adviser
who complained of Grant's drinking habits*

B. T. BATSFORD LTD

VAN NOSTRAND REINHOLD COMPANY
NEW YORK

First published 1970
© James Marshall-Cornwall 1970

Library of Congress Catalog Card Number 72-102262
SBN 7134 1206 2

Made and printed in Great Britain by
William Clowes and Sons Ltd
London and Beccles, for the publishers
B. T. BATSFORD LTD
4 Fitzhardinge Street, Portman Square, London W 1
VAN NOSTRAND REINHOLD COMPANY
450 West 33rd Street, New York, N.Y. 10001
Regional Offices:
Cincinnati Chicago Millbrae Dallas

Contents

CONTENTS

PART III ACHIEVEMENT

Illustrations

Maps

Acknowledgments

The Author wishes to express his indebtedness to three kind American friends, whose advice he has found most helpful: Boies Penrose of Philadelphia, Eric Sexton of Maine, and Henry H. Wells of Brewster, N.Y. He is also grateful for the friendly cooperation of the Librarians and Library Staffs of the Ministry of Defence and of the Royal United Service Institution.

The following gave their kind permission for illustrations to be reproduced: U.S. Signal Corps, Plates 1, 6–9, 12, 16, 18, 20–23; Prince Lithograph Co. Inc., N.Y., Plate 3 (from *The Civil War Centennial Handbook*, by William H. Price); E. P. Dutton, N.Y., Plates 4 and 5 (from *Mr. Lincoln's General*, edited and arranged by Roy Meredith); the Mansell Collection, Plates 10, 15, 25; U.S. War Department General Staff, Plates 11 and 17; the Radio Times Hulton Picture Library, Plate 19.

Author's Note

The official designations of the opposing sides in the Civil War were 'Federal' for the North and 'Confederate' for the South. Since the similarity of these names tends to cause confusion, I have throughout used the term 'Union' to denote the forces of the North, and with the same purpose the names of all Confederate leaders are printed in *italics*.

Geographical names, too, are apt to cause confusion, as they repeat themselves so frequently in the United States. For instance, there are eight towns named Columbus – in Georgia, Indiana, Iowa, Kansas, Kentucky, Ohio, Texas and Wisconsin – and in the theatre of war there were no less than seven towns named Columbia and nine named Jackson. To make identification easier, I have inserted after each place-name the postal abbreviation of its State, except in the case of Washington, D.C., and all places in Virginia.

A complete bibliography covering Grant's career would cover a great many pages. On pages 235–6 I have listed only those authorities which I have found most useful as sources.

PART I

BACKGROUND

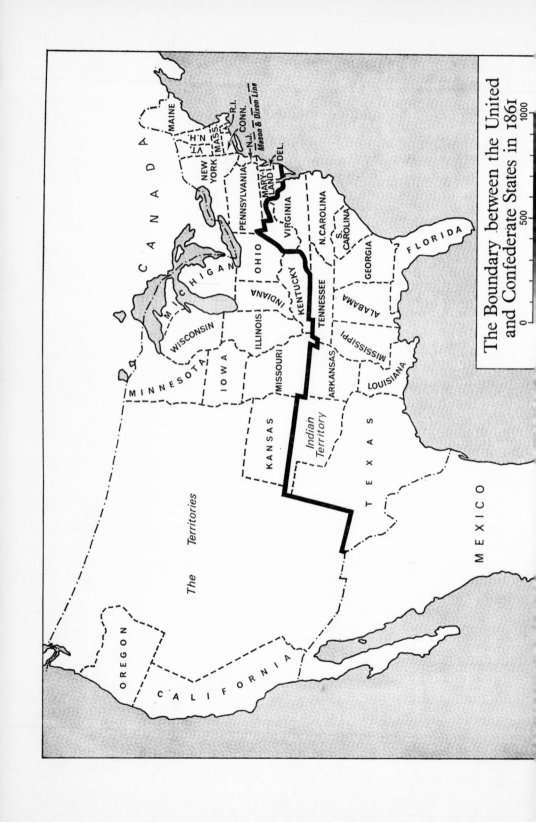

The Boundary between the United and Confederate States in 1861

I

Origins of the American Civil War

Although the causes of the Civil War may at first sight seem remote from a study of Grant's generalship, in fact those causes exercised a profound influence on the morale and temper of the combatants as well as on the grand strategy of their leaders. The real political issue between the Northern and Southern States was not so much the question of Slavery as the doctrine of States' Rights. On 4 March 1861, when Abraham Lincoln was inaugurated as sixteenth President of the United States, the eastern part of the Republic consisted of 17 Northern States in which slavery was not permitted and 15 Southern States in which slavery was legal. The political cleavage between these two sections of the country was based on compulsive economic factors. In the North, the economy of the north-eastern States depended primarily on manufacturing industry and shipping, that of the north-western ones on mining, cereal growing, stock raising and lumber. The economy of the Southern States, on the other hand, was based mainly on the cultivation of cotton which depended largely for its profitability on the practice of slave labour. In 1833 the British Government had abolished slavery in its West Indian possessions, in consequence of which the British sugar planters in the Caribbean Islands had suffered severe financial losses. The planters in the Southern States of North America were determined not to follow suit, whereas the Northerners, whose economy was not dependent on slave labour, felt that slavery was morally unjust and should be abolished throughout the country.

Legal conflicts constantly occurred when slaves who had escaped from their masters in the South took refuge in a Northern State where slavery was illegal. A further political difficulty arose as the United States acquired new territories in the Middle and Far West, and these were subsequently raised to the status of States. Was slavery to be permitted in these new States, and if so, where should the boundary be drawn between slave States and free States?

The problem was also complicated by the fact that in four of the slave

3

States – Maryland, Virginia, Kentucky and Missouri – the economy was only partially dependent on slave labour, and public opinion was divided as to whether slavery should be permitted or not. These four borderland States lay south of the traditional 'Mason and Dixon Line' which, before the American colonies obtained their independence, had separated the Northern from the Southern States. Between the years 1763 and 1767 this line had been demarcated on the ground by two British astronomers, Charles Mason and Jeremiah Dixon, in settlement of a long-standing boundary dispute between the descendants of the second Lord Baltimore and of William Penn, the Quaker. In 1632 the former had been granted by Charles I a large tract of country south of Latitude 40° North, which he named Maryland after Queen Henrietta Maria. In 1681 William Penn had been granted by Charles II the territory to the north of Maryland, but with an undefined boundary. The line demarcated by Mason and Dixon followed the parallel 39° 43′ 26·3″ and was eventually adopted as the legal boundary between the States of Pennsylvania and Maryland.[1] The territory south of that line was popularly known as 'Dixieland', where slave labour was practised in cultivating the rice, cotton and tobacco plantations, in contrast to the Puritan North where the practice of slavery was held in abhorrence.

But slavery was not the only question which caused a cleavage between the Northern and Southern States. The economy of the North depended mainly on manufacturing capacity and therefore demanded a protectionist policy of high tariffs to foster the home industries. The almost wholly agricultural South, on the other hand, favoured a free trade policy to help the export of raw cotton in exchange for foreign manufactured goods. North and South also viewed life from very different angles. The Southern planters had developed an easy and almost seigniorial way of living, differing widely from the industrial and commercial activity of the bustling Yankee North. They objected to legislative domination by a government which was, in their eyes, almost an alien one. Thus, in the South, the idea of secession gradually took root. The spirit of revolt was particularly strong in South Carolina, and in December 1860 that State seceded from the Union. Within six weeks six other States (Mississippi, Florida, Alabama, Georgia, Louisiana and Texas) followed suit and joined forces to form the 'Confederate States of America'. On 18 February 1861 *Jefferson Davis*, a native of Kentucky, was elected President of the Confederacy and the capital was set up at Montgomery (Ala).

The disparity in character between the people of the Northern and Southern States was well described by the British writer, Anthony Trollope, a shrewd observer of human nature, who travelled extensively in the United States during six months of the first year of the Civil War. He summed up the causes of Secession as follows:

1. The brass theodolite used by Mason and Dixon is now in the collection of the Royal Geographical Society, London.

The South is seceding from the North because the two are not homogeneous. They have different instincts, different appetites, different morals, and a different culture. It is well for one man to say that slavery has caused the separation; and for another to say that slavery has not caused it. Each in so saying speaks the truth. Slavery has caused it, seeing that slavery is the great point on which the two have agreed to differ. But slavery has not caused it, seeing that other points of difference are to be found in every circumstance and feature of the two people.[2]

And again:

They [the South] had become a separate people, dissevered from the North by habits, morals, institutions, pursuits, and every conceivable difference in their modes of thought and action. They still spoke the same language, as do Austria and Prussia; but beyond that tie of language they had no bond but that of a meagre political union in their Congress at Washington.[3]

The creation of a break-away Confederacy, independent of the Union, called for the adoption of a separate emblem or symbol of allegiance, under which the soldiers of the Confederate States could fight, should they have to resort to war to defend their independence. A fortnight after the election of a Confederate President and the establishment of a new capital at Montgomery (Ala), the Convention of the seven seceding States voted the adoption of a national flag, the 'Stars and Bars'. This was eventually found unsuitable; five months later a new flag, the 'Southern Cross', was adopted (see Appendix 1).

On 4 March 1861 Abraham Lincoln, a 52-year-old small-town lawyer from Illinois, was inaugurated at Washington as President of the United States. Lincoln was not a fanatical abolitionist, but he was fiercely determined to maintain the Union and to crush the rebellion in the South. As he solemnly declared: 'I believe this Government cannot endure permanently half slave and half free. I do not expect the Union to be dissolved – I do not expect the house to fall – but I do expect it will cease to be divided. It will become all one thing or all the other.' As a politician, Lincoln held the Republican ticket; but he was no mere politician; with statesmanlike vision he saw that the agricultural South and industrial North must be welded together as complementary components of one nation which, in less than a century, was destined to become the richest and most powerful in the world. That welding process required the fiery furnace of a civil war.

A month after Lincoln's inauguration matters came to a head in South Carolina, the most implacable of the secessionist States. At the beginning of April President *Jefferson Davis* summoned the Union garrison of Fort Sumter, an island blockhouse which commanded Charleston's seaward approach, to surrender the fort. The Union commander refused, and on 12 April the Confederate batteries began to bombard it. This was the first irrevocable action of the Civil War. Two days later the Union flag was lowered and the garrison

2. *Trollope*, I, 12. (See pp. 235–6 for full details of sources quoted.)
3. *ibid.*, II, 72.

surrendered, under pressure of starvation, and were allowed to withdraw to the North. No blood had been shed, but the Union flag had been violated.

Lincoln immediately called up 75,000 Militiamen for three months' service in order to suppress the rebellion, which he hoped to quell within a few weeks. Thus began a bitter struggle which was to continue relentlessly for four years. The tragedy was that each party was firmly convinced of the justice of its cause. The South entered on a fanatical struggle to preserve the liberty of States' Rights; the North was fighting to maintain the Union of the whole country as one undivided nation.

Geography of the Theatre of War

(See Maps 17 and 18 at end of book)

The American Civil War was fought over a vast area – some 620,000 square miles – three times the size of France. Consequently, its grand strategy and tactics were more profoundly influenced by the physiography of the country than was the case in any other war of modern times. The main geographical feature dominating the whole area of operations was the great Appalachian Range, which traversed the Eastern States diagonally and sharply divided the area into two separate theatres: *the eastern theatre*, covering the Piedmont and Tidewater regions of Virginia, and *the western theatre*, comprising most of the great Mississippi Basin.

Largely owing to political considerations, and to the fact that the two capitals, Washington and Richmond,[1] a mere 109 miles apart, lay in the eastern theatre, it was there that the heaviest fighting took place, and there the struggle was finally decided. Indeed, it almost seems that the war leaders, on both sides, became so engrossed with the operations east of the Appalachians that they tended at times to neglect the requirements of the western theatre, sometimes with disastrous consequences. Nevertheless, the western theatre was the scene of many fierce engagements which are of the greatest interest to the student of war, particularly as that area was geographically more adapted to amphibious operations. Grant himself was exclusively employed in the western theatre during the first three years of the war, and it was only in the final year that he was called upon to take over the supreme command in both theatres.

The Appalachian Range, roughly 100 miles wide, consists of a number of parallel ridges, which run from north-east to south-west. From the point of view of military geography, the most important of these ridges was the most easterly one, which was also the highest. This was the Blue Ridge, formed by the older igneous rocks of palaeozoic age, which runs from the neighbourhood

1. On 8 May 1861 the Confederate capital was transferred to Richmond (Va) from Montgomery (Ala).

7

of Gettysburg (Pa) south-westwards for 600 miles until it merges into the Atlanta plateau of northern Georgia. In its northern sector the Blue Ridge attains its highest point (over 4,000 feet) near Luray, where it dominates the Shenandoah Valley to the west and Piedmont Virginia to the east. Farther south-west the escarpment reaches a still higher altitude (over 6,000 feet) in the Great Smoky Mountains on the border between North Carolina and East Tennessee.

To the north-west of this main escarpment runs a parallel series of lower ridges, composed of sedimentary rocks, forming the Allegheny[2] chain. From between these ridges, known as the Clinch and Cumberland Mountains, the important Cumberland and Tennessee Rivers flow westward into the Mississippi Basin.

The Appalachian Range presented such a formidable military barrier that few attempts to cross it were made by either combatant in the Civil War; most of the fighting took place in the plains, to the east in the Virginian Piedmont region and to the west in the Mississippi Basin. The range is crossed only by one river, the Potomac, which forces its way eastward through the mountain barrier by the Harper's Ferry gap, to discharge into Chesapeake Bay. Harper's Ferry (W. Va) was one of the strategic key-points in the eastern theatre, for the Potomac Valley was also followed by the Baltimore and Ohio Railroad, which formed one of the main communication links between the eastern and western theatres. By advancing on Harper's Ferry and crossing the Potomac, *Lee*, *Stonewall Jackson* and *Jubal Early* were able on three separate occasions to paralyse the strategy of the Union leaders by a direct threat to Washington. At Harper's Ferry, too, the Potomac is joined by its right-bank tributary, the Shenandoah, which flows northward between the parallel crests of the Blue Ridge and the Massanutten Mountain. Using the Shenandoah Valley as a strategic corridor, *Stonewall Jackson*, with Napoleonic mobility, repeatedly defeated his clumsier Union opponents in the first two years of the war.

The only other railways which penetrated the Appalachian Range were:

(a) The *Manassas Gap Railroad*, which crossed the Blue Ridge by the Manassas Gap to the east of Front Royal. This branch line had little strategic value, for at the outbreak of war it had only reached a point 25 miles west of Front Royal, and did not cross the farther mountain ridges. At its eastern end this line joined the important Orange and Alexandria Railroad at Manassas Junction.

(b) The *Virginia Central Railroad* traversed the Blue Ridge at Rockfish Gap, west of Charlottesville, where it joined the Orange and Alexandria Railroad (running north) and the East Tennessee and Virginia Railroad (running south). Like the Manassas Gap Railroad, however, it had not penetrated the farther mountain ranges.

2. Formerly spelt 'Alleghany'.

(c) The *East Tennessee and Virginia Railroad* crossed the Blue Ridge west of Lynchburg, whence it ran south-west to Chattanooga (Tenn), where it was connected to the Mississippi Basin railway system by branches to Nashville and Memphis (Tenn). This vital link formed the main Confederate line of communication between the eastern and western theatres until Chattanooga fell to Grant in November 1863.

Farther south, the only railway link between the two theatres was the *Central Georgia Railroad*, which ran from Chattanooga (Tenn) southward to Atlanta (Ga), with branches running eastward to Charleston (s.c.) and Savannah (Ga) on the Atlantic coast. Thus Chattanooga and Atlanta were vital points for the interchange of Confederate reinforcements and munitions between the two theatres.

The only seaports through which the Confederates could receive armaments from abroad in exchange for their raw cotton were Wilmington (N.C.), Charleston (s.c.), Savannah (Ga), Mobile (Ala) and New Orleans (La). These ports were to a varying degree blockaded by the superior Union navy, but as this blockade had to cover 1,500 miles of Atlantic coast-line, the Confederate blockade-runners managed to maintain a precarious traffic.

East of the Appalachian Range the Piedmont region slopes gradually eastward to Tidewater Virginia, where the broad estuaries of the Potomac, Rappahannock, York and James Rivers open out into Chesapeake Bay. In their upper reaches these rivers formed successive defensive lines covering the Confederate capital at Richmond. In their lower reaches, however, this river system enabled the Union forces to threaten the Confederate eastern flank as soon as naval superiority had been gained after the duel of 9 March 1862 between the 'Monitor' and *'Merrimac'* in Hampton Roads. Had the Union leaders made more effective use of amphibious strategy in these waterways, the war might have been considerably shortened.

Turning to the western theatre, the landscape presents a very different character, for here the Appalachian Range flattens out into the great Mississippi Basin, which covers nearly one-third of the area of the United States. Rising in Minnesota, near the Canadian border, the longest of the world's rivers (if we include its right-bank tributary the Missouri) flows southward for 4,500 miles till it reaches the Gulf of Mexico below New Orleans (La). It was well named by the Algonquin natives *Missi* (great) *Sipi* (river). The Missouri joins it at St. Louis (Mo), but the river's significance in the Civil War only begins when it reaches Cairo (Ill), 125 miles farther south, the scene of Grant's first active command in 1861. At Cairo the Mississippi receives its greatest left-bank tributary, the Ohio, and 32 miles east of Cairo lies Paducah (Ky), near which the Ohio is joined by two important left-bank tributaries, the Cumberland and Tennessee Rivers, which rise in the Alleghenies.

Steamboat navigation began on the Mississippi as far back as 1811, and during the Civil War it was the most important method of transportation in the western theatre. Since then, however, its importance has greatly declined owing to the tremendous development of road and railway communications. The Mississippi itself is navigable by river steamers up to St. Louis (Mo), the Ohio up to Louisville (Ky), the Cumberland up to Nashville (Tenn) and the Tennessee up to Florence (Ala).[3] Military operations in the western theatre were therefore largely of an amphibious nature. The ultimate victory of the North indeed was greatly due to the tardiness of the Confederate leaders in appreciating the vital importance of this factor, and to the technical superiority of the Union in building river steam boats.

The Mississippi, Cumberland and Tennessee Rivers offered the main routes by which the Union forces could strike at the heart of Confederate territory. A Union advance up the two latter rivers was blocked by two strong Confederate forts, just south of the Kentucky–Tennessee border, Fort Henry on the right (east) bank of the Tennessee River and Fort Donelson on the left (west) bank of the Cumberland. The capture of these two forts formed an essential feature of Grant's first campaign in the Civil War. An advance down the Mississippi itself was also barred by fortifications between Cairo and Memphis, at Island No. 10, Fort Pillow, Fort Randolph and Fort Harris, but these defences were of less deterrent value owing to the great width of the river, which varies from half a mile to a mile.

'Ol' man river' not only kept 'rollin' along' and affording a magnificent traffic artery from north to south, but its mastery by a superior fleet of river steamers, such as the Union rapidly acquired, enabled the Northerners to split the Confederacy in two by interposing an effective barrier between the eastern Secession States and their allies west of the Mississippi in Arkansas, Louisiana and Texas. This deprived the Confederates in the eastern theatre of a potential reinforcement of 100,000 men and of a vast area of food-growing territory. The result was achieved by Grant's advance southward, coupled with Farragut's capture of New Orleans (La) at the end of April 1862.

From the point of view of military operations one of the greatest drawbacks of the Mississippi Basin was the liability of its rivers to flood, particularly after the melting of the snows in the north. This menace was especially severe in the case of the Ohio River. In recent years the danger of floods has been much lessened by the construction of regulating dams, such as those which have completely altered the geography of the Tennessee Valley, but in 1861 the flood menace was very considerable. To prevent inundation the banks of the Mississippi had, since the days of the early French settlers, been artificially raised by 'levees', or embankments, some 15 feet high, and these formed important tactical features during the war. Owing to the continual deposit of alluvium, the river banks are in many places higher than the surrounding

3. At certain seasons shallow-draft steamers could ascend as far as Chattanooga.

2 *Union sharpshooter with telescopic rifle*

3 *Small arms of Union infantry and cavalry*

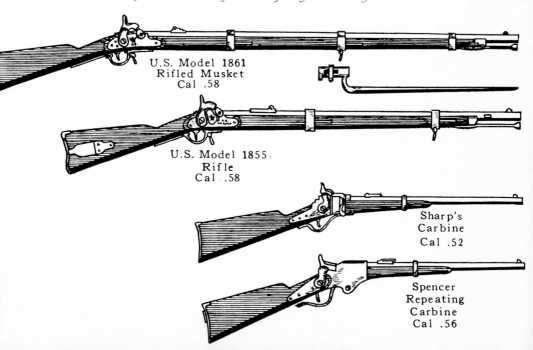

U.S. Model 1861
Rifled Musket
Cal .58

U.S. Model 1855
Rifle
Cal .58

Sharp's
Carbine
Cal .52

Spencer
Repeating
Carbine
Cal .56

4 *The Library, U.S. Military Academy,*
West Point, 1838

5 *Second Lieutenant U. S. Grant, 4th*
Infantry, 1843 (age 21)

country, so that in flood the river might attain a width of 30 miles, making navigation very difficult. The river is at its lowest in early autumn and again in early winter; the highest level occurs at the beginning of April. At the time of the Civil War the alluvial bottoms on each side of the river were frequently impassable for troops. Only the bluffs which rise at intervals afforded habitable sites and tactical objectives. These bluffs occur more frequently on the east (left) bank, as at Columbus (Ky), Memphis and Vicksburg (Tenn). These two latter towns were of major strategic importance. Memphis was 800 miles by river above New Orleans,[4] and was the junction of two vital railways: the Memphis and Ohio Railroad, running north-east to Louisville (Ky) and the Memphis and Charleston Railroad, running due east to Chattanooga (Tenn), where it connected with the Tennessee and Virginia Railroad running north-east and the Central Georgia Railroad running south to Atlanta. The Memphis and Ohio Railroad was covered by Forts Henry and Donelson in northern Tennessee, but when these forts were captured by Grant in February 1862 this line was lost to the Confederates, and Chattanooga and Atlanta then became vital to their lateral communications.

Vicksburg, the next key point on the Mississippi, lay another 400 miles down stream from Memphis,[5] half way between Memphis and New Orleans. From Vicksburg a railway ran due east through Jackson (Miss) into Alabama, but the Confederates were deprived of this lateral communication also when Vicksburg fell to Grant in July 1863.

The struggle for the possession of these vital waterways and railroad links governed the grand strategy of the whole war in the western theatre.

4. Although only 360 in a direct line.
5. Although only 200 in a direct line.

III

Relative Resources
in Manpower and Material

MANPOWER

The numerical advantage possessed by the Union over the Confederacy was overwhelming. If we exclude the two newly formed far western States of California (admitted in 1850) and Oregon (admitted in 1859), 21 Northern States with a population of 22 millions were arrayed against 11 Southern States with a population of 9 millions. But the latter figure included 3½ million negro slaves, who could hardly be enrolled as combatants against the Northerners, whose declared aim was to liberate them. The white population ratio between North and South was, therefore, more nearly 22 to 5½, or four to one. In fact, the negro slaves of the South did not rise against their masters, as might have been expected, but continued to cultivate the plantations in their owners' absence, and indeed made themselves useful in auxiliary military service as transport drivers and pioneers. In the later stages of the war the Union Government actually raised volunteer units of free negroes, but serving under white officers.

The citizens of the United States were not a warlike nation. They had indeed won their independence from the British Crown in 1776 by hard fighting, and had proved themselves to be tough and capable soldiers. Their last campaign against a major Power had been the War of 1812–14 against Britain, in which neither side had distinguished itself from a military point of view. Nor did the Mexican War of 1846–48, against a comparatively feeble enemy, evoke much military talent. Throughout the whole of this period of half a century the United States Army had been engaged in a continuous struggle with the native Indian tribes on the Western Frontier to protect the white settlers who were pushing steadily westward. This warfare, however, was of a guerrilla nature, waged against a savage and undisciplined enemy. It taught few strategic or tactical lessons which were applicable to a contest between civilized armies equipped with sophisticated weapons. There was no higher tactical formation than a regiment, and units were scattered in 52 forts covering a frontier of 1,200 miles.

The United States Regular Army was microscopic in comparison with the size of the population. In 1860, on the eve of the Civil War, it numbered 1,100 officers and 15,000 enlisted men. Of this force, 75 per cent was deployed on the Western Frontier, protecting the white settlers against Indian raids. In addition to the Regular Army there existed a force, somewhat shadowy in peacetime, known as the Militia. According to the Constitution of 1787, each State of the Union had the right to raise a local body of Militia for the defence of its territory under the general control of Congress, which was empowered:

> To provide for organizing, arming and disciplining the Militia, and for governing such part of them as may be employed in the service of the United States, reserving to the States respectively, the appointment of the officers, and the authority of training the Militia according to the discipline prescribed by Congress.

By the Militia Act of 8 May 1792, every able-bodied free, white, male citizen between the ages of 18 and 45 was liable to be called up by Presidential Decree to serve in his State Militia for no more than three months in any one year. State Governors were authorized to appoint the officers, but the appointment of General Officers was subject to Presidential approval. Thus each State Governor had at his disposal a nucleus Militia organization capable of great expansion in the event of a national emergency. The ranks of the Militia could also be reinforced by volunteers.

On the fall of Fort Sumter in April 1861, President Lincoln, under the provisions of the 1792 Militia Act, at once called up 75,000 Militiamen for three months' service. As he wished to keep the Regular Army intact, he would not allow it to be used to form training cadres, and there was no reserve of Regular officers to fall back on. The training of the raw Militia recruits could only be carried out by obtaining the services of retired Regular officers, of whom Grant was one. The State Governors were empowered to give these officers temporary Volunteer rank based on their past experience and new duties. On 3 May Lincoln called for 42,000 Volunteers, to serve for three years.

In the matter of recruiting, the South had already anticipated the North. Two days after the inauguration of President Lincoln in March 1861, which made war almost certain, the Congress of the Confederacy voted an army of 100,000 Volunteers, to be enlisted for one year. On paper, therefore, the South actually went to war with superior numbers available. On the other hand the Union could count on the bulk of the Regular Army (1,100 officers and 15,000 other ranks), the great majority of whom remained loyal to the Union flag. This was, however, less so in the case of the officers, of whom 28 per cent resigned their commissions to serve the Confederacy. Of these, the greater number had graduated at West Point, the United States Military Academy on the Hudson River (N.Y.).

Thus, on the outbreak of war, the opposing armies were approximately equal in numbers, but the enormous disparity in population soon began to tell. After

McDowell's defeat at Bull Run in July 1861 the Union Congress voted the enlistment of 500,000 Volunteers for the duration of the war, but much time was required to equip and train them. At that critical period the Union had over 300,000 men under arms; a month later this had risen to 485,000; by December 1861 the Union Army was 661,000 strong, and eventually numbered over a million.

To counter this progressive numerical increase of the Union forces, the Confederates were the first to introduce conscription. On 16 April 1862 the Confederate Congress called up all able-bodied white males between the ages of 18 and 35. Later, this age-group was extended to include those between 17 and 50. By the end of 1862 the North followed suit in introducing conscription, and on 3 March 1863 the Union Congress passed an 'Enrollment Act', conscripting all able-bodied men between 20 and 45. Two months later, however, a further gap was created by the nine-month Militiamen going home, and the heavy losses sustained at Chancellorsville had to be made good.

Eventually, the Confederates managed to put some 600,000 men into the field, of whom only one-third were conscripts. This was a fine effort for a population of only 5½ millions. By the end of the war the Confederates had mobilized 90 per cent of their military population, whereas the Union had only called on 45 per cent of the available manpower.

MATERIAL

The vast numerical superiority of the North over the South was equalled by their relative disparity in material resources. The Southern States, being almost wholly agricultural, could indeed feed themselves, but they were largely dependent on the outside world for manufactured goods and industrial products. In natural resources they possessed some copper mines in Tennessee and a minor iron and coal field in Alabama, but these were in no way comparable with the mineral riches of the North. The Southern States had no factories, apart from a few iron foundries; they had no powder-mills, ordnance workshops or textile plants; all the railway workshops and 90 per cent of the shipping yards were in the North. The main United States arms factory was at Springfield (Mass). There was indeed an important Federal arsenal, manufacturing small arms, at Harper's Ferry in West Virginia on the south bank of the Potomac, but this remained in Union hands throughout the war except for a few brief occasions, although the Confederates managed to remove the rifle-making machinery on the outbreak of war.

The most fatal inferiority of the Confederacy was in shipping and naval strength. Not only did the Union mastery of the Atlantic seaboard seriously hamper the efforts of the Confederate blockade-runners, but the powerful Union fleet of river steamers and armoured gunboats on the Mississippi and its tributaries ensured ultimate victory in the amphibious river campaigns of the western theatre, and eventually paralysed by strangulation the economic life of the Southern States.

Anthony Trollope, the British writer, visited Cairo (Ill) on 4 February 1862, just after Grant had left that base to attack Fort Henry. He recorded his impressions of these river gunboats which played such a vital part in the defeat of the Confederacy:

> Four of these gun-boats were still lying in the Ohio, close under the terminus of the railway with their flat, ugly noses against the muddy bank, and we were shown over two of them. They certainly seemed to be formidable weapons for river warfare, and to have been 'got up quite irrespective of expense'. So much, indeed, may be said for the Americans throughout the war. They cannot be accused of parsimony. The largest of these vessels, called the 'Benton', had cost £36,000 [$180,000 at that time]. These boats are made with sides sloping inwards, at an angle of 45 degrees. The iron is two-and-a-half inches thick, and it has not, I believe, been calculated that this will resist cannon shot of great weight, should it be struck in a direct line. But the angle of the sides of the boat makes it improbable that any such shot should strike them; and the iron, bedded as it is upon oak, is supposed to be sufficient to turn a shot that does not hit it in a direct line. The boats are also roofed with iron, and the pilots who steer the vessel stand encased, as it were, under an iron cupola. I imagine that these boats are well calculated for the river service for which they were built. Six or seven of them had gone up the Tennessee river the day before we reached Cairo.... The boats... will probably succeed in driving the secessionist armies away from the great river banks. By what machinery the secessionist armies are to be followed into the interior is altogether another question.[1]

The Civil War was the first one in which railway transport exercised a dominating influence on military strategy and logistics, although the rolling stock available was as yet of a primitive nature. The railway network at the disposal of the Union armies was far more highly developed than that of the Southern States, which possessed few lateral lines of communication linking the eastern and western theatres. The Confederates were further hampered by shortage of rolling stock and repair facilities.

The Civil War saw the first employment of the electric telegraph as an adjunct to military operations (see Chapter XVIII, p. 146).

Observation balloons were used in June 1862 by McClellan's Army of the Potomac, when it got within eight miles of Richmond after crossing the Chickahominy River. The balloon used was a spherical one of varnished silk, containing 26,000 cubic feet of hydrogen. It ascended to a height of 1,000 feet and gave a range of visibility of ten miles, but proved of little value for reconnaissance purposes owing to the thickly wooded nature of the country. Balloons were not used in Grant's campaigns.

The highly developed textile factories of the North gave the Union forces a great advantage in the supply of uniforms, which were largely made at the

1. *Trollope*, II, 157–8.

Schuylkill Arsenal at Philadelphia (Pa). Neither side was meticulous about dress and turn-out, and uniforms were frequently nondescript in pattern. The Union forces wore a dark-blue tunic with pale-blue trousers, as in peacetime; the headgear resembled a French *képi*, but broad-brimmed wide-awake hats were worn indiscriminately by both sides. Grant invariably wore one. The Confederates adopted a grey uniform to distinguish their troops, possibly because the West Point cadets had always been dressed in grey. Some of the Northern volunteer units indulged in fancy uniforms, such as Zouaves and Bersaglieri; there was even a New York regiment of Highlanders who wore the kilt.

The following comparison between the turn-out of Union and Confederate troops was made at the time by an intelligent French officer, fresh from the battlefields of Magenta and Solferino:

> From our first encounter, we were able to gain an idea of the outside appearance of the Confederate soldier. We noted that the question of uniform, not very well solved in the North, was not solved at all in the South. It did not seem that any attempt to regularize dress had gone beyond the distribution of a grey coat (made in Virginia, we were told) to a few groups. These 'uniforms' were in sad condition. Yet despite these rags the soldiers maintained a rather martial appearance; also, perfect order is exhibited in the camps as well as in the smallest outposts.
>
> What struck us, however, was the cavalry, very numerous, admirably mounted, and composed of splendid men.... They are proprietors' and farmers' sons, they own their own horses, and they are accustomed to outdoor life – if not to the handling of weapons. On the whole, nothing is as picturesque as the Southern cavalry. They wear the most impossible outfits: mostly rags, hats without bottoms, boots without soles.[2]

2. From the letters of Lieutenant-Colonel Camille Ferri Pisani, a.d.c. to Prince Napoleon (son of King Jérôme and nephew of Napoleon 1), who was a privileged visitor to both the Union and Confederate armies in August 1861, a few weeks after the first battle of Bull Run. Pisani's mother was the daughter of Marshal Jourdan.

IV

Command Structure and Organization

The Constitution of the United States, adopted by Congress in 1787, lays down in Article ii, Section 2, that:

> The President shall be Commander-in-Chief of the Army and Navy of the United States, and of the Militia of the several States, when called into the actual service of the United States.

In the Indian wars, which had kept the American Army busy since 1814, the United States Presidents had, naturally, delegated the actual conduct of operations to the senior Commanding General on the army establishment. In the Mexican War of 1846–48, however, President James Knox Polk had taken his *ex officio* responsibility more literally, and had personally directed the whole campaign with a fair amount of success. Polk had actually sent his senior Commanding General, Winfield Scott, to the front as a task force commander.

When the Civil War broke out in April 1861, President Abraham Lincoln similarly assumed complete control of the Union forces. It was just as well that he did so, for the professional ability of the senior officers of the U.S. Army was of a poor standard. The Commanding General at Washington was still Winfield Scott,[1] who had held that post for twenty years. A Virginian by birth, he was then 75 years old and a veteran, not only of the Mexican War, but also of the war against the British (1812–14). In his day Scott had been a good soldier, and had brought the Mexican War to a successful conclusion, under the energetic driving force of President Polk. But he had considerable limitations. He was not a West Pointer, having joined the army from the legal profession. After the war of 1812–14 he had helped to draw up a new manual of infantry training. These regulations increased the rate of marching, insisted on a high standard of musketry, and introduced the line formation in two ranks, copied

1. Popularly known in the U.S. Army as 'Old Fuss and Feathers'.

17

from the British, instead of three. Fifty years later, however, he was out of date, besides which he suffered from dropsy and was unable to mount a horse.

Scott having proved too senile to conduct operations on the scale imposed by the war with the South, Lincoln replaced him on 1 November 1861 by a much younger man, Major-General George Brinton McClellan, barely 35 years of age. McClellan was a West Pointer and had shown considerable promise as a young officer, but he proved to be totally unfitted for high command. His hesitating policy and lack of initiative infuriated the President,[2] who himself took over the active command of the forces on 11 March 1862. The war, however, continued to go badly for the Union, particularly in the eastern theatre, though in the west it was redeemed by Grant's victory at Shiloh (Tenn) and Farragut's capture of New Orleans (La).

Lincoln was a man of great vision and determination, but he had no professional qualifications for conducting a war beset with technical problems. The four months during which he personally exercised command of the Union forces were marked by a series of reverses in the eastern theatre, where *Stonewall Jackson* successively defeated the four Union commanders opposed to him, Shields, Milroy, Schenck and Frémont.

On the Confederate side President *Jefferson Davis* from the start assumed complete control of the forces in the field. He had better professional qualifications for the task than Lincoln. Not only had he been a Regular Army officer and a West Point graduate, but during the four years of Franklin Pierce's Presidency (1853–57) he had been Secretary of War at Washington. The dual task, however, of ruling the Confederacy and controlling the military operations proved too great a burden, and on 1 June 1862 he delegated the command in the eastern theatre to the capable hands of General *Robert Edward Lee*.

The heavy fighting in the eastern theatre during May and June 1862 having failed to produce a decision, in spite of very heavy Union losses, on 11 July Lincoln transferred Major-General Henry Wager Halleck from his command in the western theatre and gave him supreme command of all the Union forces. In his place Grant was given command of the Armies of the Mississippi and the Tennessee. The choice of Halleck as Commander-in-Chief was an unfortunate one. He was 47 years old, having graduated from West Point in 1839, the year of Grant's entry there. Commissioned in the U.S. Engineers, he had, like Grant, won a Brevet Captaincy in the Mexican War. Again like Grant, he had retired from the service in 1854, but he had been more successful in civilian life, having built up a good legal practice in San Francisco. On the outbreak of war Halleck volunteered to rejoin the service and was promoted to the rank of Major-General in the Regular Army, which gave him considerable seniority over Grant. In November 1861 he was given command of the Department of Missouri, where Grant served under him. Halleck was an accomplished

---

2. When it was pointed out to Lincoln that McClellan was a capable Engineer officer, the President remarked that he must have always been in charge of stationary engines.

engineer and an able administrator, but he proved incompetent as a commander in the field, for he was lacking in decision and energy. The Union successes won during his command in the western theatre in 1861 and 1862 were due largely to Grant's initiative and resolution. It was not until March 1864 that Lincoln finally realized Halleck's unsuitability as a higher commander, when he replaced him by Grant. Halleck was then transferred to the new appointment of Chief of Staff at Washington, a post for which his talents were better fitted.

A remarkable feature of the Civil War was the practice, common to both sides, of appointing to posts of high command and responsibility officers with little or no previous military experience. Thus, on the outbreak of war, President *Jefferson Davis* gave the command of all the Confederate troops in the Mississippi area to a 55-year-old bishop, who had seen no military service since his cadet days at West Point. The result, strange to say, was not so bad as might have been expected; *Leonidas Polk* proved to be quite a good corps commander, until he was killed in action in the last year of the war.

On the Union side there were still more glaring instances. Early in July 1861, President Lincoln appointed to command the Department of Missouri in the western theatre John Charles Frémont, a surveyor by profession, but not even trained at West Point. Five years earlier, however, he had been a Republican candidate for the Presidency. When his incompetence became obvious Lincoln gave him command of a division in the field. Again, when the campaign in the eastern theatre was about to open in March 1862, Lincoln appointed to the responsible post of commander of the garrison and fortifications of Washington, then within 50 miles of the front line, Brigadier-General James Samuel Wadsworth, who had no military qualifications whatsoever. The Secretary of War explained to the Commander-in-Chief that 'Wadsworth had been selected because it was necessary, for political reasons, to conciliate the agricultural interests of New York.'

These injudicious unprofessional appointments introduced an element of amateurism into the conduct of the war, at any rate in its opening phase; they also provoked considerable jealousy and intrigue among the higher commanders.

ORGANIZATION

The basic tactical unit of the United States Army, both in peace and war, was the regiment of infantry or cavalry. In peacetime no higher formation existed, so there was little scope for training officers for the responsibility of higher command.

An infantry regiment corresponded to a battalion in the British service. It consisted of regimental headquarters and ten companies. In 1861 the minimum strength of an infantry regiment was fixed at 869 officers and other ranks, the maximum permissible being 1,049. In practice an infantry regiment averaged about 900 of all ranks. Its establishment was:

Regimental headquarters: Colonel, Lieutenant-Colonel, Major, Adjutant, Quartermaster, Surgeon and 2 Assistant Surgeons, Chaplain.

Each of ten companies: Captain, Lieutenant, Second Lieutenant, First Sergeant, 4 Sergeants, 8 Corporals, 2 Buglers, 64–82 Privates.

An infantry regiment would thus have 35 combatant officers.

An infantry brigade consisted of four or five regiments, and a division of two or three brigades. An infantry division averaged between 6,000 and 7,000 of all ranks.

In both armies a corps organization was adopted in March 1862, each corps being normally composed of three divisions. Lincoln actually introduced the corps organization against the advice of his Commander-in-Chief, McClellan, and himself appointed the four corps commanders without consulting McClellan.

A cavalry regiment consisted of six squadrons, each of two companies. A cavalry division consisted of two brigades, each of several regiments. It was not until March 1864, when Grant became Commander-in-Chief, that the Union cavalry regiments were united into one cavalry corps of three divisions under Sheridan.

A field artillery battery had six guns. Batteries did not form an organic part of infantry formations, but were allotted as required, usually on the scale of three batteries to a division. Each army corps comprised an artillery brigade.

The Confederate Army was organized on much the same lines as the Union Army, but, owing to shortage of material, field batteries only had four guns.

V

Armament and Tactics

ARMAMENT

The principal United States small-arms factory was Springfield Arsenal, Massa-chusetts, which had been founded as far back as 1777 by Henry Knox, who later became the first U.S. Secretary of War (1789–94). Throughout the Civil War the Springfield Arsenal produced on average 200,000 rifles a year, so that, after the first year of war, the Union forces were able to maintain their requirements. There was a subsidiary U.S. arsenal at Harper's Ferry, Virginia, on the south bank of the Potomac, which at the outbreak of war was still in Union hands, though they soon had to evacuate it after destroying 17,000 rifles in store there. The Confederates then removed the rifle-making machinery to Richmond and Fayetteville (N.C.), so that they were able to manufacture a large proportion of the small arms they needed. In the course of the war the Confederate Government purchased some 200,000 rifles in Europe, mostly from England, in spite of the blockade, besides capturing 150,000 from the enemy.

The standard infantry weapon, common to both North and South, was the muzzle-loading Springfield percussion-cap rifled musket of ·58-inch calibre, based on the invention by the French Captain Claude Étienne Minié of an expanding bullet which, under the impact of the propellent gas, tightly en-gaged the rifled grooves of the barrel, thus acquiring increased velocity and accuracy. The Springfield rifled musket, with a 40-inch barrel, weighed just over nine pounds. This new type of small arm had been introduced into the U.S. service by the energetic *Jefferson Davis*, who had been U.S. Secretary of War from 1853 to 1857. The original model, produced in 1855, had an unsatis-factory tape primer system. An improved model was introduced in 1861, with a better percussion-cap system of ignition.

The American Civil War was the first one in which rifled small arms were used on the grand scale by both sides, and the era now dawned in which the rifle was to dominate the battlefield. The Model 1861 rifled musket had an extreme range of 1,000 yards, with an effective range of 300 yards, which was three times that of the smooth-bore musket which it superseded. In the second year of the war the Union cavalry regiments were re-equipped with the Sharps breech-loading rifled carbine of ·52-inch calibre. This weapon, which had been patented by Christian Sharps in 1848, was accurate up to 600 yards and could be fired at the rate of ten rounds a minute, three times as fast as a muzzle-loader.[1]

In the third year of the war the Union cavalry, and some infantry regiments, were re-armed with the Spencer Repeating Carbine, which had been patented in 1860 by Christopher M. Spencer of Connecticut. It had a tubular magazine in the stock, containing seven rim-fire ·52-inch cartridges made of copper. The total length of the carbine was 3 feet 3 inches, whereas the length of the Model 1861 infantry weapon was 4 feet 8 inches. This carbine was the first magazine breech-loader with metallic cartridge-cases to be used in war.

A large number of British Enfield rifled muskets of ·577-inch calibre were purchased by both sides during the war. The Enfield rifle was accurate up to 1,000 yards. The ammunition was interchangeable with that of the ·58 Spring-field weapon.

In the American Civil War telescopic sights were used for the first time, mostly by the Union infantry. They were fitted to Sharps breech-loading rifles and issued to 'sharpshooters' or snipers (see Plate 2).

On the outbreak of war, however, there were not sufficient rifled small arms to go round, and the hastily raised volunteer units on both sides were largely armed with smooth-bore muskets, either the U.S. Flintlock Musket Model 1822 or the Percussion Musket Model 1842, both of ·69-inch calibre. Their effective range was only 100 yards.

The situation as regards field artillery was equally unsatisfactory when war broke out, for the Union arsenals possessed only 163 serviceable field guns and howitzers. There was a large number of heavy cannon in the various coastal fortresses. On the outbreak of hostilities the Confederates possessed only 35 field pieces, but they controlled the U.S. Armory and Arsenal at Richmond, and quickly established another gun foundry at the neighbouring Tredegar Iron Works, which managed to supply them with 115 field guns by the middle of 1861.

The artillery weapons available were rather a mixed bag. Before the war the U.S. artillery was mainly armed with the 'Napoleon' smooth-bore muzzle-loading 12-pounder of 4·62-inch calibre. This had an extreme range of less than a mile and an effective range of 800 to 1,000 yards. It was in fact a similar weapon to that with which Napoleon had battered the British squares at Waterloo. Pre-war experiments with rifled guns had been carried out, and by 1863 half the Union artillery was equipped with the 3-inch rifled muzzle-

1. In 1857, after the Crimean War, two British cavalry regiments had been equipped with the Sharps breech-loading rifled carbine.

loading Ordnance Gun, which had an extreme range of 4,000 yards and an effective one of 2,500. Another rifled weapon used by the Union artillery was the 3-inch 10-pounder Parrott gun, designed by Captain Robert Parker Parrott of the U.S. Ordnance Department and constructed at Cold Spring Foundry on the Hudson near West Point (N.Y.), which could turn out 25 guns a week. There was also a 20-pounder Parrott (3.67-inch) and a 30-pounder (4.2-inch). Various other pieces were used by both sides, such as the 12-pounder mountain howitzer and the 24-pounder Coehorn mortar, but neither side possessed any breech-loading artillery.

TACTICS

The tactics employed by both sides were influenced by three main factors: (1) previous training; (2) nature of the terrain; (3) the weapons used.

(1) The tactical doctrine of both sides was identical, for there were a large number of West Point graduates in the Confederate army. Apart from the Mexican War, which had ended 13 years earlier, the experience of American officers was limited to the guerrilla warfare with which they were familiar on the Western Frontier. They had become expert in reconnaissance duties and fieldcraft, but lacked experience in handling artillery or in controlling the fire-power of large bodies of infantry, which they had to learn *de novo*. But the Indian wars had taught them the importance of individual manœuvre and marksmanship. This aptitude had been traditional in the U.S. Army since Revolutionary days and had enabled them to defeat the slower moving, volley-firing British battalions in the War of Independence. In this respect the Southerners had a definite advantage over their Northern opponents. Being for the most part countrymen and farmers, they were accustomed to an outdoor life and took more readily to campaigning conditions than the town-bred tradesmen and artisans who formed the bulk of the Northern troops. For the same reason the Southerners were the better horsemen and marksmen, and possessed more individual initiative.

The senior officers of the U.S. Army had been brought up on the teaching of General Winfield Scott's training manual, *Infantry Tactics*, but in 1861 this text-book was half a century old and quite outdated. Five years earlier, *Jefferson Davis*, then U.S. Secretary of War, had introduced the Springfield rifled musket into the service, and at the same time had issued to the army a modern training manual entitled *Rifle and Light Infantry Tactics*, which had just been written by a highly intelligent officer, Colonel *William Joseph Hardee*, who was then Commandant of the U.S. Military Academy at West Point. *Hardee's* manual prescribed the formation of an infantry regiment, both in attack and defence, with eight of its companies in two lines and the other two companies extended in skirmishing order. On the outbreak of war *Hardee*, a native of Savannah

(Ga), joined the Confederates and became a successful corps commander; his manual continued to be used by both sides.

(2) A more potent influence on the tactical methods of the two armies was the physical nature of the theatre of war. Just as its main geographical features, already described in Chapter II, fundamentally affected the strategic conduct of the war, so to a great extent did the micro-topography of the country determine the tactical procedure adopted by the fighting troops. The landscape of the eastern United States has, of course, changed very considerably during the past century. The populous towns of today were then villages, and much of the now cultivated areas was swampy and covered with scrub and partially cleared forest. The broken and wooded nature of the Virginian Piedmont region, where some of the fiercest fighting took place, greatly restricted the infantry field of fire and imposed point-blank ranges on the artillery. Contemporary maps of the area west of Fredericksburg and south of the Rapidan, where the Wilderness campaign was fought in May 1864, distinctly show the jungle-like nature of the country. Tangled woods and undergrowth, intersected by swampy streams, rendered impossible any movement by formed bodies of men or horses. Here the Confederates' individual self-reliance, mobility and marksmanship gave them the advantage over the slower-moving Union units.

Both the close nature of the terrain and the lack of training for that role precluded the use of shock tactics by the cavalry, which was employed either as mounted infantry or in long-distance reconnaissance and destructive raids into enemy territory.

In the western theatre, the hydrology of the country has been greatly affected by modern drainage and dam construction. The rivers are no longer so liable to flood as they were a century ago. At the time of the Civil War, every minor eminence or bluff in the Mississippi Basin was of major tactical importance. The 'bayous',[2] or creeks which intersected the riverain country, both restricted movement and afforded effective defensive obstacles.

(3) By far the most important factor influencing the tactics of both sides in the Civil War was the advent of the rifle as the infantryman's main weapon. It is true that the rifle then in use was neither a breech-loader nor a magazine-rifle,[3] and therefore the rate of fire did not exceed that of the smooth-bore musket, namely a maximum of three aimed rounds a minute. Its great superiority, however, lay in its increased effective range, which was three times that of the musket. That is to say that a body of infantry holding a defensive position could sweep with its fire a zone 300 yards in depth. If the defenders'

2. A term derived from the *boyaux*, or 'guts', as they were called by the early French settlers.

3. Toward the end of the war a few Union regiments were armed with the Spencer breech-loading rifle, which enabled them to inflict very heavy casualties on their opponents. The Union cavalry was armed with breech-loading carbines, some of them repeaters.

position were entrenched, they could withstand an assault by at least twice their own number. This gave the defence a tremendous advantage over the attack, and brought about the general adoption of field fortification. Hitherto, entrenching had been mainly resorted to as an adjunct to siege warfare; now it became an essential feature of every defensive operation. Breastworks were usually constructed of felled tree-trunks covered with earth.

This overwhelming advantage of the defence over the attack came as a sharp shock to the Union infantrymen when they attacked the Confederates' defensive position at the first battle of Bull Run, or Manassas, on 21 July 1861. The raw Union regiments were met with such a withering musketry fire that their attacks, though bravely led, broke down completely, and a disastrous panic took place. Owing to the close nature of the ground, their Regular artillery batteries, also courageously handled, could only support them by coming into action at close range in the front line. The Union gunners were then picked off by the Confederate sharpshooters, and the batteries were put out of action. Throughout the war the infantryman's rifle dominated the battlefield, and the bayonet assault ceased to be the decisive factor.

For the same reason, the cavalry charge, which had proved so effective at Salamanca and Waterloo, now became an anachronism in warfare.

PART II

APPRENTICESHIP

VI

Ups and Downs
of Grant's Early Life
1822–1860

Ulysses Grant was born on 27 April 1822 in a small township of the State of Ohio. He was the eldest son of Jesse Root Grant, who owned a farm and a tannery in the little town of Georgetown, 45 miles south-west of Cincinnati. When not at school, young Grant worked on his father's farm, took a liking to horses, and was soon at home in the saddle. At the age of 17, suddenly and somewhat fortuitously, he was pitchforked into a military career. Then, as now, each member of Congress was entitled to nominate a local lad for a cadetship at the United States Military Academy at West Point (N.Y.). This was a deliberate policy to ensure an even intake into the corps of officers from all States of the Union; the cadets thus nominated had, of course, to qualify by passing an entrance examination. Neither Grant nor his father had ever intended him for the army, but their local congressman, Thomas L. Hamer, a Democrat, was anxious to obtain the electoral support of Jesse Grant, who was a strong Whig. So, when a chance vacancy for a cadetship unexpectedly occurred, he nominated Jesse Grant's eldest son for the place.

Young Grant's name at birth, selected by his parents, had been registered as Hiram Ulysses Grant. His congressman nominator, when forwarding his recommendation to the War Department, had forgotten the correct forenames; knowing that the mother's maiden name was Hannah Simpson, he entered his nominee as 'Ulysses Simpson Grant'. When the young Hiram Ulysses reported at West Point in May 1839, the Adjutant told him that he had been officially enrolled as 'Ulysses Simpson'; to change it would involve a long correspondence with Washington. Young Grant perforce accepted the official ruling, so the name of Ulysses Simpson Grant became inscribed on the page of history. Like Napoleon's and Wellington's, his name had undergone an alteration in the course of his military career.

As a result of his newly acquired initials, young Grant was given the nickname of 'Uncle Sam Grant' by his fellow cadets. There is little to record about his four years of military education at West Point, where he was one of a class of 76. None of his class-mates achieved a noteworthy career, but neither did Grant himself display any outstanding military qualities. He appears to have disliked and rebelled against the rigid discipline and routine of West Point, where the 'plebe', or freshman, was (and still is) made uncomfortably conscious of his inferior status. He seems to have been totally devoid of any ambition to succeed in the career which had been thrust upon him. In his Memoirs, written many years later, he records of his period as a cadet:

> A military life had no charms for me, and I had not the faintest idea of staying in the army, even if I should be graduated, which I did not expect.[1]

Grant seemed to his fellow cadets to be kindly and good-natured, but shy and reserved, and rather simple-minded. The only branch of the curriculum in which he showed any real proficiency was mathematics, which had also been Napoleon's best subject. He had a fair hand for drawing. His mathematical instructor later wrote of him:

> Grant is remembered at his *alma mater* as having a cheery and at the same time firm aspect, and a prompt, decided manner.... He always showed himself a thinker and a steady worker. He belonged to the class of compactly strong men who went at their task and kept at it until they had finished. His mental machine was of the powerful, low-pressure class, which condenses its own steam and consumes its own smoke, and which pushes steadily forward and drives all obstacles before it.[2]

This encomium, however, was written more than 20 years later, after Grant had won fame in the field.

As opposed to his ability in mathematics and drawing, Grant failed lamentably in his French studies, although he managed by hard work to qualify in the passing-out examination. But if he showed little aptitude in his bookwork, he was easily the best horseman of his class. This was doubtless due to his early experiences on his father's farm, where he had acquired a love for horses and the ability to handle them. Riding had only been introduced into the West Point curriculum in the year when he joined, and many of his fellow cadets had no previous knowledge of horsemanship.

After four strenuous years at West Point, Grant passed out 21st among the 39 of his class who graduated. As his first choice, he put his name down for the cavalry, but as there were no vacancies in the only two existing dragoon regiments, he was posted to the 4th Infantry Regiment, then stationed at Jefferson Barracks, a few miles south of St. Louis (Mo). He joined his regiment as a Second Lieutenant in August 1843, but within a year the unit moved by steamer down the Mississippi and went into camp near the Mexican frontier, as relations with that country had become strained over the annexation

1. *Grant*, I, 38.
2. *King*, 53.

of Texas by the United States, which the Mexican Government refused to recognize.

When hostilities eventually broke out in March 1846, Grant's regiment formed part of the force under Major-General Zachary Taylor which crossed the Rio Grande near its mouth at Matamoros and invaded Mexican territory. He took part in the initial engagements at Palo Alto and Resaca de la Palma on 8 and 9 May, and seems to have won the approval of his commanding officer for, during the subsequent advance inland to Monterrey, he was appointed regimental quartermaster, a responsible post for a junior subaltern with only three years' service. At the battle of Monterrey in September 1846 he distinguished himself by galloping back to the wagon line under a hot fire and bringing up the ammunition when his regiment was running short of it. For this act he was awarded the brevet rank of First Lieutenant.

Grant took part in every important action of the Mexican War, except Buena Vista (February 1847). His finest exploit in the campaign was in September 1847, when Major-General Winfield Scott's column was closing in on Mexico City. After heavy fighting the Americans had stormed the fortified rocky hill of Chapultepec, which covered the two western causeways leading to the capital across the swamps which surround it. Grant's regiment formed the advanced guard of Brigadier-General William J. Worth's division, forming the left assault column. Their approach to the city along the causeway was blocked by the San Cosme Garita, a fortified guardhouse, and the causeway was swept by the Mexican artillery at close range. Although Grant should have been in rear of the column with the wagon train, he had pushed forward to the front line to see what was going on. A little to the south of the causeway stood a stone convent with a belfry. Grant made his way to this and climbed the belfry tower, from which he obtained an enfilade view of the town wall and the Mexican guns. Remembering that he had seen a mountain howitzer half a mile back along the causeway, Grant ran back and persuaded the gunners to bring it up to the convent. He helped them to manhandle the howitzer up the belfry steps, and from this platform the gunners were able to enfilade the Mexican artillery defending the city gate. Under cover of this fire the American troops stormed the San Cosme Garita and poured into the city. General Worth sent his A.D.C. to find out who was responsible for this bold initiative, and Grant was awarded the brevet rank of Captain.

Apart from some guerrilla actions on the lines of communication, the capture of Mexico City brought active operations to a close, and a treaty of peace was eventually signed at Guadalupe Hidalgo, just north of the capital, on 2 February 1848. After the ratification of the treaty in June, the United States troops evacuated Mexico and Grant's regiment spent the summer at Pascagoula (Miss). He then obtained four months' leave of absence, which he spent at St. Louis (Mo), where he had been stationed before the war. In August he married Miss Julia Dent, a lady to whom he had become engaged before leaving for the front. Their marriage was a happy one, though their life was inconvenienced by several changes of station.

In the summer of 1852 Grant's regiment was transferred to the Pacific coast, first to California and then to Oregon. The journey to the west coast was in those days a laborious one, for the Panama Canal had not been constructed and the Panama Railroad only reached as far as the Chagres River. There the troops had to detrain and proceed up the river by boat, and then march across the fever-infested isthmus to Panama. Many of them died of malaria and cholera on the way.

Life in the 'Wild West' of those days was primitive and somewhat demoralizing. California, taken over from Mexico after the war, had only become one of the United States in 1850, and Oregon was still a 'territory', where the white settlers had to struggle with the Indians for the possession of the land. The gold rush was at its height, and people were scrambling to get to the placer diggings. Drinking, gambling and lawlessness of every kind prevailed. It was no place for a respectable white woman, and Grant left his wife and children at St. Louis. Perhaps it would have been better for him had he taken them to the Pacific coast.

A grievous twilight now descended on Grant's fortunes. The truth seems to be that he took to drink during his exile on the west coast. There was plenty of inducement to that form of indulgence in his new environment. A gallon of whisky could be bought for 25 cents, and drink was the normal form of relaxation. Grant was depressed by the long separation from his family, to which he was deeply attached; he was also in financial straits. He was now serving under a new commanding officer, Lieutenant-Colonel Robert C. Buchanan, who was a strict martinet and disciplinarian, and had little sympathy for slovenly or lax conduct. Grant's biographers have produced various versions of how the break came about. His own Memoirs, written towards the close of his life, shed little light on the matter and only record the following:

> My family, all this while, was at the East. It consisted now of a wife and two children. I saw no chance of supporting them on the Pacific coast out of my pay as an army officer. I concluded, therefore, to resign, and in March applied for leave of absence until the end of the July following, tendering my resignation to take effect at the end of that time.[3]

What is certain is that Brevet Captain Grant resigned from the U.S. Army with effect from 31 July 1854.

On returning to civil life at the age of 32, he took up farming, the only vocation of which he had any knowledge. His wife owned some rough, uncleared land 12 miles from St. Louis. Grant set to work with a will, cleared the timber and undergrowth and, with his own hands, built a log cabin for his family to live in. It was a hard struggle, and his father did little to help him financially, but he kept at it for the next three years. Then in the winter

3. *Grant*, I, 210.

of 1857–58 misfortune struck again, laying him low with fever and ague, so that he had to abandon farming. When he recovered he tried his hand at various jobs, such as running an agency in real estate, but without success. Finally, in May 1860, now 38 years old, he moved to the lead-mining township of Galena (Ill), where his father owned a leather store, which was being managed by his younger brothers. There he took on a clerk's job at the meagre salary of $800 a year.

In that winter of 1860–61 Grant's fortunes had reached their nadir. He was slovenly and unkempt in appearance; he had not shaken off his drinking habits; his father and younger brothers despised him and refused to lend him money; he was generally regarded as one of life's failures. Nobody would have dreamt that from this shabby chrysalis would emerge, within the next four years, the triumphant victor of the Civil War.

VII

Back to the Army again
1861

The outbreak of war in April 1861 found Grant plying his humble trade in the little town of Galena (Ill). The State of Illinois is bounded on the west by the upper Mississippi, which separates it from the State of Missouri, and on the south-east by the Ohio River which separates it from Kentucky. Illinois lay in the area where hostilities might be expected to open, for it was one of those borderland States intersected by the Mason and Dixon Line, where the sympathies of the people were divided as to joining Union or Confederacy.

In all the three adjacent States, Missouri, Illinois and Kentucky, the outbreak of war brought political uncertainty and confusion. In Missouri, which contained large cotton plantations and many slave owners, the State Governor, Claiborne F. Jackson, was bent on joining the South. When Lincoln called up 75,000 Militiamen to fight the Secession States, and Missouri was summoned to provide its quota, Governor Jackson insolently replied that his State 'would not furnish one man to carry on such an unholy crusade'. He attempted to hand over to the Confederates the arms in the local U.S. arsenal, but this move was foiled by the prompt action of the Union military authorities. Desultory fighting of a guerrilla nature ensued in central Missouri during the following months, and the Confederate forces were eventually compelled to withdraw into Arkansas. Missouri's adherence to the North was thus secured, but regional loyalties remained divided. In the course of the war the State furnished 100,000 recruits to the Union, but 50,000 joined the Confederate Army.

In Kentucky too, public opinion was divided as to which side to join. As in the case of Missouri, the State Governor, Beriah Magoffin, was a strong adherent of the South, though he was only supported by about one-fourth of the members of the State Legislature. When Lincoln called on Kentucky to enrol four regiments for Union service, Governor Magoffin scornfully refused, with the words: 'Kentucky will furnish no troops for the wicked purpose of subduing her sister Southern States.' On 20 May the Kentucky

Legislature declared its neutrality in the war, which position was accepted for the time being by both the Union and Confederate Governments.

The fact that Missouri and Kentucky, both south of the latitude of the Mason and Dixon Line, failed to join the Confederacy was of very great importance, strategically and economically. The adherence of these two States to the South would have added nearly two millions to the population of the Confederacy.

Illinois, sandwiched between Missouri, where active operations were already in progress, and Kentucky which had declared itself neutral, was thus in a somewhat delicate position. Governor Richard Yates, however, was a staunch Unionist and his lead was followed by an overwhelming majority of the citizens. As soon as Lincoln issued his call for 75,000 Militiamen, thousands flocked to Springfield,[1] the State capital, to volunteer for military service. Among those enrolled on 23 April was the humble clerk of Jesse R. Grant & Sons' leather store in Galena. The State Militia office was overwhelmed with applications and was in a state of chaos. Someone told the Governor that Grant had held a Regular commission for eleven years and had seen active service, so Captain Grant was engaged as an assistant in the Adjutant-General's office at three dollars a day. His efficiency and knowledge were soon noticed, and Governor Yates gave him the job of mustering some of the newly formed units in southern Illinois. On 15 May at Mattoon he mustered into State service the 21st Illinois Regiment, though he found it in a deplorable condition of indiscipline and disorder. Realizing now that his own military experience could be of use to his country, Grant was fired by the ambition to obtain an active command. On 24 May he addressed the following modest application to the authorities in Washington:

Sir,
Having served for fifteen years in the regular army, including four years at West Point, and feeling it the duty of every one who has been educated at the government expense to offer their services for the support of the government, I have the honor very respectfully to tender my services until the close of the war, in such capacity as may be offered.

I would say in view of my present age and length of service, I feel myself competent to command a regiment, if the President in his judgment should see fit to intrust one to me. Since the first call of the President I have been serving on the staff of the Governor of this State, rendering such aid as I could in the organization of our State Militia, and am still engaged in that capacity. A letter addressed to me at Springfield, Illinois, will reach me.

I am, very respectfully, your obedient servant,

U. S. GRANT[2]

The Secretary of War had doubtless more urgent matters to attend to, for Grant received no reply. His prospects, however, now became brighter. State Governors were empowered to commission officers up to the rank of Colonel

1. Not to be confused with Springfield (Mo) or Springfield (Mass).
2. *Grant*, 1, 239–40.

of Volunteers; promotions above that rank had to be made by the President. Governor Yates, who had not failed to notice Grant's abilities, now offered him a Colonelcy, to command the 21st Illinois Regiment, then in camp near Springfield. This was the unruly unit which Grant had mustered at Mattoon a month previously, and which no commanding officer had succeeded in disciplining.

On 17 June Colonel Grant took over command of the Twenty-First, which numbered 36 officers and more than 900 other ranks. He at once asserted his authority over the 'Mattoon mob', and soon licked them into shape. A disturbance broke out one evening in their camp shortly after his arrival. The regimental bully, a well-known trouble maker, had returned from town fighting drunk and raising hell. Grant quietly walked up to him, and with one blow knocked him flat, then gagged his mouth with a bayonet, and had him tied up and removed to the guardroom. One day Grant discovered that his men were in the habit of filling up their water-bottles with whisky. On the next route-march he suddenly halted the regiment and ordered every man to empty his water-bottle into the sand. Grant was not unacquainted with the effects of hard liquor, but he was determined that it should not undermine the discipline of troops under his command. However, he was no martinet as regards dress and turn-out; he was no believer in 'spit and polish'. Indeed, he was extremely casual about his own dress and deportment. After a month's strenuous training under his leadership the 21st Illinois became a well-disciplined and efficient unit. It was only just in time, for the newly raised Union regiments were now called upon to take the field.

Early in July President Lincoln appointed Major-General John Charles Frémont to command the 'Department of the West', which included the States of Illinois and Missouri. Frémont took over his new command on 25 July and established his headquarters at St. Louis (Mo), on the right bank of the Mississippi. Lincoln's choice of Frémont as an area commander was unfortunate, for he had neither military experience nor soldierly qualifications. Frémont's father was a Frenchman[3] who had settled in South Carolina. The son started life as a teacher of mathematics and engineering. At the age of 25 he obtained a commission in the Topographical Corps, and in the early 1840s had done excellent work in surveying and exploring the Rocky Mountains, where he had marked out the overland trails to the far North-West. After having been dismissed the service on a disciplinary charge, Frémont became a Republican politician, and even stood as a candidate for the Presidency in 1856. Indeed, his appointment as a Major-General in the U.S. Army was entirely due to political influence. During the three months of his tenure of command in the western theatre the Union forces suffered serious reverses in the south-west section of Missouri, largely owing to his incapacity and in-

3. General Frémont was very proud of his French origin, and always insisted on his name being spelt with an acute accent on the e.

decision. He had 56,000 troops under his command, but they were scattered in small detachments all over Missouri and Illinois without any tactical purpose.

Under the orders and counter-orders of Frémont, Grant's regiment was moved about from pillar to post in northern Missouri, either guarding railway lines or dealing with suspected rebel outbreaks. On 7 August, to his great astonishment, Grant suddenly heard that the War Department had promoted him to the rank of Brigadier-General. His name was nineteenth in a batch of 37 Brigadiers, the first list of those appointed in the Civil War. Other names of those who were later to serve under him, included in the same list, were Buell, Hurlbut, McClernand, Pope, Prentiss, Sherman and Sigel.[4]

On 8 August Frémont appointed Brigadier-General Grant to command the South-eastern District of Missouri. His command comprised three regiments stationed in and around Ironton, 75 miles south of St. Louis. His orders were to entrench his posts, send out reconnaissances and submit daily reports. Grant's first situation report, sent in on the following day, is of considerable interest, as it illustrates his ability to appreciate the situation rapidly and to foresee what was required:

> I arrived here yesterday. Since that time I have studied the nature of the ground it may become necessary for me to defend, the character of the troops, and the means to do it with. From all that I have yet learned, from spies and loyally disposed citizens, I am led to believe there is no force within 30 miles of us that entertains the least idea of attacking this position, unless it should be left so weak as to invite an attack. It is fortunate, too, for many of the officers seem to have so little command over their men, and military duty seems to be done so loosely, that I fear at present that our resistance would be in inverse ratio to the number of troops to resist with.
>
> Spies are said to be seen every day within a few miles of our camp; marauding parties are infesting the country, pillaging Union men, within 10 miles of here. At present I can spare no force; in fact, have no suitable troops to drive these guerrillas out and afford to Union citizens of this place or neighborhood the protection I feel they should have.
>
> Artillery and cavalry are much needed, and the quartermaster's department is yet quite deficient. The number of teams would scarcely suffice for the use of this as a military post without making any forward movement, and the horses of those we have are many of them barefoot and without forage. But I have taken steps to remedy those latter defects.

Frémont can have had few officers serving under him who could give him such a clear and straightforward picture of the situation.

Shortly after taking over command of his brigade at Ironton, Grant was ordered to move his headquarters farther south to Cape Girardeau on the right bank of the Mississippi, 100 miles south-south-east of St. Louis. This was an important strategic point, as it commanded the great waterway leading southward into the heart of Confederate territory. Grant remained there only from 30 August to 2 September, when he was ordered to occupy Cairo, at the

4. These promotions were all antedated to 17 May 1861.

southern extremity of the State of Illinois. Cairo was a still more vital point than Cape Girardeau, for it was the railhead of the Illinois Central Railroad and also a main centre of navigation, being situated at the confluence of the Mississippi and Ohio Rivers. Here Grant first made contact with the officers of the U.S. Navy, with whom he was to collaborate so successfully in his forthcoming amphibious campaigns. Facing him, on the opposite bank of the river, lay the neutral State of Kentucky.

The whole military situation was now suddenly transformed by the action of the opposing Confederate commander, Major-General *Leonidas Polk*. This officer, a nephew of James Knox Polk who had been U.S. President during the Mexican War, was an interesting and picturesque character. He had started life as a military cadet, but on leaving West Point had resigned from the Army to become a clergyman in the Episcopal Church. For the last 20 years he had been Bishop of Louisiana, but on the outbreak of war at once threw off his surplice and at the age of 55 joined the Confederate Army. President *Jefferson Davis* made him a Major-General and gave him command of the Confederate troops in the area east of the Mississippi. *Polk* was an intelligent man, and quickly saw the advantage the Confederates would gain by seizing Cairo (Ill) and Paducah (Ky), 32 miles farther east. Not only would the occupation of these two places give the Confederates navigational control of the Mississippi, Ohio, Tennessee and Cumberland Rivers, but it might also induce the neutral State of Kentucky to join the South. To achieve this object, *Polk* advanced into Kentucky territory on 3 September and occupied Columbus on the left (east) bank of the Mississippi, 20 miles below Cairo. The 'bishop's move', strategically sound, proved politically disastrous. The Kentucky Legislature, which had a pro-Union majority, abandoned its neutrality and joined the North.

Grant at once appreciated both the political and military significance of *Polk*'s violation of Kentuckian neutrality. On 5 September he telegraphed from Cairo to the Speaker of the Kentucky Legislature at Frankfort:

> I regret to inform you that Confederate forces in considerable numbers have invaded the territory of Kentucky, and are occupying and fortifying strong positions at Hickman and Chalk Bluffs.

For this action Grant incurred an official reprimand from Frémont, perhaps deservedly, for it is no part of a Brigadier's duty to correspond directly with political authorities. However, he no doubt felt that the end justified the means.

But Grant went one step further; on the same day he crossed the Ohio River and entered Kentucky himself, occupying Paducah, 45 miles up stream from Cairo. On the previous evening he had telegraphed to Frémont that he was about to occupy Paducah unless he received orders to the contrary. Paducah was even more important to the Union than Cairo, for it commanded the junction of the Tennessee and Cumberland Rivers with the Ohio, thus giving access to the heart of Tennessee State, where the bulk of the Confederate forces in the western theatre were assembling. By Grant's seizure of Paducah *Polk* was forestalled in his project of occupying that vital confluence of waterways. In this, Grant not only displayed strategic insight, but also showed that he had the initiative and daring to take prompt advantage of an opportunity without waiting for orders. He knew only too well the hesitating and lethargic character of his Commander-in-Chief, who at the time was preoccupied by other hostile threats in western Missouri.

Grant now had under his command 15 infantry regiments, seven troops of cavalry and three batteries of field artillery, amounting to some 14,000 men, the strength of two divisions. But of this force only one-third was concentrated with him at Cairo, the remainder being dispersed in holding seven separate strategic points in Illinois, Kentucky and Missouri. During the next few weeks he was busily engaged in inspecting and training his troops in their scattered cantonments and at the same time in sending out reconnaissances, both across country and by river steamer, to ascertain the Confederate dispositions and intentions. He even worked out a plan for forcing the enemy to evacuate Columbus, which *Polk* was now fortifying and arming with heavy artillery, and where he had concentrated 13 infantry regiments.

Grant, it must be remembered, was still faced with the task of training and disciplining his raw levies, both officers and men. The Militiamen called up in April for three months had now gone home, and his units were composed of the Volunteers who had joined the colours in May and July, and were therefore hardly yet fit for active operations. All the Regular units of the U.S. Army had been retained by Lincoln in the eastern theatre for fear of a Confederate threat to Washington.

On 29 September Grant reported to Frémont as follows:

Everything here is quiet and no rumors to disturb it. The cold season is now so nearly at hand, that it is time to think of providing winter quarters for the garrison. Log huts could be cheaply built, but even they would call for the outlay of some money. Credit will not do at this place longer. I understand that the credit of the Government has been already used to the extent of some hundred thousand dollars, and no money ever paid out. This causes much murmuring among the citizens, and unless the paymaster is soon sent to pay off the troops, the same may be expected from the soldiers.

He was apparently not getting much help from the administrative staff of his incompetent Commander-in-Chief. He was, however, resourceful enough to find other means of obtaining firewood for his troops. On 11 October he recorded:

I sent the gunboats down near Columbus today, not so much for the purpose of reconnoitering as to protect a steamer sent after wood belonging to Hunter, who is with the Southern Army. About 100 cords were brought up.

Meanwhile he continued to send out reconnaissance patrols and organized an efficient intelligence service. The troops under his command were now reduced, as he had been ordered to reinforce Charles Ferguson Smith, the Brigadier on his left flank in Kentucky, and to send other units to assist the troops on his right in Missouri, leaving him with a force of only 11,000, which he organized in five tactical brigades. But his units were still very inadequately equipped. On 27 October he reported to Frémont:

> I am not prepared for a forward movement. My cavalry are not armed nor my artillery equipped; the infantry is not well armed, and transportation is entirely inadequate to any forward movement.

Despite these shortcomings, the static quiescence of Grant's command was suddenly disturbed on 1 November by the following warning order from Frémont, who was still trying to cope with the Confederate columns which had invaded south-west Missouri:

> You are hereby directed to hold your whole command ready to march at an hour's notice, until further orders.... You are also directed to make demonstrations with your troops along both sides of the [Mississippi] river towards Charleston, Norfolk and Blandville, and to keep your columns constantly moving back and forward against these places, without, however, attacking the enemy.

On the following day Grant was ordered to send a force south-westwards from Cape Girardeau to assist in driving the Confederates across the border into Arkansas. He at once despatched a brigade group of 3,000 men under Colonel Richard James Oglesby with that object, and on 5 November he received orders to make an immediate demonstration against Columbus, which was still strongly held by *Polk*. Grant needed no further spur to launch his first offensive operation against the enemy. On the afternoon of 5 November he embarked his force of five infantry regiments, two cavalry companies and two field-guns, a little over 3,000 men. As dusk fell, the flotilla, escorted by two gunboats, steamed southward down stream and anchored during the night off the Kentucky shore, some three miles above Columbus.

The expedition had been organized with the greatest secrecy. The troops had been issued with two days' rations, but had no idea where they were going. Grant's first operation order was issued on board the steamer 'Belle of Memphis' at 2 a.m. on 7 November. He divided his force into two brigades, commanded respectively by Brigadier-General John Alexander McClernand and Colonel Henry Dougherty.

The objective of the attack was a Confederate encampment on the right (west) bank of the Mississippi immediately opposite *Polk*'s fortress at Columbus. The river is here 800 yards wide, and the Confederate camp was sited on a low flat known as Belmont, formed by a bend of the river and clothed with forest, partially cleared to make room for a few fields of corn. The camp was occupied by a brigade of 2,500 men under Brigadier-General *Gideon Johnson*

Pillow, which had been ordered by *Polk* to advance westward to intercept Colonel Oglesby's column operating in Missouri.

At 8 a.m. the four Union transports landed the force on the Missouri shore three miles above Belmont at a point previously selected by Captain Henry Walke, Grant's senior Naval Officer. Leaving five companies of Dougherty's brigade to guard the landing place and the transports, Grant led the remainder of his force through the forest towards the Confederate camp three miles to the south. Meanwhile Walke's two wooden gunboats, 'Tyler' and 'Lexington', steamed down stream to engage the Columbus batteries which overlooked Belmont. When within a mile of the camp, Grant deployed his column, McClernand on the right and Dougherty on the left. Control of the action was now rendered difficult by the thick woods, but by noon the Union troops converged on the camp and stormed it without much difficulty, the defenders fleeing in confusion to the river bank.

As soon as *Polk* at Columbus heard of the landing at Belmont, he rushed reinforcements across the river to succour *Pillow*, and supported their counter-attack with the fire of two field batteries from the high ground on the left bank, which commanded the Belmont camp at a range of under 1,000 yards. By this time, unfortunately, the Union troops had got completely out of hand. Grant had ordered the Confederate camp to be burnt. This was too much for his raw troops. Elated by their comparatively easy victory, they scattered in an orgy of looting and the officers lost all control of their men. Indeed, as Grant recorded, 'Some of the higher officers were little better than the privates.' *Pillow* now landed two of his reinforcing regiments a mile up stream and launched a counter-attack on Grant's disorderly rabble. Finding his retreat threatened, Grant managed to collect his scattered troops about 2 p.m. and led them back to the landing place, closely pursued by the Confederates. He himself displayed considerable courage and was the last to leave the Missouri shore. As the final transport was preparing to cast off, his horse slithered down the steep river bank with him and trotted across the gang-plank on board the steamer.

It was a sad ending to a well-conceived and daring plan. Bonaparte, in his first Piedmont campaign, had suffered similar set-backs from the ill-discipline of his troops; both Bonaparte and Grant learnt a lesson which they never after-wards forgot.

The 'battle of Belmont' was the first action in which Grant had actively engaged the enemy in combat. It was, of course, no more than a large-scale raid, but it served to illustrate the possibilities of amphibious warfare, which was to form so important a feature of Grant's future campaigns. Both sides claimed Belmont as a victory; the Union troops suffered 485 casualties, but they inflicted 641 on their opponents. Apart from his sound planning and organiza-tion of the expedition, Grant showed himself to be a capable leader in action. He certainly made several tactical mistakes. He advanced through difficult,

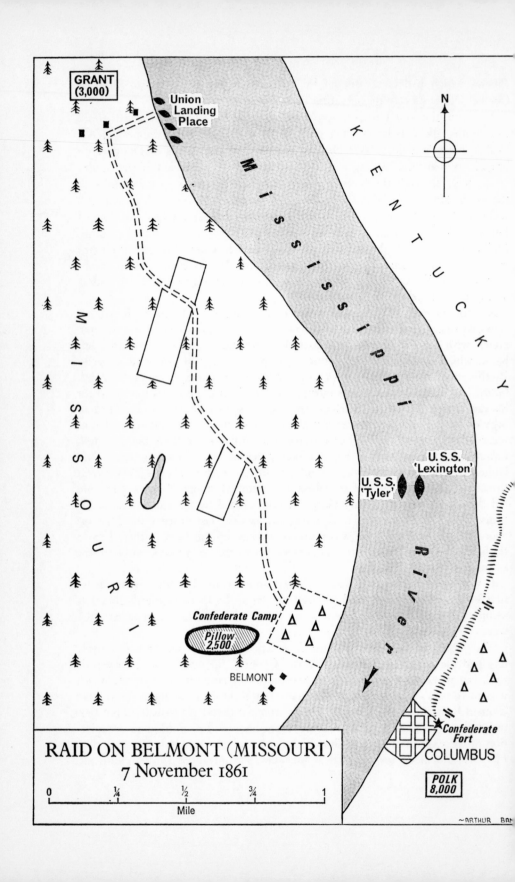

GRANT (3,000)

Union Landing Place

N

K E N T U C K Y

M i s s i s s i p p i

M
I
S
S
O
U
R
I

U.S.S. 'Lexington'

U.S.S. 'Tyler'

Confederate Camp

Pillow 2,500

BELMONT

R i v e r

Confederate Fort

COLUMBUS

POLK 8,000

RAID ON BELMONT (MISSOURI)
7 November 1861

0   ¼   ½   ¾   1
Mile

~ARTHUR BAN

wooded country, with untried troops, without making any preliminary re-connaissance; had he done so, of course, he might have sacrificed the element of surprise. The attack on the camp was made with his whole force, apart from the rearguard left at the landing place, without retaining any tactical reserve for eventualities. The operation taught Grant many lessons; *en forgeant on devient forgeron*.

It has been alleged that Grant undertook the expedition without any authority from headquarters, and that it led to an unnecessary waste of life. Perhaps the best answer to this is given by Grant himself in his Memoirs:

> The two objects for which the battle of Belmont was fought were fully accomplished. The enemy gave up all idea of detaching troops from Columbus. His losses were heavy for that period of the war.... Belmont was severely criticized in the North as a wholly un-necessary battle, barren of results, or the possibility of them from the beginning.
> If it had not been fought, Colonel Oglesby would probably have been captured or destroyed with his three thousand men. Then I should have been culpable indeed.[5]

After Belmont, both sides in the Mississippi area settled down to reorganize and equip their forces, and no further operations took place during the re-maining weeks of 1861. The first nine months of the war had not gone too well for the Union. In the eastern theatre, Major-General *Pierre Gustave Beauregard* had soundly thrashed Irvin McDowell's more numerous Army of the Potomac in the first battle of Bull Run, or Manassas, on 21 July, and the Confederate Army was firmly established in Virginia within 30 miles of Washington. Confederate morale was in consequence very high. In the western theatre, the Confederate forces had, with considerable difficulty, been finally driven out of Missouri, and Kentucky had acceded to the Union, but a large slice of Kentucky was still occupied by the Confederates. At no point had Union troops been able to penetrate into Confederate territory, except in western Virginia, west of the Alleghenies, where the young Major-General George Brinton McClellan, commanding the Army of the Ohio, had expelled a minor Confederate detachment in July, as a result of which West Virginia seceded from Virginia on 20 August, and was later incorporated into the Union as a separate State.

President Lincoln had good reason to be dissatisfied with the results achieved by his senior commanders, and he now made important changes in the higher posts. At the beginning of November he replaced the elderly Winfield Scott as Commander-in-Chief by the youthful and showy McClellan, popularly known as 'the young Napoleon'. Unfortunately, McClellan merely mimicked the mannerisms of his model without displaying any of his talents, and Lincoln later regretted his choice. At the same time Lincoln removed the incompetent Frémont from the Department of Missouri,[6] replacing him first by David

5. *Grant*, I, 280-1.
6. Grave charges concerning fraudulent contracts for the purchase of rifled carbines and

Hunter, and a few weeks later by Henry Wager Halleck. In the Department of the Ohio, William Tecumseh Sherman was replaced by Don Carlos Buell.

On 21 November Grant, at Cairo, submitted to his new chief, Halleck, at St. Louis, a memorandum describing the miserable equipment of his troops:

> The condition of this command is bad in every particular except discipline. In this latter I think they will compare favorably with almost any volunteers. There is a great deficiency in transportation. I have no ambulances. The clothing received has been almost universally of an inferior quality and deficient in quantity. The arms in the hands of the men are mostly the old flintlock repaired . . . and others of still more inferior quality.
>
> My cavalry force are none of them properly armed. . . . Eight companies are entirely without arms. . . .
>
> The Quartermaster's Department has been carried on here with so little funds that Government credit has become exhausted. I would urgently recommend that relief in this particular be afforded.

Whatever Halleck's faults were as a commander, and they were many, he was an efficient administrator, and he doubtless took steps to remedy these defects before active operations were resumed.

---

for the fortification of St. Louis were made against General Frémont by a Congress committee of inquiry in December 1861. Owing to his political influence, however, no action was taken against him; at the end of March 1862 Lincoln transferred him to command a corps in the Alleghenies, where he was outmanœuvred in June by *Stonewall Jackson* at Cross Keys. Frémont resigned from the army at the end of that month on being superseded by Pope, his junior, in the command of the Army of Virginia.

VIII

Personalities and Planning
in the Western Theatre
1861–1862

The military operations of 1861 having resulted in a deadlock, despite the superiority of the North in numbers and resources, it was evident that Union strategy had been gravely at fault. Strategy, of course, must always be the handmaid of national policy, but so far President Lincoln's conduct of the war had been influenced, not only by national policy, but by home politics. This tendency had already produced unhappy results in his selection of military commanders. Lincoln, as an astute politician, realized that, in order to pursue the war successfully and maintain a united North, he must conciliate both the Republican and Democratic parties in Congress. Hence the inappropriate appointment of individuals like Frémont and Halleck to important posts; the latter had few, and the former had no military qualifications at all. On the Confederate side, too, the same practice was to be seen, witness President *Davis*'s appointment of *John Buchanan Floyd* to command the 18,000 beleaguered troops in Fort Donelson, which resulted in the disaster described in the next chapter.

Still more unfortunate than Lincoln's selection of leaders was his choice of strategic objectives. Before his retirement, the elderly Commander-in-Chief, Winfield Scott, had advocated what was known as the 'anaconda plan', which was to hold back the Confederates in the eastern theatre, while operating offensively down the Mississippi Valley in order to crush the Southern States by economic and military strangulation. This was an eminently sound policy, which eventually had to be in part adopted. But in the early stages of the war it was unacceptable from the political point of view, owing to the vulnerability of the Union capital. Throughout 1861 there had been acute anxiety about a Confederate thrust at Washington, and after the defeat at Bull Run this became an imminent peril. The loss of Washington, with a disaffected Maryland in its rear, might have spelt the disruption of the Union. Consequently, the North expended a disproportionate amount of energy and resources in attempting to throw back the Confederate Army in Virginia, while neglecting the western theatre. President *Davis* indeed fell into the same error, for he devoted his major military effort to the defence of Richmond at the expense of the Mississippi Valley. The Confederacy could equally well have been governed from Alabama, where its capital had been originally established. Thus both sides wasted their energies in the endeavour to reach their opponent's capital, instead of concentrating on the destruction of his field army.

President Lincoln was also obsessed by the idea of gaining the adherence of the border States. Neutral Kentucky had joined the Union owing to *Polk*'s unwise incursion, and the Union had gained a military foothold there thanks to Grant's prompt initiative. Similarly, West Virginia had seceded from its parent State after McClennan's military success in the Alleghenies. Lincoln's eye now turned to the neighbouring region of East Tennessee. Tennessee had been the last State to secede from the Union, indeed not until two months after the outbreak of war, and it was divided politically on regional lines. Geographically, the State ran from west to east through eight degrees of longitude for 450 miles. Its western boundary was the Mississippi and its eastern the crest of the Alleghenies. The western half belonged to the cotton belt, but East Tennessee was an upland region where sympathies lay more with the North. Lincoln hoped that a military move southward through Kentucky would detach East Tennessee from the Confederacy.

A cardinal defect in the command structure of the Union forces in the western theatre at the close of 1861 was the lack of a centralized army headquarters, parallel with the 'Army of the Potomac' in the east. The west, by contrast, was split into three independent territorial commands named 'Departments'. From west to east these were called the Departments of Kansas (Hunter), Missouri (Halleck) and the Ohio (Buell), each communicating separately with McClellan at Washington. The Kansas Department was now purely administrative, being outside the zone of operations. The two important commands were those of Halleck at St. Louis (Mo) with 90,000 men and Buell at Louisville (Ky) with 45,000. Halleck was a Major-General, but Buell only a Brigadier-General. These two commanders were as jealous of each other as cats, and would not cooperate. Halleck, with some reason, constantly begged McClellan to give him the chief command in the west, which McClellan refused to do, being a personal friend of Buell and doubtful of Halleck's fitness for the post.

Under Halleck's command were Samuel Ryan Curtis and John Pope, each with about 15,000 men in Missouri, now more or less pacified, and in front line Grant with 20,000, holding the important confluences of the Tennessee and the Cumberland with the Ohio. Farther east in Kentucky were the five divisions of Buell.

On the Confederate side the higher command was more logically organized. In September President *Davis* had appointed Major-General *Albert Sidney*

Johnston as supreme commander in the western theatre. His front was divided into two sectors by the Cumberland River, which in fact coincided with the boundary between the commands of Halleck and Buell on the opposing side. *Johnston's* western sector was commanded by Major-General *Leonidas Polk* with 28,000 men, and the eastern by Major-General *William Joseph Hardee* with 22,000. Owing to their inferior numbers the Confederates were restricted to a defensive strategy, their main object being to block the waterways leading southward and to cover their forward line of lateral communication, the Memphis and Ohio Railroad, which ran south-westward from Bowling Green (Ky) to the important centre of Memphis (Tenn) on the Mississippi.

The Union strategic policy in the western theatre at that time was less clearly defined; in fact it was chaotic. Under political pressure by the President, McClellan ordered Buell, at Louisville (Ky) on the Ohio, to move southward and invade East Tennessee. His directive, dated 3 December, shows a peculiar disregard for military considerations:

> The best strategical move in this case will be that dictated by the simple feelings of humanity. We must preserve these noble fellows from harm; everything urges us to do that – faith, interests, and loyalty. For the sake of the eastern Tennesseans who have taken part with us I would gladly sacrifice mere military advantages.

Buell, with a more practical outlook, suggested that it would be as well if his advance were supported by a forward movement by Halleck to cover his right flank. Halleck, on being appealed to by McClellan, replied that he had no troops to spare, and that in any case they were not yet properly equipped.

In fact, no cooperation could be expected from these two Department commanders owing to their mutual jealousy. Halleck had graduated from West Point two years earlier than Buell, and both had been promoted to Brevet Captain for their services in the Mexican War, but Halleck had retired from the army in 1854, and had practised as a lawyer until the outbreak of war, when Lincoln made him a Regular Major-General. Buell, on the other hand, had served continuously as a Regular officer, with considerable experience on the staff, and had reached the rank of Lieutenant-Colonel when war broke out; he was then promoted as Brigadier-General of Volunteers. There is no doubt that he was a far more experienced and capable officer than Halleck. Buell was the first person to produce an intelligent strategic plan for the forthcoming operations. On 29 December he wrote to McClellan, who was then on the sick list:

> It is my conviction that all the force that can possibly be collected should be brought to bear on that front of which Columbus and Bowling Green may be said to be the flanks. The center, that is, the Cumberland and Tennessee where the railroad crosses them, is now the most vulnerable point. I regard it as the most important strategical point in the whole field of operations.

Buell had hit the nail on the head, and it was on this strategic point that Grant's first major operation was to be directed shortly. The President in Washington now realized that there was a lack of harmony between his two commanders in the west; on 31 December he telegraphed to each of them: 'General McClellan is sick. Are you in concert?' Buell replied:

> There is no arrangement between General Halleck and myself. I have been informed by General McClellan that he would make suitable disposition for concerted action.

Halleck replied:

> I have never received a word from General Buell. I am not ready to cooperate with him. Hope to do so in a few weeks. . . . Too much haste will ruin everything.

The nearest historical parallel seems to have been the lack of mutual assistance between the Earl of Chatham and Sir Richard Strachan at Walcheren, 52 years earlier.

Halleck continued to stick his toes in, pleading lack of troops, although he had 90,000 under his command. Finally, on 7 January 1862, Lincoln lost patience and telegraphed to both commanders:

> Please name as early a day as you safely can on or before which you can be ready to move southward in concert. Delay is ruining us.

Halleck replied that he was short of weapons. On 13 January McClellan wrote personally to Buell:

> You have no idea of the pressure brought to bear here upon the Government for a forward movement. It is so strong that it seems absolutely necessary to make the advance on Eastern Tennessee at once.

Buell complied and ordered his best divisional commander, Brigadier-General George Henry Thomas, to advance southward towards the Cumberland Gap in the Alleghenies, which was held by a Confederate brigade commanded by Brigadier-General *Felix Kirk Zollicoffer*. Thomas, a Virginian fighting for the North, was one of the most efficient officers in the Union Army. On 19 January he encountered the enemy at Mill Springs on the upper Cumberland River and routed them, *Zollicoffer* being killed. There was, however, no corresponding move by Halleck.

This minor success on the east flank of the Confederate position in Kentucky had little bearing on the major purpose of cutting the Memphis and Ohio Railroad and invading Tennessee. McClellan was most anxious to get this operation started, either by advancing down the Mississippi, which was blocked by *Polk*'s fortress at Columbus, or by pushing up the Tennessee and Cumberland Rivers, which the Confederates had now fortified by the construction of two strong earthworks, at Fort Henry on the right (east) bank of the Tennessee and Fort Donelson, eleven miles further east, on the left (west) bank of the Cumberland. Until these two forts had been stormed by land operations supported by river gunboats, no large-scale southward advance could be made.

After further prodding, Halleck at last consented to undertake this amphibious operation. But he continued to raise objections. On 20 January he wrote to McClellan:

> The idea of moving down the Mississippi by steam is, in my opinion, impracticable, or at least premature.... A much more feasible plan is to move up the Cumberland and Tennessee, making Nashville the first objective point. This would turn Columbus and force the abandonment of Bowling Green.... But the plan should not be attempted without a large force, not less than 60,000 effective men.

But now an important piece of information reached Washington, which caused the Union leaders to accelerate their plans. On 29 January McClellan telegraphed to Halleck and Buell:

> A deserter just in from the rebels says that ... he heard officers say that *Beauregard* was under orders to go to Kentucky with fifteen regiments from the Army of the Potomac.

This was indeed vital intelligence; *Beauregard* had defeated McDowell at Bull Run six months earlier. On the following day Halleck replied:

> Your telegraph respecting *Beauregard* is received. General Grant and Commodore Foote will be ordered to immediately advance, and to reduce and hold Fort Henry, on the Tennessee River.

Grant was thus precipitately launched on his first major offensive campaign.

IX

Grant invades Tennessee
February 1862

Before describing Grant's first major offensive campaign, it is essential to examine his personal relations with his immediate superior, Henry Wager Halleck, for a clash between their very different personalities was soon to produce serious discord. Grant was a man of resolute character, rather simple-minded but completely straightforward, and intensely practical. Halleck's character presented an exact antithesis to these qualities. He was more of a jurist than a general, having devoted more effort to the practice of the law than to that of soldiering. In his whole career he had never done a day's regimental duty, nor had he ever commanded troops. General Fuller has characterized him as 'a witless pedant', but that is hardly fair; a pedant he certainly was, but he had plenty of intelligence; his nickname in the U.S. Army was 'Old Brains'. Halleck had graduated from West Point in 1839, being in the Senior Class when Grant was a 'plebe', and passed out so high that he obtained a commission in the U.S. Engineers and was immediately appointed assistant instructor in engineering at West Point. Two years later he was transferred to the Board of Engineers at Washington and was employed in constructing the coast defences of New York. When the Mexican War broke out he was sent with an expedition to California, where he served on the staff and displayed considerable administrative ability. In 1853 he was employed in fortifying the Pacific coast, but in the following year he resigned from the army and turned to the law, in which he built up a successful practice, eventually becoming President of the Pacific and Atlantic Railroad. On the outbreak of war in 1861, Lincoln made him a Regular Major-General, along with Frémont and McClellan, and in November he replaced the incompetent Frémont in command of the Department of Missouri.

The relations between Halleck, the theoretical pundit, and Grant, the practical soldier, were never cordial. Halleck's personality did not invite friendly cooperation, for his manner was harsh and forbidding, while his nature was jealous and devious. In 1854 he had been serving on the administrative staff in San Francisco at the time when Grant was obliged to resign his commission, and the memory of those circumstances may have prejudiced him against his new subordinate from the start.

However that may be, Halleck must have been impressed by Grant's ability to command and train his troops, for on 16 December he extended Grant's Cairo District eastwards to include Paducah and Smithland in Kentucky, together with the division commanded by Brigadier-General Charles Ferguson Smith. Corps formations had not yet been adopted in the Union Army, but this in effect gave Grant the status of a corps commander, for he now had three divisions under command, amounting to 20,000 men. These divisions were commanded respectively by C. F. Smith, Lewis Wallace, and John Alexander McClernand, three officers of very different background and qualities.

The senior of them, Charles Ferguson Smith, was a man of exceptionally fine character and soldierly abilities. He was 15 years older than Grant, and had been his Chief Instructor in Tactics at West Point. Grant had then looked up to him as a model of the perfect officer. Smith had distinguished himself in the Mexican War, obtaining three brevet promotions. In August 1861 he was promoted Brigadier-General of Volunteers, but ranking three months junior to Grant, under whom he was now serving.

Lew Wallace was a much younger man, being five years younger than Grant. He had served as a Volunteer in the Mexican War and was a talented writer, being the author of *Ben Hur* and other historical novels.

John Alexander McClernand was without any previous military experience, being one of the political Generals. He was ten years older than Grant and a lawyer by profession, having been called to the bar in 1832. Purely on political grounds, he had been promoted Brigadier-General of Volunteers in the same batch as Grant, but ranking junior to him. His baptism of fire had been in the Belmont raid three months earlier, when his brigade had formed the right wing of Grant's force. McClernand was of an intriguing disposition, and Grant had to remove him from command a year later.

The only other officer serving under Grant whom it is necessary to mention here was Captain John Aaron Rawlins, his Assistant Adjutant-General, or administrative staff officer. When Grant was first promoted Brigadier-General, he was entitled to select one staff officer and two A.D.C.s. Having few friends at that time, Grant had selected as his personal staff officer the young lawyer who acted as legal adviser to his father's leather business. Without any military experience, Rawlins proved to be an excellent staff officer and was popular with all ranks. He served Grant as Chief of Staff faithfully throughout the war, eventually reaching the rank of Major-General.

At Cairo Grant acted in close cooperation with the senior naval officer, Flag-Officer Andrew Hull Foote, who in September had been placed in command of all 'Naval operations upon the Western waters'. Foote was a conscientious and experienced seaman. When war broke out he was Superintendent of the Brooklyn Navy Yard, and as soon as he was transferred to the West he assumed command of a number of river steamers, some of which had been converted into iron-clad gunboats in the building yards at St. Louis (Mo) and Cincinnati (Ohio) by Commander John Rodgers. With this naval flotilla he was placed under Halleck's command for combined operations. After discussing matters with Foote, Grant was convinced that he could force his way up the Tennessee and Cumberland Rivers, capture the barrier defences at Fort Henry and Fort Donelson, and cut the Memphis and Ohio Railroad by destroying the railway bridge over the Tennessee, 15 miles above Fort Henry. This would sever the lateral communications between *Hardee* and *Polk*, who commanded the two wings of *Johnston*'s army.

On 6 January Grant asked Halleck's permission to visit him at St. Louis in order to outline his plans for this operation. His first meeting with his new Commander-in-Chief was not an auspicious one. He describes it in his Memoirs as follows:

> The leave [to go to St. Louis] was granted, but not graciously. I had known General Halleck but very slightly in the old army, not having met him either at West Point or during the Mexican War. I was received with so little cordiality that I perhaps stated the object of my visit with less clearness than I might have done, and I had not uttered many sentences before I was cut short as if my plan was preposterous. I returned to Cairo very much crestfallen.[1]

One can picture the owlish and pedantic Halleck crushing Grant's enthusiasm with frigid disdain. However, Halleck's neighbouring commander, Buell, had been pressing the same strategic plan on McClellan at Washington, and the latter now ordered Halleck to have reconnaissances made up the Tennessee and Cumberland Rivers in order to prevent Confederate reinforcements being sent to Brigadier-General *Simon Bolivar Buckner* at Bowling Green. Halleck was thus forced to instruct Grant to undertake these reconnaissances. Grant took immediate action, as recorded in his Memoirs:

> I at once ordered General Smith to send a force up the west bank of the Tennessee to threaten Forts Heiman and Henry; McClernand at the same time with a force of 6,000 men was sent out into west Kentucky, threatening Columbus with one column and the Tennessee River with another. I went with McClernand's command. The weather was very bad; snow and rain fell; the roads, never good in this section, were intolerable. We were out more than a week splashing through the mud, snow and rain, the men suffering very much. The object of the expedition was accomplished. The enemy did not send reinforcements to Bowling Green, and General George H. Thomas fought and won the battle of Mill Springs [19 January] before we returned.[2]

1. *Grant*, 1, 287.
2. *ibid.*, 1, 286.

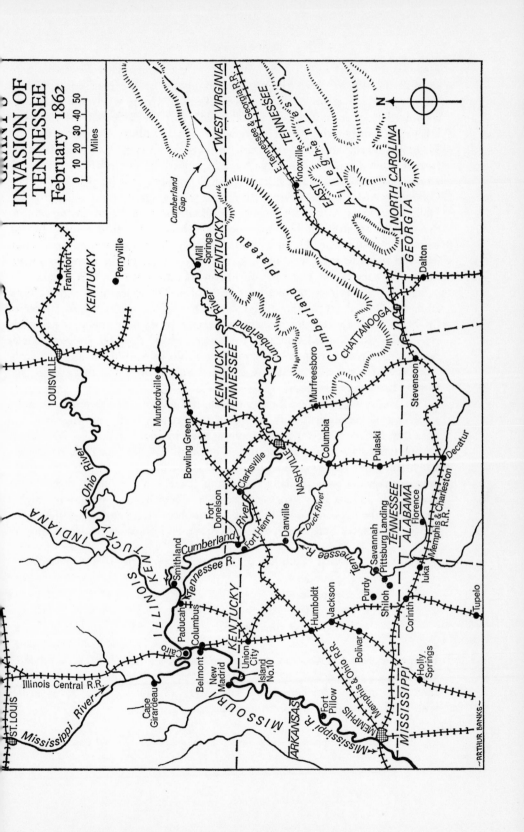

GRANT'S
INVASION OF
TENNESSEE
February 1862

Miles
0 10 20 30 40 50

N

~ARTHUR BANKS~

Here we see Grant on his toes and ready to take immediate offensive action, making no excuses about the weather conditions or the poor equipment of his troops. As a result of these reconnaissances, Grant was more than ever convinced that prompt action would enable him to carry out his cherished scheme of cutting the Memphis–Bowling Green railway by capturing Fort Henry. Halleck, however, still remained inactive. On 28 January, risking a further snub from his chief, Grant telegraphed to Halleck: 'If permitted, I can take and hold Fort Henry on the Tennessee', and he persuaded Flag-Officer Foote to back him up with a similar message. On the following day Halleck received McClellan's telegram about the transfer of *Beauregard* to the western theatre. Halleck may not have been a practical soldier, but he was an ambitious one. He now saw his chance of being given supreme command in the west if he were to win a striking victory. He hesitated no longer. On 1 February Grant received full instructions to move on Fort Henry.

During the previous summer the Governor of Tennessee, under instructions from the Confederate authorities, had constructed on the northern border of his State a strong redoubt to bar the passage of each of the two navigable rivers, the Cumberland and the Tennessee, which flow on parallel courses northward through Kentucky to join the Ohio at Smithland and Paducah. The one barring the Tennessee was named Fort Henry, and that barring the Cumberland, Fort Donelson.

Fort Henry was sited on the right (eastern) bank of the Tennessee, 50 miles south-east of Paducah, but its position had been very badly chosen, for it was on a low flat on the river's edge, commanded by high ground on both banks within small-arms range of the fort. The work had been started in summer when the river was low, but in early February the river was rising and the powder-magazine was in danger of being flooded. When these defects were discovered, an auxiliary work named Fort Heiman was started on higher ground on the opposite bank, but this had not been completed when the Union attack took place. Fort Henry had a fairly powerful armament, consisting of:

    1 10-inch 'Columbiad', throwing a projectile of 128 pounds[3]
    2 42-pounders
    8 32-pounders
    5 18-pounders
    1 6-inch rifled gun

Except for the latter weapon, all were smooth-bores. The fortress commander was Brigadier-General *Lloyd Tilghman*, a capable Regular officer, with less than 3,000 men under command. They were all raw recruits, poorly armed with flintlock muskets and sporting rifles.

3. The 'Columbiad' was a bronze coast defence gun, smooth-bore and muzzle-loading.

Grant's men, although better armed, were also largely composed of raw levies. Anthony Trollope, who arrived at Cairo the day after Grant's expedition had started for Fort Henry, describes vividly the appearance of two regiments which were embarking to reinforce him:

Two regiments passed through the place during the time, getting out of one steamer on to another, or passing from the railway into boats. One of these regiments passed before me down the slope of the river-bank, and the men as a body seemed to be healthy. Very many were drunk, and all were mud-clogged up to their shoulders and very caps. In other respects they appeared to be in good order. It must be understood that these soldiers, the volunteers, had never been made subject to any discipline as to cleanliness. They wore their hair long. Their hats or caps, though all made in some military form and with some military appendance, were various and ill-assorted. They all were covered with loose, thick, blue-gray great-coats, which no doubt were warm and wholesome, but which from their looseness and colour seemed to be peculiarly susceptible of receiving and showing a very large amount of mud. Their boots were always good; but each man was shod as he liked.[4]

These volunteer recruits, though deficient in 'good order and military discipline', were by no means a rabble. They were imbued with a fiercely patriotic spirit, and fought gallantly at Fort Donelson a fortnight later.

On 3 February, the day after receipt of their orders, Grant and Foote started off on their expedition, with 17,000 men embarked in transports. These, however, were only sufficient to convey one division at a time. They were preceded by Foote's flotilla of four armoured gunboats ('Essex', 'Cincinnati', 'Carondelet' and 'St. Louis') and three wooden gunboats ('Tyler', 'Conestoga' and 'Lexington'). The gunboats were armed with 8–inch 70–pounders, rifled 42-pounders, 32-pounders and 12-pounder boat-howitzers, 51 guns in all, being three times the number of guns mounted in Fort Henry.

Heavy rain had fallen and the river was rising rapidly. Although the strong current impeded the river-craft, it in fact favoured the Union flotilla, as the flood-water swept away the mines and boom which the Confederates had laid in the fairway. On the following day the flotilla anchored six miles below Fort Henry and the leading division, McClernand's, disembarked on the right bank. The transports were then sent back to Paducah to collect Smith's division, which was landed on the left bank. On 6 February both divisions set off on a six-mile march across difficult swampy country, McClernand's division moving on Fort Henry and Smith's on Fort Heiman.

Meanwhile, without waiting for the army, Foote's seven gunboats steamed up stream until Fort Henry became visible at a range of a mile. At 11.30 a.m. the gunboats opened fire and the guns of the fort promptly replied. The Union gunboats were struck repeatedly, but their armour saved them from serious damage. They gradually closed the range and with their heavier metal knocked

4. *Trollope*, II, 156.

out all 17 guns of the fort, which surrendered at 2 p.m. The sailors lost only seven killed and 32 wounded and missing.

Brigadier-General *Tilghman* had realized from the beginning that he was out-gunned and outnumbered. In order to avoid a useless sacrifice of life he wisely sent off 2,500 of his garrison across country to Fort Donelson, 11 miles to the east, while he himself with less than 100 men remained to man the guns of Fort Henry. Grant rode in at 3 p.m. to take possession, but the victory had been won by the U.S. Navy.

As soon as Fort Henry fell, three gunboats under Commander S. L. Phelps were dispatched up stream to destroy the railway bridge which formed the link between the two wings of *Johnston*'s army. On 8 February these gunboats penetrated southward as far as Florence (Ala), spreading panic in the rear of the Confederate forces. The capture of Fort Henry at the cost of so few casualties caused great satisfaction at Washington. On 7 February McClellan telegraphed his congratulations to Halleck, adding: 'Please thank Grant and Foote and their commands for me.' Two days later Halleck passed on this message to Foote, but not a word to Grant.

The swift capture of Fort Henry was indeed no great achievement on Grant's part, for the advance of the two land columns had been badly synchronized with the action of the gunboats. Grant had, however, learnt some lessons from his earlier operation at Belmont. On this occasion he had sent Colonel Joseph Dana Webster, his Chief of Staff, to carry out a preliminary reconnaissance of the approaches to Fort Henry, and he had taken care to retain a brigade of Smith's division as a reserve.

Grant's next objective was Fort Donelson on the Cumberland, but he does not seem to have realized that it would be a much tougher nut to crack than Fort Henry, for he reported to Halleck:

> I shall take and destroy Fort Donelson on the 8th and return to Fort Henry with the forces employed, unless it seems feasible to occupy that place with a small force that could retreat easily to the main body. I shall regard it more in the light of an advance grand guard than as a permanent post.

In accordance with this intention he ordered McClernand and Smith to advance eastward with their divisions on two parallel dirt tracks, and sent off a senior engineer officer with a cavalry escort to carry out a preliminary reconnaissance. But he now found that it would take at least a week for Foote's gunboats to get back to Paducah, repair the damage they had sustained at Fort Henry, and then move up the Cumberland to support him. The weather was also very bad. On 8 February he reported to Halleck:

> At present we are perfectly locked in by high water and bad roads, and prevented from acting offensively, as I should like to do. . . . I contemplated taking Fort Donelson today with infantry and cavalry alone, but my troops may be kept busily engaged in saving what we now have from the rapidly rising water.

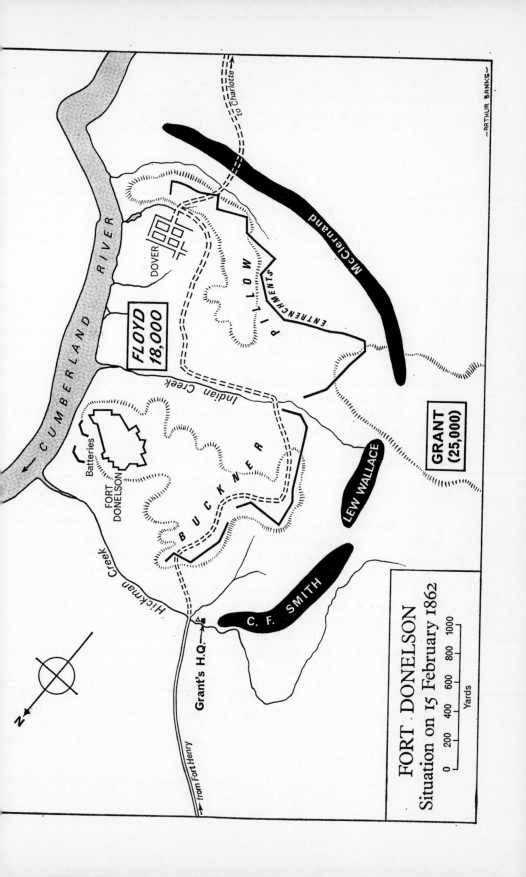

~ARTHUR BANKS~

CUMBERLAND RIVER

to Charlotte

McClernand

DOVER

ENTRENCHMENTS

PILLOW

FLOYD
18,000

Indian Creek

GRANT
(25,000)

Batteries

FORT
DONELSON

BUCKNER

LEW WALLACE

Hickman Creek

C. F. SMITH

N

Grant's H.Q.

from Fort Henry

FORT DONELSON
Situation on 15 February 1862

0   200   400   600   800   1000
Yards

On the 12th the weather improved, and Grant's two columns began their advance. In the afternoon his advanced guards encountered and drove back the enemy outposts, and by the evening he deployed his force in a wide semi-circle to envelop the Confederate defences, McClernand's division on the right and Smith's on the left.

Fort Donelson was a far more formidable defensive position than Fort Henry. Its nucleus was a large earthwork redoubt, about 25 acres in area,[5] sited on the northern spur of a plateau some 120 feet high on the left bank of the Cumberland River. On the forward slope of this spur, just below the fort, were sited two batteries, one 20 feet above the water's edge, the other 50 feet higher, which enfiladed a straight stretch of the river for a mile down stream. In these two batteries were mounted:

> 1 10-inch 'Columbiad'
> 1 rifled converted 'Columbiad'
> 1 8-inch howitzer
> 10 32-pounders
> 2 9-pounders

Though fewer in number than those at Fort Henry, these guns were far more effectively sited, as their plunging fire could penetrate the decks of armoured vessels, and the upper battery was at such an elevation that the gunboats could only hit it with their mortars.

On the north and south the fort was protected by two streams, Hickman Creek and Indian Creek, which at this time were impassable, being filled with back-water from the Cumberland. The western escarpment of the plateau crowned by the fort was protected by a strong line of rifle-pits and entrench-ments, covered by an abatis of felled trees, which barred the mile of open ground between the two creeks. These earthworks extended southward for another mile and a half beyond Indian Creek as far as the bank of the Cum-berland, and included within the perimeter the village of Dover, situated on a hill overlooking the river. The defensive perimeter was 4,500 yards in extent.

The Confederate theatre commander, Major-General *Albert Sidney Johnston*, had been so shaken by the swift capture of Fort Henry that he at once evacuated Bowling Green and withdrew all *Hardee*'s troops to Nashville, the State capital of Tennessee, on the upper Cumberland. At the same time, in order to save Fort Donelson from a similar fate, he reinforced its previous garrison of 6,000 with 12,000 additional men under three senior officers, Brigadier-Generals *John Buchanan Floyd*, *Gideon Johnson Pillow* and *Simon Bolivar Buckner*. The senior of them, *Floyd*, was not a professional soldier at all. In 1857 he had succeeded *Jefferson Davis* as Secretary of War at Wash-

---

5. Not 100 acres, as stated by Grant in his Memoirs, an error repeated by many his-torians; the whole defended area was about 400 acres.

ington under James Buchanan's Presidency. During his tenure of office he had been indicted for maladministration of army funds, and the investigation of this charge was still proceeding when war broke out. *Jefferson Davis* then gave him a military command out of political loyalty.

The next senior officer was *Pillow*, against whom Grant had fought at Belmont. He also was a lawyer turned soldier, but had slightly more military experience than *Floyd*, as he had been given a command in the Mexican War by President Polk. As Grant records in his Memoirs:

> I had known General *Pillow* in Mexico, and judged that with any force, no matter how small, I could march up to within gunshot of any intrenchments he was given to hold.[6]

The third of the trio of Fort Donelson's defenders was a Regular officer, *Buckner*, the only one of them with any military ability. He was a year younger than Grant, having been in the term below him at West Point, and he had befriended Grant when the latter had been overtaken by adversity in California.

On 14 February Grant's two leading divisions were deployed facing the western and southern sectors of the outer defences of Fort Donelson. These were manned by the whole of *Floyd*'s infantry, *Buckner*'s division on the right and *Pillow*'s on the left. No attempt had been made to interfere with Grant's approach march or deployment. On the same day Brigadier-General Lew Wallace's division arrived from Fort Henry and took over the Union centre sector, with C. F. Smith's division on its left and McClernand's on its right. The investment of Fort Donelson was now complete on the landward side. Grant established his headquarters on the high ground overlooking Hickman's Creek, behind the left flank of Smith's division, where he could watch the approach of the Union gunboats.

During the night of the 13th/14th Flag-Officer Foote arrived with his flotilla, having previously sent forward on the 12th Commander Henry Walke with the 'Carondelet' to draw the fire of the shore batteries at long range. Expecting to repeat his easy victory at Fort Henry, at 3 p.m. on the 14th Foote steamed up the river with his four armoured gunboats in line abreast, 'Louisville', 'St. Louis', 'Pittsburgh' and 'Carondelet', followed at half a mile distance by the unarmoured 'Tyler' and 'Conestoga'. At 3.30 p.m. Foote opened fire with the bow guns of his flagship 'St. Louis' and the rest of the flotilla joined in. The Confederate batteries replied with every gun, and the gunboats were hit repeatedly. Foote boldly closed in to within 400 yards of the fort, but the shore batteries were well protected by earth ramparts and had a tremendous advantage in their height above the water-line. The struggle was an unequal one, and all the gunboats sustained serious damage, the 'Carondelet' being hit 54 times. Foote himself was severely wounded, and the flotilla was forced to withdraw with a loss of 11 killed and 43 wounded. The Confederate batteries suffered no casualties.

6. *Grant*, 1, 294.

The repulse of the naval flotilla was a great disappointment to Grant, who had watched the action from the high ground above Hickman's Creek. He felt that he would now have to settle down to siege operations. He has been criticized for not launching an assault on the land defences to synchronize with the naval attack, but he had hoped that the gunboats would be able to run the gauntlet of the batteries and take station up stream from the fort, when he would close in from the south and west to cut off the enemy's retreat. That night the weather, which had been mild, turned bitterly cold, with snow and wind, the temperature dropping to 12° Fahrenheit, and the ground was frozen hard. The troops on both sides suffered severely.

In spite of the success of the Confederate batteries, the faint-hearted *Floyd* decided on the 14th that he could not hold Fort Donelson against Grant's force with less than 50,000 men. He held a council of war with his divisional and brigade commanders, when it was unanimously decided that they should break out southward by the Dover–Charlotte road to unite with *Hardee* at Nashville. *Pillow*'s division was to attack McClernand's investing lines early on the 15th and clear the escape road, while *Buckner*'s division acted as rear-guard.

During the night of the 14th/15th Grant received an urgent message from Foote, who was lying seriously wounded in his flagship at anchor three miles down stream, asking him to visit him to decide on further action, as the gunboats would have to go back to Paducah to refit. Grant rode off early on the 15th to meet the Flag-Officer, apparently without nominating any senior officer to command the troops in his absence.

Shortly after dawn *Pillow* launched his attack with 8,000 men against McClernand's sector south and west of Dover. The Union troops were completely surprised and were driven back in disorder, the fugitives being pursued by the Confederate cavalry under Lieutenant-Colonel *Nathan Bedford Forrest*. By 11 a.m. *Pillow* had opened up the Dover–Charlotte escape route. McClernand's division was scattered and in disarray, but Lew Wallace extended to his right to form a flank and checked the Confederate onrush. Overpowered by his success, *Floyd* now lost his head and, instead of carrying out the southward withdrawal which had been planned, sent off a telegram to *Johnston* announcing a decisive Confederate victory. He then ordered *Buckner* to advance on the right and attack Lew Wallace's division.

At this moment Grant arrived from his visit to Foote. He found Wallace and McClernand in consultation and at once appreciated the critical situation. As Lew Wallace has related:

In his ordinary quiet voice he said, addressing himself to both officers, 'Gentlemen, the position on the right must be retaken'. With that he turned and galloped off.

Grant galloped straight to Smith's headquarters on the left and ordered him to deliver a frontal assault on the trenches covering Fort Donelson in order

Major-General J. C. Frémont (1813–1890)

7 Lieutenant-General H. W. Halleck (1815–1872)

9 Brigadier-General W. S. Rosecrans (1819–1898)

Major-General D. C. Buell (1818–1898)

to create a diversion in favour of the counter-attack being prepared on the right. Smith had already detached a provisional brigade of two regiments to support McClernand on the right; putting himself at the head of four regiments, he led the assault up a glacis slope under a withering fire from the Confederate rifle-pits and also from the guns of the fort. 'No flinching now, my lads', shouted the veteran Brigadier-General. 'Here, this is the way! Come on!' With his cap on the point of his sword, Smith led his men through the tangled abatis and stormed the Confederate trenches, within half a mile of the fort. *Buckner* counter-attacked with his division, but failed to dislodge Smith's men. At the same time the counter-attack by Wallace and McClernand on the Union right drove *Pillow* back and retook the lost positions, including the Dover–Charlotte road. By nightfall the Confederates were back in their original position.

During the night *Floyd* held another council of war in the village of Dover. This time the Confederate leaders realized that their situation was hopeless and that they had no alternative but to surrender. The two lawyer-generals, *Floyd* and *Pillow*, were determined not to fall into Union hands; *Floyd* knew that he might have to face a charge of embezzlement. They handed over command of the garrison to *Buckner*, their junior, and shortly before daylight embarked on river steamers with two Virginian regiments and escaped to Nashville. Another Confederate officer decided to escape captivity; Lieutenant-Colonel *Forrest* had been a successful plantation owner in Mississippi, but was without military or any other education. On the outbreak of war he enlisted as a trooper at the age of 40, and was now commanding a cavalry regiment of 1,500 men. Being a tough and hardy horseman, he collected his troopers before dawn and broke out along the river-bank, plunging through the frozen marshy creeks. He lived to fight another day, and made his name as a dashing cavalry leader.

At daybreak on 16 February the unfortunate *Buckner* sent a flag of truce to Grant to ask for terms. Grant's reply has become famous:

> No terms except an unconditional and immediate surrender can be accepted. I propose to move immediately upon your works.[7]

Buckner, protesting at such 'ungenerous and unchivalrous terms', had no option but to submit; 14,623 prisoners and 40 cannon fell into Union hands. The Confederates also suffered some 2,000 casualties in the course of the fighting; the total Union losses were 2,886.

Lew Wallace, who could wield the pen as well as the sword, has left us

---

7. Grant's demand for an 'unconditional surrender' was doubtless in the mind of President Franklin D. Roosevelt when, on 20 January 1943 at the Casablanca Conference with Churchill, he proposed to apply the same formula at the capitulation of Germany and Japan.

10   *Union gunboats attacking Fort Henry, Tennessee River, 6 February 1862* a vivid and detailed account of the capture of Fort Donelson. It contains the following graphic description of his chief[8]:

> From the first his silence was remarkable. He knew how to keep his temper. In battle, as in camp, he went about quietly, speaking in a conversational tone; yet he appeared to see everything that went on, and was always intent on business. He had a faithful assistant adjutant-general, and appreciated him; he preferred, however, his own eyes, word, and hand. His aides were little more than messengers. In dress he was plain, even negligent; in partial amendment of that his horse was always a good one and well kept.

8. *Battles and Leaders of the Civil War*, 1, 398–428.

Hd Qrs. Army in the Field

Camp near Donelson, Feby 16th 1862

Gen. S. B. Buckner,
Confed. Army.

Sir; Yours of this date proposing Armistice, and appointment of Commissioners to settle terms of Capitulation is just received. No terms except an unconditional and immediate surrender can be accepted.

I propose to move immediately upon your works.

I am Sir; very respectfully
Your obt. svt.
U. S. Grant
Brig. Genl.

Facsimile of the original 'unconditional surrender' ultimatum from Grant to Buckner at Fort Donelson

X

Frustration and Eclipse
February–March 1862

The capture of Fort Donelson with its numerous garrison was the first substantial victory won by the Union forces in the first nine months of the war. It roused the greatest enthusiasm throughout the North, and Grant suddenly became a popular hero. The public fancy too was tickled by the term 'unconditional surrender', which Grant had insisted on, and the coincidence of his initials caused him now to be known as 'Unconditional Surrender Grant'. Directly President Lincoln heard of the capture of Fort Donelson, he promoted Grant to the rank of Major-General of Volunteers[1] and appointed him to command the new Military District of the Tennessee, still of course under Halleck's command, where he ranked on a par with Pope, who was still a Brigadier-General, as was Buell, who was independent of Halleck.

Grant's promotion at once aroused Halleck's jealousy of his subordinate, whose success seemed to be stealing the limelight. On the following day he telegraphed to McClellan:

> Make Buell, Grant and Pope Major-Generals of Volunteers and give me command in the West. I ask this in return for Forts Henry and Donelson.

On 19 February he also recommended that C. F. Smith should be promoted Major-General, adding: 'Honor him for this victory'. From these recommendations it is obvious that Halleck was determined to deprive Grant of any individual credit for the victories he had achieved. Buell with 50,000 men had remained inactive at Louisville without making any contribution to Grant's success. Pope, under Halleck's orders, was commanding the troops in Missouri and had rendered Grant still less assistance. Both Buell and Pope had been senior to Grant as Brigadier-Generals, but Grant's promotion had now made them his juniors.

---

1. He was not promoted to Major-General in the Regular Army until July 1863, after the capture of Vicksburg.

On 20 February Halleck again telegraphed to McClellan:

> I must have command of the armies in the West. Hesitation and delay are losing us the golden opportunity. Lay this before the President and Secretary of War. May I assume command? Answer quickly.

McClellan, who disliked Halleck and knew his limitations, replied frigidly:

> Buell at Bowling Green knows more of the state of affairs than you at St. Louis.... I shall not lay your request before the Secretary until I hear definitely from Buell.

Meanwhile Grant was anxious to exploit his success and push up the rivers to drive the enemy out of west Tennessee. In this he was strongly supported by Flag-Officer Foote, now partially recovered from his wounds. In reporting to Halleck the fall of Fort Donelson, Grant told him that, unless he received contrary instructions, he intended to occupy Clarksville (40 miles up the Cumberland from Fort Donelson) on 21 February and Nashville (another 50 miles up the Cumberland) by 1 March. In accordance with this plan he sent Smith's division up river by steamer to occupy Clarksville. The jealous and timorous Halleck, however, was not anxious to see his successful subordinate gain further laurels; on the 18th he telegraphed to Grant:

> Don't let gunboats go higher up than Clarksville. Even there they must limit their operations to the destruction of the bridge and railroad, and return immediately to Cairo, leaving one at Fort Donelson.

Buell, on Grant's left, was equally anxious to push on, now that Grant had opened the road. He had four divisions under his command, amounting to 50,000 men, and had sent forward one of them under Brigadier-General William Nelson to support Grant. Nelson reached Nashville on 24 February, shortly followed by another of Buell's divisions under Ormsby McKnight Mitchel.[2]

The loss of both Fort Donelson and Nashville was a shattering blow to the Confederate Commander-in-Chief in the western theatre, General *Albert Sidney Johnston*. He was 59 years old and had a great reputation as a fighting soldier. On the outbreak of war *Jefferson Davis* had made him a full General and given him command of all the forces west of the Alleghenies. He had committed a serious error in sending the incompetent *Floyd* with 12,000 men to reinforce *Buckner* at Fort Donelson. Now, with only 20,000 men, he was forced to retreat to Murfreesboro (32 miles south-east of Nashville) in order to preserve his railway link with Chattanooga. He also ordered *Polk* to abandon his strongly fortified outpost at Columbus (Ky) and fall back to Jackson (Tenn), where Major-General *Gustave Beauregard* had now arrived from the eastern

---

2. Mitchel was more distinguished as an astronomer than as a soldier; he died of yellow fever eight months later.

theatre. The two wings of the Confederate Army in the west were thus separated by a distance of 140 miles, with the Tennessee River in between. Had there been a Napoleon commanding the Union forces, *Johnston* and *Beauregard* would have been destroyed in detail. But Halleck was no Napoleon; he was still sitting at St. Louis, 200 miles to the north; the most he did was to send his Chief of Staff, Brigadier-General George Washington Cullum, to Cairo to form an advanced report centre, but he neither visited the front himself, nor sent liaison officers forward to keep in touch.

There now arose a series of mutual misunderstandings between Grant and his chief which caused confusion in the Union higher command during the following fortnight. The main cause of these misunderstandings seems to have been that the telegraph operator at Grant's advanced headquarters deserted to the Confederates, taking with him his file of telegrams, so that it became impossible to ascertain which messages were actually sent or received. The trouble appears to have started with a reprimand sent to Halleck by McClellan from Washington on 21 February:

> You do not report either often or fully enough. Unless you keep me fully advised, you must not expect me to abandon my own plans for yours.

Stung by this rebuke, Halleck decided to make Grant the scapegoat. On 25 February he ordered Grant to send Smith's division from Fort Donelson to Fort Henry. Unknown to Halleck, however, Grant had already sent Smith's division up to Clarksville, and from there Buell had sent it forward to support his own troops at Nashville. In order to clear up the confused situation, Grant went up to Nashville on the 27th for a consultation with Buell and returned on the following day to Fort Donelson. On 1 March Halleck wrote to McClellan:

> I have had no communication with General Grant for more than a week. He left his command without my authority and went to Nashville. His army seems to be as much demoralized by the victory of Fort Donelson as was that of the Potomac by the defeat of Bull Run. It is hard to censure a successful general immediately after a victory, but I think he richly deserves it. I can get no returns, no reports, no information of any kind from him. Satisfied with his victory, he sits down and enjoys it without any regard to the future. I am worn out and tired with this neglect and inefficiency. C. F. Smith is almost the only officer equal to the emergency.

To which McClellan sent a somewhat unkind reply on the 3rd:

> Do not hesitate to arrest him at once if the good of the service requires it, and place C. F. Smith in command. You are at liberty to regard this as a positive order if it will smooth your way.

On the following day Halleck wrote a further letter to McClellan, complaining of Grant's 'neglect of my often-repeated orders', and added:

A rumor has just reached me that Grant has resumed his former bad habits. I do not deem it advisable to arrest him at present, but have placed General Smith in command of the expedition up the Tennessee.

He then telegraphed to Grant, who was at Fort Donelson:

You will place Major-General C. F. Smith in command of the expedition, and remain yourself at Fort Henry. Why do you not obey my orders to report strength and positions of your command?[3]

To this Grant wrote the following dignified reply:

Your dispatch of yesterday is just received. Troops will be sent under command of Major-General Smith as directed. . . . I am not aware of ever having disobeyed any order from headquarters – certainly never intended such a thing. I have reported almost daily the condition of my command and reported every position occupied. . . . My reports have nearly all been made to General Cullum, chief of staff, and it may be that many of them were not thought of sufficient importance to forward more than a telegraphic synopsis.

Grant's strength return forwarded with this letter shows that his command consisted of 46 infantry regiments, three cavalry regiments, ten field batteries, in all some 27,000 men. This firm but temperate reply produced a still more spiteful letter from Halleck on 6 March, enclosing an anonymous accusation about frauds in the disposal of captured enemy property at Forts Henry and Donelson. On the 7th Grant replied, expressing his indignation at Halleck's insinuations, and ending with the request: 'I respectfully ask to be relieved from further duty in the Department.' This correspondence continued acrimoniously until the matter finally reached the ear of President Lincoln, who on 10 March demanded an enquiry to establish the exact facts. The Adjutant-General at Washington wrote to Halleck as follows:

It has been reported that soon after the battle of Fort Donelson, Brigadier-General Grant left his command without leave. By direction of the President, the Secretary of War desires you to ascertain and report whether General Grant left his command at any time without proper authority, and if so, for how long; whether he has made to you proper reports and returns of his force; whether he has committed any acts which were unauthorized or not in accordance with military subordination or propriety, and, if so, what.

Halleck, being an astute lawyer, now realized that he had a bad case and would be unable to substantiate any of the misdemeanours which he had ascribed to Grant, and so decided to climb down. On 13 March he telegraphed to Grant:

You cannot be relieved from your command. There is no good reason for it. . . . Instead of relieving you, I wish you as soon as your new army is in the field to assume the immediate command and lead it on to new victories.

3. *Grant*, 1, 326.

On the 15th he replied to the Adjutant-General's demand with a soft-soapy letter, explaining that Grant had gone to Nashville 'with good intentions' and had acted throughout with 'praiseworthy but mistaken zeal'. No further action should be taken in the matter as 'there never has been any want of military subordination.'

Matters were thus patched up between the two men, but Grant never forgave Halleck for the affront to his self-respect.

Meanwhile, in Washington, Lincoln had become increasingly impatient with 'the young Napoleon's' conduct of the war, and decided to assume the supreme command of military operations in both theatres himself. On 11 March he sent McClellan to take command of the Army of the Potomac in the eastern theatre, and gave command of the western theatre to Halleck, being the senior officer in that region, which was now divided into three District commands under Buell, Grant and Pope. Thus Halleck, through no merit of his own, achieved his ambition of becoming supreme commander in the West. Lincoln was right enough in simplifying the command structure there, but unfortunately he chose the wrong man to be Commander-in-Chief. He only realized his mistake later.

11 *Union armoured gunboat 'St. Louis' on the Cumberland River (Flag Officer Foote's flagship in attack on Fort Donelson)*

12 *Union transports on the Tennessee River*

*13 Battle of Shiloh: Union camp surprised by Confederate attack, Sunday morning,
6 April 1862*

14 Battle of Shiloh: Confederate attack repulsed at 'Hornet's Nest', 6 April 1862

XI

The Battle of Shiloh
April 1862

The capture of Forts Henry and Donelson had shaken the whole structure of Confederate defence in the western theatre, and their forces were now dangerously scattered. They had completely evacuated Kentucky and had lost Nashville, the State capital of Tennessee. Halleck, who had been appointed Commander-in-Chief of the Union forces in this theatre on 11 March, was in a strong position, thanks to Grant's energy and successful leadership, and he now held the strategic initiative. Halleck had three armies under his orders, commanded respectively by Pope (25,000), Grant (40,000) and Buell (50,000), poised to advance southward by the three waterways leading into the heart of the Confederacy: the Mississippi, the Tennessee and the Cumberland.

To oppose the threat of this triple thrust, *Johnston*, the Confederate Commander-in-Chief, was isolated at Murfreesboro with 17,000 men, while *Polk*, also with 17,000, was withdrawing southward from Columbus (Ky) to Jackson (Tenn), where *Beauregard* from the eastern theatre had arrived on 16 February. A reinforcement of 10,000 men under Major-General *Braxton Bragg* from Mobile (Ala) was hurrying northward to join *Beauregard*. Had Halleck possessed the energy and vision to push forward at the beginning of March, he could have defeated these scattered forces in detail. Halleck's hesitation to act enabled *Johnston* to concentrate some 45,000 men in the neighbourhood of Corinth by the last week in March. The little town of Corinth in northern Mississippi was an important strategic objective, for it was the junction between two railways vital to the Confederate communications: the line running south from Jackson (Tenn) to Mobile (Ala) and the line from Memphis (Tenn) running east to Chattanooga (Tenn) and Charleston (s.c.).

Farther west, Pope's advance down the Mississippi was barred by the Confederate fortifications at Island No. 10, near New Madrid (Mo), and at Fort Pillow, Fort Randolph and Memphis, all in Tennessee. *Beauregard* should have realized the futility of leaving these garrisons isolated, for they were bound in the long run to suffer the same fate as had befallen Forts Henry and Donelson. However, these forts did delay Pope for some weeks, leaving Halleck with only Grant and Buell available for the main drive southward.

Meanwhile, in accordance with orders issued by Halleck on 1 March the divisions of C. F. Smith and William Tecumseh Sherman, escorted by armoured gunboats, had steamed up the Tennessee River under Smith's command for 100 miles without opposition. By the middle of March they had established themselves on the left bank at Pittsburg Landing, where they had discovered a good defensible position, eight miles above the village of Savannah (Tenn) and 20 miles north-east of Corinth. This position was intended to form a secure base for an overland expedition to seize the railway junction at Corinth and cut the Memphis and Charleston Railroad. At Savannah, unfortunately, Smith sustained a severe accident, from the effects of which he never recovered, and he died five weeks later. The command of his division was taken over by his senior Brigadier, William Harvey Lamb Wallace (not to be confused with Lew Wallace, who commanded another of Grant's divisions).

His misunderstandings with Halleck having been finally cleared up, Grant left Fort Henry on 15 March and reached Savannah on the 17th. Here he proceeded to reorganize his army, now increased to six divisions by the addition of three newly raised ones, commanded respectively by Stephen Augustus Hurlbut, Benjamin Mayberry Prentiss and William Tecumseh Sherman. Like Grant, all three had been promoted to the rank of Brigadier-General in May 1861. Hurlbut and Prentiss, however, were Illinois lawyers without Regular Army experience, whereas Sherman, two years older than Grant, had been senior to him as a cadet at West Point, but had left the army at the age of 33 to become a successful banker. Sherman's future career was to be closely linked with Grant's, and he proved to be a firm friend and loyal supporter of his chief, besides becoming one of the outstanding leaders of the Civil War.

Grant's army now numbered 35,000 infantry, 3,000 cavalry and more than 100 guns. His divisions were located as follows:

1st Division	William H. L. Wallace	Savannah
2nd „	John A. McClernand	„
3rd „	Lew Wallace	Crump's Landing
4th „	Stephen A. Hurlbut	Pittsburg Landing
5th „	William T. Sherman	„ „
6th „	Benjamin M. Prentiss	Savannah

During the last week of March Grant moved the 1st, 2nd and 6th Divisions up to Pittsburg Landing, preparatory to the advance on Corinth.

Grant's instructions from Halleck were to remain on the defensive and to avoid any general engagement until Buell's army on his left could come up to his support. Buell at that time had 40,000 men at Columbia (Tenn), 85 miles north-east of Pittsburg Landing, but his advance was badly delayed by the flooded state of the country and also because the Confederates had burnt the bridges over the Duck River, a right-bank tributary of the Tennessee, now swollen by the heavy rains. Buell's army consisted of five divisions under G. H. Thomas, A. McD. McCook, W. Nelson, T. L. Crittenden and T. J. Wood.

Grant was anxious to press on to his immediate objective, which was to seize the railway junction at Corinth before the Confederates there should be reinforced, but he was restrained by a further order from Halleck, dated 16 March:

> As the enemy is evidently in strong force, my instructions not to advance so as to bring on an engagement must be strictly obeyed.

The cautious Halleck was obviously anxious to put a brake on Grant's impetuosity, for two days later he followed this up with a further admonition:

> By all means keep your forces together until you connect with General Buell, who is now at Columbia (Tenn), and will move on Waynesboro with three divisions. Don't let the enemy draw you into an engagement now. Wait till you are properly fortified and receive orders.

This message only reached Grant on the 22nd, as the telegraph did not operate farther south than Fort Henry. Halleck's instructions were perfectly sound, for the Union commanders had no reliable information as to the strength or intentions of the Confederates. Grant, however, paid little heed to his chief's injunctions and proceeded to concentrate his divisions on the west bank of the river in readiness for the advance to Corinth. Although he had 3,000 cavalry at his disposal, he neglected to send out any reconnaissance patrols to gain contact with the enemy, nor, in spite of Halleck's orders, did he make any attempt to entrench his exposed forward position, beyond instructing his Chief Engineer, Lieutenant-Colonel James Birdseye McPherson,[1] to reconnoitre a general line of defence. Grant records his own frame of mind at the time as follows:

> When all reinforcements should have arrived I expected to take the initiative by marching on Corinth, and had no expectation of needing fortifications, though this subject was taken into consideration.[2]

The area just west of Pittsburg Landing in which five of Grant's divisions were now camped had originally been selected by Sherman, who described it thus in a message to Grant:

1. McPherson later became one of Grant's favourite and most successful subordinates. He was killed in July 1864 near Atlanta while commanding the Army of the Tennessee under Sherman.
2. *Grant*, I, 332.

I am strongly impressed with the importance of the position, both for its land advantages and its strategic position. The ground itself admits of easy defense by a small command, and yet affords admirable camping ground for a hundred thousand men.... The only drawback is that at this stage of water the space for landing is contracted too much for the immense fleet now here discharging.

The area was indeed eminently suitable from a defensive point of view. It consisted of a plateau rising to a height of 200 feet above the river, uninhabited, heavily timbered and intersected by streams, which were now swollen with the back-water from the Tennessee. The plateau was roughly triangular in shape, each side of the triangle measuring about four miles. On the east it was bounded by the Tennessee River, here 500 yards wide, and by its tributary the Lick Creek; the north-western face was well protected by the deep and swollen Snake Creek and its smaller tributary, Owl Creek; the south-western side was more open, being only partially protected by two smaller streams, Oak Creek and Locust Grove Creek. This south-western face of the triangle was traversed by the road running from Pittsburg Landing to Corinth, 20 miles to the south-west, where *Johnston*'s army was already assembled. The south-western face of the plateau was thus by far the most vulnerable, though its flanks were well protected, on the left by Lick Creek and on the right by Owl Creek and Oak Creek. On the ridge above Oak Creek, where the Corinth road crossed it, stood a log-built church named Shiloh, the only building in the whole area, except for the log-house at Pittsburg Landing.

Grant had established his headquarters at Savannah, eight miles below Pittsburg Landing and on the opposite side of the river. There he intended to await the arrival of Buell's army. Lew Wallace's division was on the left bank at Crump's Landing, three miles farther up stream, watching the road to Purdy, where some Confederate troops had been reported. The remaining five divisions of Grant's army were encamped on the plateau west of Pittsburg Landing, Sherman and Prentiss on the south-west face astride the Corinth road, and behind them the divisions of McClernand, Hurlbut and William Wallace. In Grant's absence at Savannah, McClernand, now a Major-General, was the senior officer in command of the troops, though Grant had little confidence in his abilities. Grant appears to have given him no instructions, either about entrenching the exposed front or for the collection of intelligence. Sherman and Prentiss, being in the front line, should have taken some steps on their own initiative; both their divisions consisted of raw recruits, untrained in field fortification or in outpost duties.

It cannot be said that Grant's intelligence service was efficiently organized. On 3 April Sherman's division captured an enemy scout who was sent back to Grant for interrogation, but no information about hostile movements was obtained. Again on 5 April Sherman's troops captured a Confederate patrol of ten men, with equally negative results.

We can now switch to the 'other side of the hill' to follow the Confederate

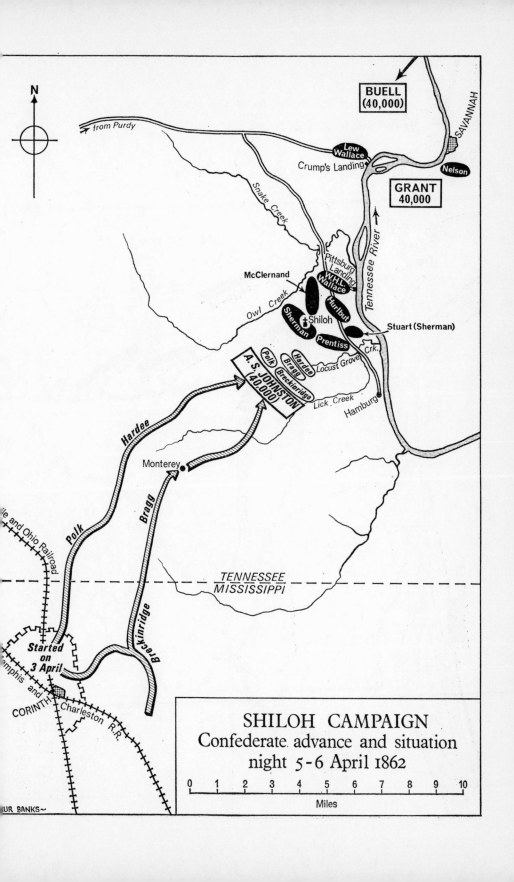

N

from Purdy

BUELL
(40,000)

SAVANNAH

Lew
Wallace

Crump's Landing

Nelson

Snake Creek

GRANT
40,000

Pittsburg
Landing

McClernand

W.H.L.
Wallace

Tennessee River

Owl Creek

Hurlbut

Sherman

✝Shiloh

Prentiss

Stuart (Sherman)

Crk.

Polk

Hardee

Bragg

Breckinridge

Locust Grove

A. S. JOHNSTON
(40,000)

Hardee

Lick Creek

Hamburg

Bragg

Monterey

Breckinridge

Polk

TENNESSEE
MISSISSIPPI

le and Ohio Railroad

Started
on
3 April

mphis and

CORINTH

Charleston R.R.

UR BANKS~

SHILOH CAMPAIGN
Confederate advance and situation
night 5-6 April 1862

0 1 2 3 4 5 6 7 8 9 10

Miles

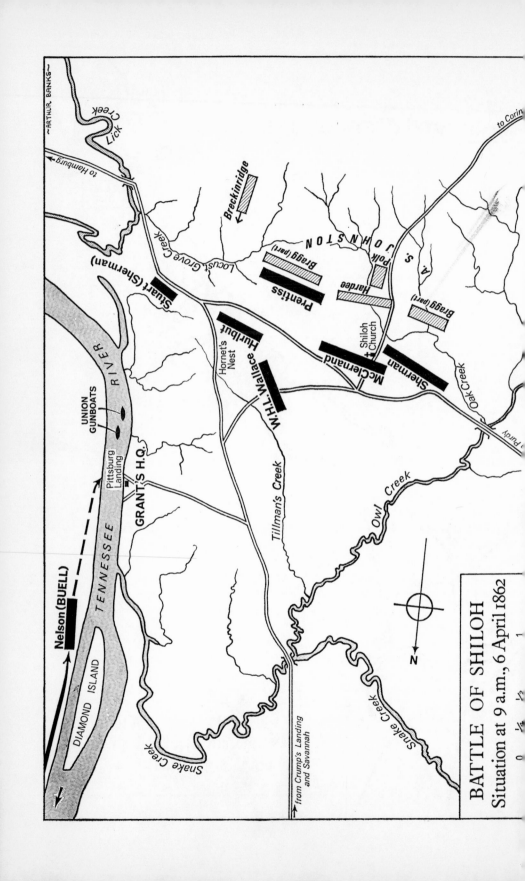

BATTLE OF SHILOH
Situation at 9 a.m., 6 April 1862

movements, which Grant had so strangely ignored. The surrender of Fort Donelson with its large garrison had come as a shock to the whole of the South, and a public outcry arose for the removal of General *Albert Sidney Johnston*. President *Davis* refused to accede to this demand, but *Floyd* and *Pillow* were, naturally, removed from their commands. After Buell's capture of Nashville, *Johnston* with *Hardee*'s corps retired southward from Murfreesboro (Tenn) into Alabama and then moved westward to Corinth (Miss), where in the last week of March he joined forces with *Gustave Beauregard*, who had under his command the troops of *Leonidas Polk*, *Braxton Bragg* and *John Cabell Breckinridge*, in all some 40,000 men. *Johnston* appointed *Beauregard* as his second-in-command and organized his army into three corps under *Hardee*, *Polk* and *Bragg*, all West Point graduates.

The Confederates, operating in their own country, were well informed about the Union movements. On 2 April *Johnston* learnt that Buell was advancing south-west from Columbia (Tenn) to unite with Grant. He realized that the latter's army was in an exposed position at Pittsburg Landing with the river at his back. He decided therefore to advance immediately and crush Grant's force before Buell's arrival. The main attack was to be directed on the Union left flank, resting on Lick Creek, so as to drive Grant's force away from Pittsburg Landing and cut off its retreat.

The Confederate advance began on 3 April, following two parallel dirt tracks which led north-eastward through thickly forested country. Progress was slow owing to the miry state of the roads, and it was not until 4 p.m. on 5 April that the Confederate columns halted within two miles of the Union encampment. *Hardee*'s corps had led the advance, followed by *Bragg* and *Polk*, with *Breckinridge*'s division in reserve, but when the Confederate army deployed for action at dawn on Sunday, 6 April, the units had become very mixed up owing to the faulty orders issued by *Beauregard*. The corps deployed in line with *Hardee* and *Polk* on the left, facing Shiloh Church, and *Bragg* in the centre; the right wing, facing Locust Grove Creek, was formed by *Breckinridge*'s division, which *Johnston* had meant to hold in reserve.

The Confederate attack came as a complete surprise to the Union troops, who indeed were asleep in their tents when they were roused by musketry fire at close range. Sherman's division was encamped on the Shiloh Church ridge overlooking Oak Creek, with Prentiss's camp east of him, and David Stuart's brigade, detached from Sherman's division, still further to the east, facing Locust Grove Creek. McClernand's and Hurlbut's divisions were camped further in rear, with William Wallace's just west of Pittsburg Landing. Sherman's failure to give his chief any warning of the impending attack cannot be explained or excused. On 5 April his outposts had made contact with Confederate patrols and had even captured some prisoners. Yet on that day he reported to Grant:

The enemy is saucy, but got the worst of it yesterday, and will not press our pickets far. I will not be drawn out far unless with certainty of advantage, and I do not apprehend anything like an attack on our position.

The camps of Sherman, Prentiss and Stuart were quickly overrun by the Confederate assault, and a general stampede to the rear took place. Both divisions were composed of raw recruits who had never been in action before. The Union troops were driven back for a distance of one to two miles, but the more experienced divisions of McClernand and William Wallace were rushed up to their support, and by noon a new front was stabilized. Five of Grant's divisions were now in line and heavily engaged, with Sherman on the extreme right, next to him McClernand, then William Wallace, Prentiss and Hurlbut, though the units were very much intermingled. Lew Wallace's division, five miles away at Crump's Landing, was sorely needed.

At 6 a.m., when the Confederate attack was launched, Grant was having breakfast in his steamer 'Tigress' at Savannah, eight miles down stream from Pittsburg Landing. Had he anticipated any attack, he would of course have been in the forward area with his troops, but in order to meet Buell he and his staff had been spending the night back at Savannah. Buell's leading division, commanded by William Nelson, had in fact reached Savannah on 5 April, after an exhausting march, and Grant had ordered it to continue its march up the east bank of the Tennessee to a point opposite Pittsburg Landing, where it would be ferried across the river. Buell himself arrived at Savannah on the evening of the 5th, but just missed Grant who was on board his steamer. On the morning of the 6th Grant's breakfast was interrupted by the sound of heavy firing from the south, so he at once started off up stream, stopping on the way at Crump's Landing to give Lew Wallace verbal orders to move his division forward. Unfortunately Wallace thought that the gun-fire came from the direction of Purdy, far to the west, so he marched off inland from the river, and only reached the battlefield by a circuitous détour after dark, too late to be of any assistance.

Between 8 and 9 a.m. Grant with his staff disembarked at Pittsburg Landing, where they were horrified to see thousands of fugitives who had fled from the firing-line and were seeking shelter. Grant at once mounted his horse and rode from one divisional command post to another, seeing the divisional commanders and endeavouring to stabilize the line. He also reorganized the ammunition supply and made efforts to collect the stragglers and send them back to their units. Between 1 and 2 p.m. he rode back to Pittsburg Landing, where he met Buell, who had just arrived there by steamer. The relations between the two army commanders were, unfortunately, not as cordial as they should have been. Buell was four years older than Grant and had far greater military experience. He had won a Brevet Majority in the Mexican War, and had held many staff appointments in the Regular Army. He was a competent and meticulous officer and a strict disciplinarian. Buell had previously as a Brigadier-General ranked senior to Grant, but Grant's immediate promotion after Fort Donelson had now made him by five weeks senior to Buell, who resented taking orders from one of whom he did not quite approve. Grant and Buell have each left very different accounts of the battle of Shiloh, and it is evident that Buell considered that Grant's army had got itself into a thorough mess, and that he was not anxious to have his own mixed up with it. However, it was arranged between them that Nelson's division should cross the river and reinforce Grant's left wing, which was now under extreme pressure.

The battle raged fiercely all day, the Union left flank being gradually pressed back to the bluff above Pittsburg Landing, which was the main Confederate objective. Sherman's division on the Union right was driven back beyond Tillman's Creek, but held on to the ridge north of it which covered the vital bridge across Snake Creek, by which Lew Wallace's division was expected to arrive at any minute. In the centre there was desperate fighting round the salient known as the 'Hornet's Nest', where the divisions of William Wallace and Prentiss were outflanked and virtually surrounded. About 5 p.m. Prentiss, with more than 2,000 of his men, was forced to surrender, and Wallace was mortally wounded. Hurlbut extended his right to fill the gap, and the timely arrival of Colonel Jacob Ammen's brigade of Nelson's division, which had now crossed the river, saved the situation and the left flank held. On the bluff covering Pittsburg Landing, Grant's Chief of Staff, Colonel Joseph Dana Webster, an artillery officer, brought ten field batteries into action to defend this key point. The two Union gunboats, 'Tyler' and 'Lexington', also gave artillery support from the river, though it was largely ineffective owing to the elevation of the bluffs.

Although the Confederates had gained much ground, it was only at the cost of shattering losses, most of the firing having been at point-blank range. Their Commander-in-Chief, *Johnston*, had fallen, mortally wounded early in the afternoon while, rather unnecessarily, leading one of his brigades into action. The command then devolved on *Beauregard*. Towards nightfall the battle ground to a standstill, both sides being completely exhausted. The Confederates had now lost their chance of a resounding victory. They had committed all their troops from the start in a frontal assault without retaining any reserves. They had suffered heavy casualties in launching repeated attacks on the 'Hornet's Nest', so stoutly defended by Prentiss and Wallace, instead of working round the Union left flank near the river. As dusk fell, *Beauregard* ordered his troops to break off the fight and bivouac on the ground won.

The tide had now turned in favour of the Union. Lew Wallace's division arrived after dark, to reinforce the right flank, having wasted much time by taking an unnecessarily long route. The remainder of Nelson's division crossed the river to reinforce the left flank, and during the night Buell's three other divisions, under Crittenden, Wood and McCook, disembarked at Pittsburg

Landing from Savannah. Grant and Buell now had a considerable numerical superiority over *Beauregard*.

During the night of 6/7 April torrential rain fell, which the Confederates endured with less discomfort, since they were occupying the camps from which they had driven the Union troops. Early on the following morning Grant and Buell separately ordered their divisions to take the offensive; the whole Union line advanced, Grant's four surviving divisions forming the right wing, and Buell's four comparatively fresh ones on the left. The Southerners, now greatly outnumbered, fought stubbornly, but were gradually driven back. By 3 p.m. the Union troops had regained all the ground lost on the previous day. *Beauregard* realized that it was useless to prolong the struggle, as his troops were completely worn out and in considerable disorder. He ordered a retreat to Corinth. There was no pursuit by the Union troops.

Thus ended the battle of Shiloh, one of the fiercest combats of the Civil War. The total Confederate casualties were 10,699, while the Union losses amounted to over 13,000, of which nearly 11,000 were suffered by Grant's Army of the Tennessee and more than 2,000 by Buell's Army of the Cumberland. These figures compare approximately with those for Napoleon's *Grande Armée* and the Russians at the battle of Friedland (14 June 1807).

Controversy has raged during the past century over the leadership displayed by Grant at Shiloh. One could say that more ink has been expended in discussing the pros and cons than all the blood which was shed on the battlefield. Grant and Buell have each left their own personal narratives; Grant's is a modest and fairly factual account, but somewhat evasive with regard to the main charges laid against him. Buell's story, 'Shiloh reviewed',[3] is a more detailed and professional composition, but it was written 23 years after the occurrence of the events, and is unfortunately tainted with personal jealousy and recrimination. He ends his narrative with the following disparaging comment on Grant's conduct of the battle:

> And of Grant himself – is nothing to be said? The record is silent and tradition adverse to any marked influence that he exerted upon the fortune of the day. . . . If he could have done anything in the beginning, he was not on the ground in time. The determining act in the drama was completed by 10 o'clock.

Buell felt strongly that his own army should have been given more credit for winning the battle and for rescuing Grant's army from destruction; he was indignant that Grant appeared to belittle the assistance rendered by the Army of the Cumberland, and he resented that fact that Grant then went on to climb to the top of the military ladder while he himself had to be content with lesser laurels.

Unfortunately, America's greatest military historian, Dr. John Codman

3. *Battles and Leaders*, 1, 486–536.

Ropes, has been largely influenced by Buell's biased narrative. His verdict is as follows:

> In regard to General Grant's management in this severe action, it is to be noted that he at no time made any attempt to unite the disconnected portions of his army and establish a line of battle. It may be that this could not have been effected. . . . But it is certain that General Grant made no effort to accomplish any such result. In fact, he can hardly be said to have undertaken to perform on this day the functions of a commander of an army. He left the division-commanders entirely to themselves.[4]

This is a grossly erroneous judgment, easy enough to make from the arm-chair of an academic historian who has never been faced with the task of piecing together the disintegrated fragments of a broken battle-front. Grant's situation was similar to that with which General Sir Hubert Gough was confronted on 18 March 1918. All the evidence shows that, throughout the battle, Grant visited in turn each of his divisional commanders, and inspired them with his own fierce determination to resist the enemy's onslaught. He also supervised their replenishment with ammunition, organized artillery support and endeavoured to stem the rearward rush of thousands of fugitives from the front. Here is Grant's account of the condition of his troops:

> Three of the five divisions engaged on Sunday were entirely raw, and many of the men had only received their arms on the way from their States to the field. Many of them had arrived but a day or two before, and were hardly able to load their muskets according to the manual. Their officers were equally ignorant of their duties. Under these circumstances it is not astonishing that many of the regiments broke at the first fire. In two cases, as I now remember, colonels led their regiments from the field on first hearing the whistle of the enemy's bullets. In these cases the colonels were constitutional cowards, unfit for any military position; but not so the officers and men led out of danger by them.[5]

That Grant succeeded in restoring confidence and the will to resist amid these scenes of panic and disorder is sufficient evidence of his powers of leadership. At no moment did he relax his efforts; as he reports:

> During the whole of Sunday I was continuously engaged in passing from one part of the field to another, giving directions to division commanders.

Besides, all this was accomplished in spite of continuous physical pain. On the evening of 4 April, while he was riding back to Pittsburg Landing in the dark after visiting his divisions, his horse had fallen on the muddy track, pinning him to the ground and severely crushing his leg; it was like Massena's mishap on the eve of Wagram. Grant records of the night of the 6th/7th:

> My ankle was so much swollen from the fall of my horse the Friday night preceding, and the bruise so painful, that I could get no rest.

4. *Ropes*, ii, 82–3.
5. *Grant*, i, 342.

79

There was nothing more that Grant could have done in the heat of the conflict, as he had no reserve troops under his hand with which to influence the battle. He did, in fact, send two staff officers to hasten the approach of Lew Wallace who, like d'Erlon between Quatre Bras and Ligny, was wandering several miles away to the west of the battlefield. Wallace's absence was due partly to his mistaken idea of the direction from which he heard gun-fire, partly perhaps to imprecise verbal orders given to him by Grant earlier in the day at Crump's Landing. One can find little to criticize in Grant's handling of the battle once it had started. His absence from the battlefield when the Confederate attack was first launched was unfortunate, but was due to his anxiety to meet Buell at the earliest possible moment in order to plan concerted action.

We must, however, condemn Grant's lack of foresight in his initial disposition of his troops. Halleck was partly to blame for what happened, since he was still at St. Louis, more than 300 miles away, too far to exercise proper control of his army commanders. He had ordered Grant to disembark at Savannah, entrench himself there and await the arrival of Buell; after that their combined forces were presumably to advance on Corinth, but no precise orders were given to that effect. Instead, Grant had pushed all six of his divisions across the broad Tennessee River, where five of them were peacefully encamped on a site reported by Sherman to be easily defensible. This, Grant considered, would make a suitable springboard for the advance on Corinth, but he made no effort to visit the front line, or to see that the forward divisions were patrolling the ground ahead of them, although the enemy was known to have 40,000 men only 20 miles away. Grant knew also that three of his divisions were newly recruited and badly trained, yet two of these were posted in closest proximity to the enemy. Grant further omitted to nominate McClernand, his senior divisional commander, to assume command of the army when he himself was absent at Savannah, eight miles away from Pittsburg Landing.

And what of Grant's cavalry? We hear nothing about their employment before the battle, when they should have been sent forward to reconnoitre to the south-west, where the Confederate cavalry were patrolling actively. Of their use during the action Grant has only this to say:

The nature of this battle was such that cavalry could not be used in front; I therefore formed ours into line in rear, to stop stragglers, of whom there were many.[6]

No mention is made of using the cavalry to follow up the beaten enemy on the evening of 7 April, although Grant admits that:

An immediate pursuit must have resulted in the capture of a considerable number of prisoners and probably some guns.

6. *Grant*, I, 343–4.

Grant has given us the following excuse for his neglect to order a pursuit:

> I wanted to pursue, but had not the heart to order the men who had fought desperately for two days, lying in the mud and rain whenever not fighting, and I did not feel disposed to positively order Buell, or any part of his command, to pursue. Although the senior in rank at the time, I had been so only a few weeks.[7]

Both these excuses are feeble ones. The Confederate troops had also been fighting desperately and had been lying in the mud and rain. A vigorous pursuit by the fresh troops of Lew Wallace and by Buell's comparatively fresh army would have turned the Confederate retreat into a disastrous rout. Buell, like Blücher at Waterloo, could have offered to carry out the pursuit, leaving Grant's exhausted divisions to rest and recuperate. But Buell was no Blücher. He evades the issue by putting the responsibility on to Grant's shoulders in the following words:

> If General Grant meant to imply that I was responsible that the pursuit was not made, I might perhaps answer that it is always to be expected that the chief officer in command will determine the course to be pursued at such a juncture, when he is immediately upon the ground.[8]

The personal relations between these two army commanders were, as we have seen, far from cordial. Grant, by the chance of promotion, had recently acquired five weeks' seniority over Buell, whom he still regarded as his superior in military knowledge and experience, and hesitated to give him a direct order which might not have been readily obeyed. Doubtless Grant showed too much delicacy in this matter, and should have exerted his authority more positively, but his nature was modest and unassuming, whereas Buell made no attempt to conceal his disapproval of their relative status. For instance, Buell thus describes his attitude towards Grant at the close of the first day's fighting:

> I had had no consultation with General Grant, and knew nothing of his purpose. I presumed that we should be in accord, but I had been only a few hours within the limits of his authority, and I did not look on him as my commander, though I would have zealously obeyed his orders.[9]

Grant may well have hesitated to issue orders to such an unwilling collaborator.

The battle of Shiloh had produced many lessons, both in the exercise of command and in the conduct of operations.

7. *Grant*, I, 354-5.
8. *Battles and Leaders*, I, 533-4.
9. *ibid.*, I, 519.

XII

Further Frustration after Shiloh
April–June 1862

On the same day that *Beauregard* retreated to Corinth after his defeat by Grant and Buell on the blood-stained field of Shiloh, Halleck's right wing, under Major-General John Pope, won an important but bloodless victory on the banks of the Mississippi, the capture of the strongly fortified Island No. 10, just south of New Madrid, where the Confederate garrison of 7,000 men with 160 guns was forced to surrender. This success was due not so much to the leadership of Pope as to the gallantry of Commander Henry Walke of the U.S. Navy, whose two gunboats ran the gauntlet of the shore batteries and cleared the way for the crossing of Pope's divisions. The capture of Island No. 10 opened up America's greatest waterway to the southward advance of the Union forces.

Three weeks later the U.S. Navy, thanks to the resourceful daring of Flag-Officer David Glasgow Farragut, won another striking victory for the Union by the capture of New Orleans, which opened up vast possibilities for future offensive operations in the western theatre. New Orleans, with its population of 170,000, was the largest city of the Confederacy and the most important seaport remaining to the South. Lying 110 miles up the Mississippi from its mouth, New Orleans gave the Union a secure base for an advance up river to join forces with Halleck's army moving down stream. As Lincoln said at the time:

> The Mississippi is the backbone of the Rebellion; it is the key to the whole situation. But we must have troops enough not only to hold New Orleans, but to proceed at once toward Vicksburg, which is the key to all that country watered by the Mississippi and its tributaries. If the Confederates once fortify the neighboring hills, they will be able to hold that point for an indefinite time, and it will require a large force to dislodge them.

Lincoln's wise words outlined the objective of the whole Union strategy in the western theatre. Had Halleck possessed any real military talent, he would have marched directly to Corinth and then turned westward to capture Vicks-burg, 90 miles away.

After the twin and simultaneous victories of Shiloh and Island No. 10, Halleck at last moved his headquarters southward and established himself at Pittsburg Landing on 11 April, to assume personal command of his army of over 100,000 men, which he now proceeded to reorganize. Although Grant, who had borne the brunt of the Shiloh battle, was the senior commander serving under him, Halleck now broke up his command and removed Grant from any executive functions. The veteran divisions of McClernand and Lew Wallace, which had fought at Fort Donelson and Shiloh, were withdrawn into reserve and placed under McClernand's command. Grant's other divisions were handed over to Major-General George Henry Thomas, the victor of Mill Springs, formerly serving under Buell, Thomas now being given command of the right wing of the army. Buell was given command of the centre, with his four remaining divisions, while Pope, who arrived on 21 April from Island No. 10, formed the left wing at Hamburg, five miles south of Pittsburg Land-ing. These three forces were now designated as army corps; Grant was thus squeezed out of the command structure, being given the nominal status of Second-in-Command, but with no responsibility, for he was never even con-sulted by Halleck.

It is difficult to fathom the motive underlying Halleck's treatment of Grant at this juncture. It may have been personal jealousy; on the other hand, Halleck may have genuinely held a poor opinion of Grant's abilities as a commander, and may have gained the impression that the battle of Shiloh had been won by Buell's efforts rather than by Grant's. Whatever the reason, Halleck's re-organization of the army was a bitter blow to Grant, who, after having been in command of six fighting divisions, now found himself the fifth wheel of the coach. Between these two men there existed a deep mutual antipathy, and they also regarded military problems from widely different angles. Grant felt strongly that, with 100,000 men under command, the Union leader had only to advance swiftly southward in pursuit of the defeated *Beauregard* and seize the key-point of Corinth, the main objective of the campaign, only 20 miles away. Not so the hesitant Halleck; having marshalled his huge army, he delayed his start until 30 April, and then moved cautiously southward, en-trenching his position at the end of each day's march.

Halleck took four weeks to cover the 20 miles to Corinth. By that time *Beauregard* had been reinforced by Major-General *Earl Van Dorn's* corps, which increased his strength to 50,000, and he threw up strong entrenchments for the defence of Corinth. Realizing, however, that he was heavily outnum-bered, he abandoned Corinth on 29 May, after removing all his stores and equipment, and slipped away unmolested to Tupelo (Miss), 50 miles further south, based on the Mobile and Ohio Railroad. *Beauregard's* health had been failing for some weeks, and President *Davis*, greatly disappointed by the loss of Corinth, replaced him on 27 June by Major-General *Braxton Bragg*.

The loss of Corinth was a severe blow to the fortunes of the Confederates. Not only did it involve the abandonment of the important Memphis and Ohio Railroad, but it forced them to evacuate Fort Pillow, their most northerly barrier fort on the Mississippi after the capture of Island No. 10. This enabled the Union river flotilla to move down stream as far as Memphis, an important river port and railway junction. Flag-Officer Foote had been forced to retire after the severe wound which he had received at Fort Donelson, and the Union river fleet was now commanded by Commodore Charles Henry Davis. The Union gunboats quickly overpowered the less heavily armed Confederate ones, only one of which escaped destruction, and Davis took possession of Memphis on 6 June. The river was now open as far down as Vicksburg, 400 miles farther south, which Farragut, coming up from New Orleans, had already reached on 18 May. Thus, for the first time, the whole length of the Mississippi, from St. Louis to the Gulf of Mexico, was dominated by the Union navy.

The occupation of Corinth and the capture of Memphis should have enabled the Union Commander-in-Chief to advance rapidly on Vicksburg and finish the campaign in the western theatre. That would have brought the war to an end at least a year earlier. But there was nothing Napoleonic in Halleck's make-up, and he continued to sit immobile at Corinth, contenting himself with the repair of roads and railways, a more important objective to his engineer's mind than the destruction of the enemy's forces. He instructed Pope, who was cautiously following *Beauregard* southward, not to risk an engagement, saying: 'I think the enemy will continue his retreat, which is all I desire.' President Lincoln was still anxious to liberate the pro-Union population of eastern Tennessee so, under pressure from Washington, on 10 June Halleck sent Buell with 30,000 men eastward toward Chattanooga, the important railway centre in the Cumberland Mountains, which was still in Confederate hands.

Halleck's inaction during and after the advance to Corinth infuriated Grant who, besides his embitterment at his own impotent position, hated to see such golden opportunities being thrown away. He has recorded his exasperation as follows:

For myself I was little more than an observer. Orders were sent direct to the right wing or reserve, ignoring me, and advances were made from one line of intrenchments to another without notifying me. My position was so embarrassing in fact that I made several applications during the siege [of Corinth] to be relieved. . . . I had suggested to the commanding general that I thought if he would move the Army of the Mississippi at night, by the rear of the centre and right, ready to advance at daylight, Pope would find no natural obstacle in his front and, I believed, no serious artificial one. The ground, or works, occupied by our left could be held by a thin picket line, owing to the stream and swamp in front. To the right the troops would have a dry ridge to march over. I was silenced so quickly that I felt that possibly I had suggested an unmilitary movement. . . . After the capture of Corinth Buell was sent east, following the line of the Memphis and Charleston Railroad. This he was ordered to repair as he advanced – only to have it destroyed by small guerrilla bands or other troops as soon as he was out of the way. If he had been sent directly to Chattanooga as rapidly as he could march, ... he could have arrived with but little fighting, and would have saved much of the loss of life which was afterwards incurred in gaining Chattanooga.[1]

An interesting sidelight on Grant's feelings of frustration is given by the following extract from the Memoirs of Sherman who was then serving under Thomas, the right wing commander:

A short time before leaving Corinth I rode from my camp to General Halleck's headquarters ... where we sat and gossiped for some time, when he mentioned to me casually that General Grant was going away the next morning. I inquired the cause, and he said that he did not know, but that Grant had applied for a thirty days' leave, which had been given him. Of course we all knew that he was chafing under the slights of his anomalous position, and I determined to see him on my way back. ... I found him seated on a camp-stool, with papers on a rude camp-table; he seemed to be assorting letters, and tying them up with red tape into convenient bundles. I inquired if it were true that he was going away. He said, 'Yes.' I then inquired the reason, and he said: 'Sherman, you know. You know that I am in the way here. I have stood it as long as I can, and can endure it no longer.' ... I then begged him to stay. I argued with him that ... if he remained, some happy accident might restore him to favor and his true place. ... Very soon after this ... I received a note from him, saying that he had reconsidered his intention, and would remain.[2]

The 'happy accident' occurred shortly after. On 11 July Grant, who was then at Memphis, received a telegram from Halleck, ordering him to report immediately at Department headquarters at Corinth and take over command there. Grant did so, and found that Halleck had been called to Washington to take over the supreme command of all the Union armies. Halleck left Corinth on the 17th, leaving Grant, as next senior in rank, to command the Armies of the Mississippi and the Tennessee, but with no other instructions.

The sudden transfer of Halleck to Washington resulted from the series of reverses suffered by the Army of the Potomac in the eastern theatre. It will be remembered that on 11 March President Lincoln had personally taken over direct comand of the Union forces, and had sent McClellan, the previous Commander-in-Chief, to command the Army of the Potomac. McClellan, however, bungled the subsequent campaign in the Richmond Peninsula, and during May and June *Stonewall Jackson* in the Shenandoah Valley, by brilliant tactical manœuvre, had defeated in turn all the Union leaders sent to oppose him. Lincoln then realized that his command structure was faulty. On 26 June he created a new Army of Virginia under Pope, withdrawn from the western theatre, to deal with the Shenandoah Valley and the protection of Washington, leaving McClellan with the Army of the Potomac to handle the operations against Richmond. Finding the control of so many armies too

1. *Grant*, 1, 377–84.
2. *Sherman*, 1, 282.

burdensome on top of his political responsibilities, on 11 July Lincoln summoned Halleck, the senior officer in the western theatre, to take over the supreme command. Lincoln was right enough to hand over the duties of Commander-in-Chief to a professional soldier, but again he chose the wrong man for the post.

Thus, fortuitously, Grant found himself the senior commanding General in the western theatre. It was certainly not due to any recommendation on the part of Halleck. After Fort Donelson and Shiloh, however, Lincoln was beginning to appreciate Grant's fighting qualities. When Edwin McMasters Stanton, his Secretary of War, laid before him a report alleging Grant's unsuitability for high command, all the President said was: 'I cannot spare this man – he fights.'

XIII

Army Commander in the West
July–October 1862

(See Map 19 at end of book)

On Halleck's promotion to the chief command in Washington, Grant was left as senior army commander in the western theatre, although the area of his command now only covered the valleys of the Mississippi and the Tennessee. A month before Halleck's transfer, Buell's Army of the Cumberland (also referred to as the Army of the Ohio), 25,000 strong, had been diverted eastward to capture the important railway junction at Chattanooga, 200 miles east of Corinth, which was held by the Confederate commander, *Edmund Kirby Smith*, with some 2,000 men detached from his main body at Knoxville. Halleck had dispatched Buell eastwards on 10 June in accordance with Lincoln's policy of directing the strategic *Schwerpunkt* of operations in the western theatre towards East Tennessee in order to liberate the pro-Union population of that region. This was a purely political objective with no military potential value, the only worthwhile strategic objective in that area being Chattanooga itself, which was a vital link in the Confederate lines of communication; any further advance into the Alleghenies would have involved a dangerous dispersal of force.

Thus Buell's command was entirely divorced from Grant's, both commanders taking their orders directly from Washington. Owing to Lincoln's obsession with East Tennessee, the Mississippi Valley was for the time being relegated to the status of a secondary theatre, although that waterway offered the most direct approach to the heart of the Confederacy. Halleck's mind, however, was completely sterile as regards strategic conception, and the only directive which Grant could extract from him was to keep his forces concentrated and be ready to reinforce Buell. Grant's last order from Halleck was to dispatch G. H. Thomas's division of 6,000 to join Buell; in August he was ordered to send two more divisions to Buell (Eleazer A. Paine and Robert B. Mitchell) and in September yet another (Gordon Granger), so that by mid-September the army of 64,000 which he had taken over from Halleck had been whittled down to 46,000, while Buell's had been increased to over 50,000. Nor could Grant's army be readily concentrated for any offensive action. He was now operating in hostile territory; intelligence of the enemy's movements was diffi-cult to obtain, and a large portion of his troops had to be employed in guarding the lines of communication. As the Mississippi and Tennessee Rivers were now at their lowest level, they could only be navigated by shallow-draught steamers, so that the bulk of his army's supplies had to be forwarded by rail, and the railways were being constantly sabotaged by Confederate guerrilla raiders. The important railhead at Corinth was still practically in the front line, so Grant moved his headquarters back to Jackson (Tenn) on the Colum-bus–Corinth railway. Profiting by the lesson learnt at Shiloh, he protected Corinth with a strongly entrenched perimeter, a precaution which was shortly to prove its value.

Grant's campaign in north-eastern Mississippi in the fall of 1862 has received comparatively little attention by military historians, but these operations are worthy of detailed study as they were the first which he undertook as an inde-pendent army commander. In the course of them we see his powers of leadership rapidly developing, based on his experiences at Belmont, Fort Donelson and Shiloh. But to see this campaign in its proper perspective we must first review the military situation in the eastern theatre and also follow the operations of Buell's Army of the Ohio on Grant's immediate left flank.

During the early summer of 1862 the Union forces in Virginia had achieved no positive results. President Lincoln had himself in March assumed supreme command of the Union forces, after sending McClellan to command the Army of the Potomac, but McClellan had proved a disappointment as an army com-mander and Lincoln himself said that he 'had the slows'. McClellan's hesitating and dilatory tactics certainly failed to make any progress against the much weaker Confederate forces opposed to him in the Yorktown Peninsula and in front of Richmond, while *Stonewall Jackson*'s skilful manœuvring in the Shenandoah Valley repeatedly outwitted his opponents. The 'Seven Days' Battles' east of Richmond at the end of June had led to no positive results in spite of 16,000 Union casualties, and in the second Battle of Bull Run at the end of August *Lee* out-manœuvred the greatly superior forces of McClellan and Pope, inflicting 14,500 casualties on the Union troops. *Lee* followed up this success in early September by crossing the Potomac with 55,000 men and in-vading Maryland, thus offering an imminent threat to Washington.

Meanwhile, west of the Alleghenies, Buell's Army of the Ohio had also been out-manœuvred by the Confederates and driven back on the defensive. When *Braxton Bragg* took over command from *Beauregard* at the end of June, he at once determined to profit by the wide dispersal of the Union forces con-fronting him and passed to the offensive. Leaving *Earl Van Dorn* with 16,000 men and *Sterling Price* with another 16,000 to threaten Grant's key position at Corinth, *Bragg* moved his main body (35,000) back by rail from Tupelo

(Miss) to Mobile (Ala) and thence north by the Central Georgia Railroad to Chattanooga (Tenn), which he reached on 29 July, thus forestalling Buell who was advancing slowly eastward toward the same objective.

The slowness of Buell's advance on Chattanooga was due partly to his habitual caution and lack of energy, partly to the instructions given him by Halleck. Although the best line of communication for the supply of Buell's army was the railway running south from Louisville (Ky) through Nashville and Murfreesboro (Tenn), Halleck had insisted on his using the railway running eastward from Memphis via Corinth (Miss) to Decatur (Ala). This ran parallel to the enemy's front and in fact was almost in the front line, and was therefore subject to constant interruption by Confederate raids, which greatly retarded Buell's progress and forced him to disperse his divisions in order to protect his line of communication. The tardiness of Buell's advance left the road wide open for *Bragg*'s invasion of Kentucky, which the Confederates hoped to detach from the Union. Seizing the initiative, *Bragg* pushed north from Chattanooga during the month of August, preceded by the cavalry regiments of *John H. Morgan* and *Nathan B. Forrest*, who raided far and wide into Kentucky. Crossing the Cumberland River unopposed at Carthage and Gainesville, *Bragg* captured Munfordville by the middle of September, thus cutting Buell off from his base at Louisville on the Ohio. Meanwhile, further east, *Kirby Smith* with a column of 10,000 men advanced north on a parallel course from Knoxville on the upper Tennessee. On 30 August he captured Lexington and pushed on to Frankfort, the State capital of Kentucky, where *Bragg* attempted to set up a Confederate Legislature. Buell's left flank was thus enveloped, and he was forced to fall back on his base at Louisville.

We can now turn back to Grant's army in northern Mississippi, where his position had become somewhat precarious owing to Buell's retreat. As Grant has recorded in his Memoirs:

> The most anxious period of the war, to me, was during the time the Army of the Tennessee was guarding the territory acquired by the fall of Corinth and Memphis and before I was sufficiently reinforced to take the offensive. The enemy also had cavalry operating in our rear, making it necessary to guard every point of the railway back to Columbus, on the security of which we were dependent for all our supplies.[1]

Before leaving Corinth, Halleck had dispatched Lew Wallace's division westward across the Mississippi into Arkansas. Grant had now established his headquarters at Jackson (Tenn), where he had a reserve of 6,000 men under McClernand, and detachments amounting to 9,000, including Hurlbut's division, guarding the railway back to Columbus. His remaining forces were organized in three mobile groups: the right wing under Sherman (7,000) was at Memphis, guarding the Mississippi waterway against *Van Dorn*'s stronger

1. *Grant*, I, 395.

corps between Vicksburg and Holly Springs; the centre under Edward Otho Cresap Ord (8,000) was distributed between Humboldt, Jackson and Bolivar, while the left wing (9,000) at Corinth was commanded by William Starke Rosecrans, who had taken over from Pope on the latter's transfer to an army command in the eastern theatre.

Rosecrans, who was now serving under Grant for the first time, commanded the largest striking force in his army. Three years older than Grant, Rosecrans had graduated from West Point a year earlier and, like Halleck, had been commissioned in the U.S. Engineers. In the following year he was appointed Assistant Instructor in Fortification at West Point and thus missed the Mexican War. In 1854, like Grant, he resigned from the army and went into business at Cincinnati; in June 1861 he was promoted Brigadier-General in the Regular Army. Rosecrans seems to have had an inflated view of his own abilities and resented taking orders from Grant, so that trouble soon arose between them.

In early September Grant's key position at Corinth was threatened by the two Confederate corps of *Earl Van Dorn* and *Sterling Price*, each some 16,000 strong. *Van Dorn* was watching the Lower Mississippi with his headquarters at Holly Springs, 50 miles west-south-west of Corinth, while *Price* was concentrated at Tupelo, the same distance due south of Corinth. Were these two to join forces, they would greatly outnumber the mobile troops at Grant's disposal, namely those under Rosecrans and Ord, some 17,000 in all, for Sherman on the right wing could not leave Memphis unguarded, and the remainder of Grant's troops were tied down to the protection of his lines of communication.

Bragg's successful drive during August northward from Chattanooga had now turned Buell's left flank; in order to prevent Grant from detaching any more troops to reinforce Buell, *Bragg* had ordered *Van Dorn* and *Price* to make a combined attack on Corinth. *Van Dorn* at first demurred, as he felt that his primary objective was to protect the Mississippi waterway. On 1 September *Bragg* ordered *Price* at Tupelo to launch an immediate attack against Grant as Buell was in full retreat to Nashville. *Price* consequently advanced northward through Baldwyn with his two divisions numbering 14,000 men. On 14 September his leading division, commanded by *Henry Little*, occupied the little village of Iuka on the Memphis and Charleston Railroad, 25 miles south-east of Corinth. The Union garrison consisted of the 8th Wisconsin Regiment under Colonel R. C. Murphy, who abandoned Iuka and all the military stores there without a fight, much to Grant's indignation. Grant realized that he must act at once to crush *Price* before he could be reinforced by *Van Dorn*. His plan was to annihilate *Price* with a pincer movement, by Rosecrans advancing through Jacinto from the south-west, while Ord converged on Iuka from the north-west. Rosecrans had two divisions numbering 9,000, while Ord's force numbered 8,000, so when combined they would outnumber *Price*. It was a sound plan, but,

> The best-laid schemes o' mice an' men
> Gang aft a-gley,

either owing to adverse weather conditions or the ineptitude of subordinates, as Wellington had experienced at Sabugal half a century earlier.

On the morning of 18 September Ord's force entrained at Corinth and detrained at Burnsville, 18 miles to the east down the railway, and Grant moved his tactical headquarters from Corinth to Burnsville, from which place he could maintain touch with his two force commanders by mounted dispatch riders. Ord's divisions then marched across country to an assembly position three miles north of Iuka, from which he was to attack the village at dawn the next day, in conjunction with Rosecrans's simultaneous attack from the south, which was to be delivered along the Fulton–Iuka road, so as to block the enemy's line of retreat.

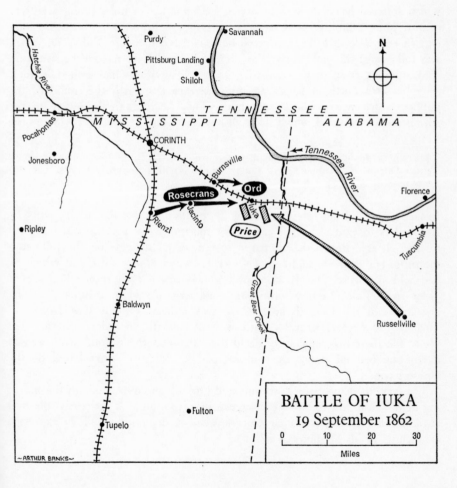

BATTLE OF IUKA
19 September 1862

0   10   20   30
Miles

~ARTHUR BANKS~

After midnight on the 18/19 September Grant was greatly disappointed at receiving a message from Rosecrans saying that his column had been delayed, but he hoped to reach Iuka by 2 p.m. on the 19th. Grant, therefore, immediately instructed Ord to cancel his dawn attack and to wait until he heard the sound of gunfire from the south, when he would attack in concert with Rosecrans. The whole plan, however, now miscarried. Instead of turning north along the Fulton–Iuka road, the head of Rosecrans's column turned north two miles short of it. About 4 p.m. his leading division, commanded by Charles Smith Hamilton, encountered the Confederate pickets two miles south-west of Iuka, and heavy firing broke out. The Confederate commander, *Henry Little*, deployed his division and galloped to the front, but was shot dead. *Price* himself then came up and took command. As he reported in his dispatch: 'The fight began, and was waged with a severity I have never seen surpassed.' The Confederates advanced southward, enveloping the head of Hamilton's column, which suffered heavily and was driven back for half a mile, losing a battery of nine guns. Hamilton sent repeated messages to Rosecrans, who was a long way in rear, asking to be reinforced by David Sloan Stanley's division which was following; this only arrived as night fell, too late to restore the situation.

Meanwhile, from dawn onwards, Ord's two divisions had waited in their assembly area north of Iuka, straining their ears to catch the sound of the gunfire which was to mark zero hour. They heard nothing, owing to the strong north-east wind which blew all day. As Grant records in his Memoirs:

> The wind was still blowing hard and in the wrong direction to transmit sound towards either Ord or me. Neither he nor I nor any one in either command heard a gun that was fired upon the battlefield.[2]

In fact Grant did not receive news of the battle until late that night, when he sent orders to Ord to attack early next morning, and rode forward himself to take charge. Both sides prepared to renew the struggle on the following morning, and *Price* brought up *Dabney Herndon Maury*'s division which he had held in reserve. Shortly after midnight, however, *Price* received an urgent order from *Van Dorn*, whom *Bragg* had now placed in command of the operations in the Corinth area. *Price* was ordered to join *Van Dorn* immediately at Ripley, 30 miles south-west of Corinth, in order to attack that place. He therefore reluctantly decided to abandon the ground won, and at dawn marched off down the Fulton road to Baldwyn, unmolested by the Union troops.

The combined forces of Rosecrans and Ord advanced on Iuka on the morning of the 20th, but found the place evacuated. Grant was extremely annoyed at the indifferent way in which Rosecrans had carried out his task; he expressed his feelings in his Memoirs as follows:

2. *Grant*, I, 412.

Rosecrans, however, had put no troops on the Fulton road, and the enemy had taken advantage of this neglect and retreated by that road during the night. Word was soon brought to me that our troops were in Iuka. I immediately rode into town and found that the enemy was not being pursued even by the cavalry. I ordered pursuit by the whole of Rosecrans' command and went on with him a few miles in person. He followed only a few miles after I left him and then went into camp, and the pursuit was continued no further. I was disappointed at the result of the battle of Iuka – but I had so high an opinion of General Rosecrans that I found no fault at the time.[3]

Grant's plan to crush *Price* at Iuka was a complete failure, for which the blame must largely be laid on Rosecrans. Firstly, he was slow in carrying out his approach march from Jacinto; he only had 18 miles to march, but reached his assembly area ten hours late. He also took the wrong approach road, leaving the Iuka–Fulton road open for the enemy's withdrawal. Rosecrans marched in rear of his leading division instead of at its head, so failed to deploy his second division to outflank *Price*'s position. Finally, he failed to carry out an energetic pursuit. Admittedly, the ground was swampy, even in September, and movement off the roads was difficult, but Rosecrans was familiar with the local topography, as his headquarters had previously been at Iuka, and he had had a survey made of the neighbourhood. As Grant pointed out:

He was personally familiar with the ground, so that I deferred very much to him in my plans for the approach.[4]

Iuka, in fact, was a disappointing battle; Rosecrans's casualties were 790, while the Confederates lost about 700, including the sick and wounded whom they were forced to leave behind. *Price* marched south to Baldwyn and then west to Ripley, where on 28 September he joined forces with *Van Dorn*.

After the indecisive battle of Iuka Grant returned to his main headquarters at Jackson (Tenn), 58 miles north of Corinth, leaving the latter railway junction to be held by Rosecrans, with four divisions under his command (McKean, Davies, Stanley and Hamilton), in all 18,500 men, including 2,500 cavalry. But Grant also had another important point to protect, Bolivar on the Tennessee and Ohio Railroad, 40 miles north-west of Corinth, which was attacked on 22 September by Confederate cavalry who damaged the railway. To protect that railhead Grant posted there Hurlbut's division (6,500), while retaining in reserve at Jackson the division of James Birdseye McPherson, who had previously been his Chief Engineer. Sherman's 7,000 men could not be removed from the key point of Memphis on the Mississippi, which was an essential river base for any further southward advance.

Van Dorn, who had been joined by *Price* at *Ripley* on 28 September, now had 22,000 men under command, with good rearward lines of communication, both by rail and river. He was therefore in a favourable position to strike with

3. *Grant*, I, 413.
4. *ibid.*, I, 408.

superior force at either of the three objectives, Memphis, Bolivar or Corinth. He discarded Memphis, owing to the Union preponderance in gunboats; he also rejected Bolivar, as the Hatchie River afforded the Union troops a strong defensive line. He therefore decided to attack Corinth, in the hope of driving Rosecrans back to the Tennessee River and cutting him off from Grant; he could then cross the Tennessee himself and join *Bragg* in the envelopment of Buell's army.

Having decided on this ambitious plan, *Van Dorn* moved rapidly on Corinth. He advanced northward from Ripley on 29 September, and on 2 October occupied Pocahontas on the Memphis and Charleston Railroad, thus placing himself half-way between Bolivar and Corinth and leaving Grant in the dark as to his objective. *Van Dorn* then turned eastward along the railway, where he was met by Rosecrans's cavalry patrols. Rosecrans sent out a brigade of McKean's division to make contact with the enemy, and with the remainder of his force manned the outer ring of old Confederate trenches which had been constructed by *Beauregard* earlier in the year to resist Halleck's advance, about three miles distant from Corinth on the north and north-east.

The Confederate attack was launched at 10 a.m. on 3 October against the north-west sector of the Corinth defences by all three divisions in line, commanded by *Mansfield Lovell, Dabney Maury* and *Louis Hébert*. It was pressed home with such vigour that the Union troops, though resisting stubbornly, were driven out of their forward entrenchments and forced back for two miles to the newer line of works close to Corinth which Grant had previously ordered Rosecrans to construct. These lines were incomplete, but comprised several strong earthwork redoubts which formed emplacements for heavy artillery, including some 30-pounder Parrott guns and an 8-inch howitzer. Rosecrans had all four of his divisions extended on a two-mile front, with Hamilton and Davies on the right sector north of Corinth, and Stanley and McKean to the west of the Mobile and Ohio Railroad. Fierce fighting continued all day, but the Confederates were unable to pierce the Union line. They had marched ten miles over dusty roads before launching their attack in very hot weather, and they were short of water. Both sides were physically exhausted and night brought an end to the struggle. The opposing lines bivouacked within 600 yards of each other.

Grant, 58 miles away at Jackson, received no news of the battle until late in the evening. He immediately entrained his reserve division, under McPherson, with orders to detrain as near as possible to the scene of action at Corinth. Now that he knew that Corinth was *Van Dorn*'s objective, he ordered Hurlbut at Bolivar to march 25 miles to Pocahontas in order to cut off *Van Dorn*'s retreat. The Confederates would thus be trapped between the three Union forces.

On the morning of the 4th *Van Dorn* and *Price* renewed their attack on the Union lines. The Confederate left wing at first made progress in spite of heavy

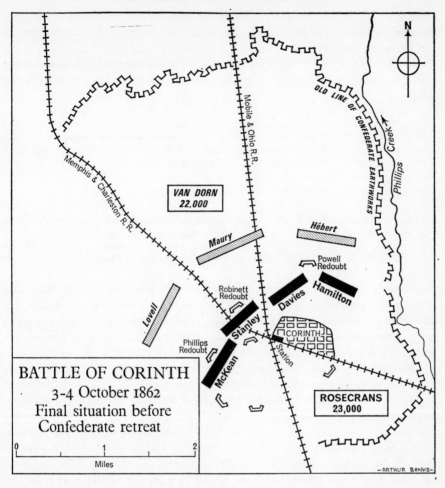

BATTLE OF CORINTH

3-4 October 1862
Final situation before
Confederate retreat

VAN DORN
22,000

ROSECRANS
23,000

artillery fire at close range, and the Powell Redoubt, immediately north of Corinth, was captured. On the right, however, they were less successful, and the Robinett Redoubt, west of the town, withstood a series of fierce assaults. Rosecrans then ordered a counter-attack by a brigade of Hamilton's division on the right flank, and the Powell Redoubt was retaken after a hard struggle. Neither side had any more troops in reserve, and the day was again extremely hot – Rosecrans estimated the shade temperature at 94°. *Van Dorn* realized that his attack had failed, and about 2 p.m. ordered a withdrawal westwards to Pocahontas, only just in time to evade Grant's intended encirclement, for at 4 p.m. McPherson, with five regiments and a field battery, began to detrain north of Corinth.

Both sides had fought with great courage and tenacity; the Confederates, in particular, displayed extreme gallantry in launching repeated assaults against previously entrenched defensive positions, and consequently suffered heavier casualties. Their losses amounted to 4,838 (24 per cent), while those of the Union troops were over 3,000 (17 per cent).

As after the action at Iuka, Rosecrans made no attempt to follow up the enemy's withdrawal, in spite of the following extract from his account of the battle:

> Our pursuit of the enemy was immediate and vigorous, but the darkness of the night and the roughness of the country, covered with woods and thickets, made movement impracticable by night and slow and difficult by day. General McPherson's brigade of fresh troops with a battery was ordered to start at daylight and follow the enemy.[5]

Grant's Memoirs throw a different light on the matter:

> Rosecrans, however, failed to follow up the victory, although I had given specific orders in advance of the battle for him to pursue the moment the enemy was repelled. He did not do so, and I repeated the order after the battle.... Rosecrans did not start in pursuit until the morning of the 5th and then took the wrong road.[6]

Rosecrans's extravagant account of his personal activities during the battle impairs his credibility as a witness. The facts are that *Van Dorn's* retreat started at 2 p.m. on 4 October; McPherson's division reached Corinth at 4 p.m., but the pursuit only began at 6 a.m. on the 5th, so that the Confederates got away with a start of 16 hours.

The retreating Confederates reached the crossing of the Hatchie River near Pocahontas on 5 October, but found their road blocked by Hurlbut's division (6,500), so after a short skirmish they turned south to Ripley and eventually reached Holly Springs on the Mississippi Central Railroad. There now arose a further clash between Rosecrans and his Commander-in-Chief. The former, on reaching Jonesboro on 7 October, heard that his advanced guard had occupied Ripley, already evacuated by the Confederates. Having failed to catch up with *Van Dorn,* Rosecrans now hoped to enhance his reputation by advancing far into enemy territory. Grant, however, felt that the chance of a decisive victory having eluded him, it would be wiser to collect his scattered forces and reorganize his communications in order to move west into the Mississippi Valley. As he has recorded,

> I now regarded the time to accomplish anything by pursuit as past and, after Rosecrans reached Jonesboro, I ordered him to return. He kept on to Ripley, however, and was persistent in wanting to go farther.[7]

On receipt of Grant's order, at midnight on 7/8 October Rosecrans telegraphed back:

5. *Battles and Leaders,* II, 753.
6. *Grant,* I, 417–18.
7. *ibid.,* I, 419.

Yours 8.30 p.m. received. Our troops occupy Ripley. I most deeply dissent from your views as to the manner of pursuing. We have defeated, routed and demoralized the army which holds the Lower Mississippi Valley.... All that is needful is to continue pursuing and whip them.... I beseech you, bend everything to push them while they are broken and hungry, weary and ill-supplied.[8]

Grant exercised exemplary patience in dealing with his refractory subordinate:

I thereupon ordered him to halt and submitted the matter to the general-in-chief, who allowed me to exercise my judgment in the matter, but enquired 'why not pursue?' Upon this I ordered Rosecrans back. Had he gone much farther he would have met a greater force than *Van Dorn* had at Corinth and behind intrenchments or on chosen ground, and the possibilities are he would have lost his army.

Here we see Grant's rapidly developing powers as a leader. At Shiloh, six months earlier, he himself had failed to realize the necessity for field fortification and for the immediate exploitation of success. He had also seen how Halleck, after the occupation of Corinth, had thrown away the chance of decisive victory by a wide dispersal of his forces. He was determined to repeat none of these errors. Rosecrans had now twice let him down by failing to carry out an immediate tactical pursuit; further, Rosecrans had disputed Grant's definite orders, regardless of the logistic and strategic situation, and Grant would have been justified in removing him from his command. Grant, however, was by nature fair-minded and tolerant, 'slow to chide and swift to bless'. He referred the matter to his chief at Washington, and when given complete discretion he stuck to his cautious policy and refused to be seduced by Rosecrans's wild-cat schemes. Rosecrans was neither a good strategist nor a competent tactical leader. During the battle of Corinth he had issued to his hard-pressed divisional commanders a stream of incoherent and unintelligible orders, one of which, to Charles Smith Hamilton, was sent back to him, endorsed on the reverse: 'Respectfully returned. I cannot understand it.'[9]

Grant's later reflections on the battle of Corinth are worth repetition:

This battle was recognized by me as being a decided victory, though not so complete as I had hoped for, nor nearly so complete as I now think was within the easy grasp of the commanding officer at Corinth. Since the war it is known that the result, as it was, was a crushing blow to the enemy, and felt by him much more than it was appreciated at the North. The battle relieved me from any further anxiety for the safety of the territory within my jurisdiction, and soon after receiving reinforcements I suggested to the general-in-chief a forward movement against Vicksburg.[10]

8. *Battles and Leaders*, II, 754-5.
9. *ibid.*, II, 757.
10. *Grant*, I, 420.

XIV

Grant's first Advance on Vicksburg
November 1862–January 1863

Lincoln had from the beginning realized the prime importance of the Mississippi waterway as a strategic corridor leading to the heart of the Confederacy, the control of which would cut off from the eastern States the three important western ones, Arkansas, Louisiana and Texas. He had, however, been deflected from this primary strategic objective by the political lure of liberating the pro-Union population of eastern Tennessee. After the occupation of Corinth at the end of May and the capture of Memphis by Union gunboats in June, there had been nothing to prevent Halleck from moving at once on Vicksburg, the next vital point, which was then only weakly garrisoned and had not yet been strongly fortified. Grant had experienced the frustration of standing idly by during the summer months while Halleck neglected his golden opportunity of seizing this key point on the waterway.

On 16 October, after the battle of Corinth, Lincoln confirmed Grant's appointment as commander of the 'Department of the Tennessee', which in fact did not alter his status as he already commanded all the troops between the Tennessee and Mississippi Rivers. At the same time he removed Buell, somewhat unjustly, from command of the Army of the Ohio, and replaced him by Rosecrans, having over-estimated the latter's performance at the battle of Corinth.

Grant fully realized the necessity for making Vicksburg his next objective. As he has recorded in his Memoirs:

Vicksburg was important to the enemy because it occupied the first high ground coming close to the river below Memphis. From there a railroad runs east, connecting with other roads leading to all points of the Southern States. A railroad also starts from the opposite side of the river, extending west as far as Shreveport, Louisiana. Vicksburg was the only channel . . . connecting the parts of the Confederacy divided by the Mississippi. So long as it was held by the enemy, the free navigation of the river was prevented. Hence its importance.[1]

1. *Grant*, I, 422.

In order to reach Vicksburg, Grant had to lead his army through one of the most impassable regions of the American Continent for military operations. Its geography, and particularly its hydrology, has been well described as follows:

> Of all the great rivers of the world, the Mississippi is perhaps the crookedest. A ship sailing over its waters will often travel a distance of thirty miles to reach a point eight or ten miles distant from its starting-place.... The Mississippi flows through a soft alluvial soil, in which it cuts fresh channels to right or left at the occurrence of the slightest obstacle to its direct progress. It is thus continually leaving its old bed for a new one, so that its long course is marked by countless swampy islands and peninsulas, while on either side may be seen stagnant crescent-shaped lakes, the remnants of its abandoned channels.... The land on either side is intersected by a network of bayous or sluggish streams as crooked as the river itself, and sometimes so long and deep as to be navigable for miles by vessels of considerable size. The strip of country thus creased and channelled in every direction averages some forty miles in width. It is filled with cypress swamps, interspersed with dense forests of cottonwood, sweet gum, magnolia, sycamore and tulip, beneath which the ground is thickly covered with impenetrable masses of creeping vines. In such a country operations with an army are quite impracticable; at no season is it possible for a large body of men to secure a foothold.[2]

Grant appreciated that, before invading this swampy jungle to get at Vicksburg, he must first destroy *Van Dorn*'s field army, now reinforced to 24,000, which had retreated south-westward from Corinth to Holly Springs on the Mississippi Central Railroad, its main line of supply. Grant had also to consider that his own southward advance would extend his line of communications, rendering it more vulnerable to raids by the enemy cavalry. After allowing sufficient troops for its protection he would only have available 30,000 men, which gave him a slender margin of superiority over *Van Dorn*.

Grant's plan of operations was to move down the Mississippi Central Railroad from Grand Junction (half-way between Memphis and Corinth) and establish an advanced base at Holly Springs (Miss), with the object of crushing *Van Dorn*'s mobile force, and then to push on to the important railway junction of Jackson (Miss), where he would be in a position to attack Vicksburg from the east. He would thus avoid the swampy labyrinth of bayous which protected Vicksburg from the north. So far, however, he had received from Washington no strategic directive. On 26 October, therefore, he wrote to Halleck, outlining his plan, and requesting permission to move south:

> You never have suggested to me any plan of operation in this Department.... With small reinforcements at Memphis I think I would be able to move down the Mississippi Central [rail]road and cause the evacuation of Vicksburg and to be able to capture and destroy all the boats in the Yazoo river.

Getting no reply from Washington, Grant on 2 November telegraphed to Halleck:

2. *Fiske*, 179-81.

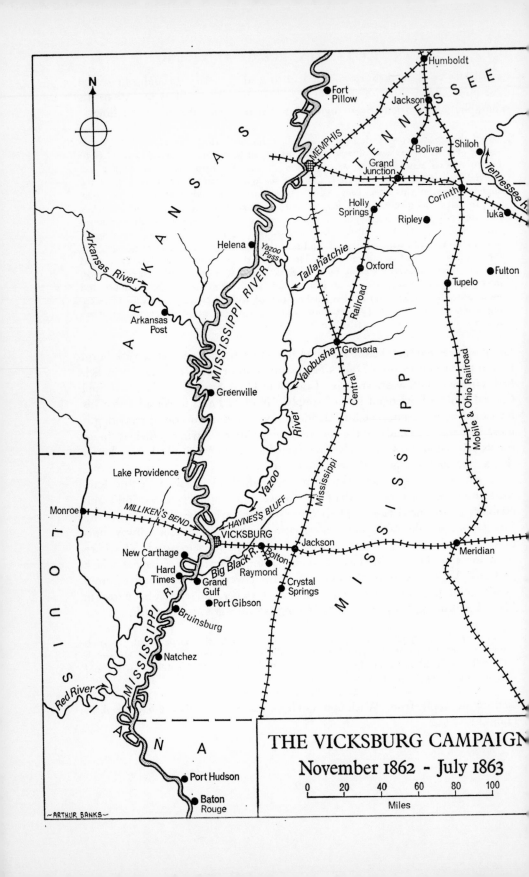

THE VICKSBURG CAMPAIGN
November 1862 - July 1863

I have commenced a movement on Grand Junction, with three divisions from Corinth and two from Bolivar. Will leave here tomorrow, and take command in person. If found practicable, I will go to Holly Springs, and, may be, Grenada, completing railroad and telegraph as I go.

Grant, as we have already seen at Belmont a year earlier, was always ready to act on his own responsibility and take the initiative when left without orders. His army was now organized in three groups: Sherman on the right at Memphis, C. S. Hamilton[3] in the centre at Bolivar and McPherson on the left at Corinth. His troops moved off on the 2nd and Grand Junction was occupied on the 8th, *Van Dorn* falling back 35 miles to the Tallahatchie River, where he entrenched his army in a strong position on the south bank. Grant's cavalry occupied Holly Springs on the 13th, and he decided to move his railhead there from Columbus (Ky), now 150 miles behind him. Sherman's two divisions were ordered to move south from Memphis in the last half of November and join the rest of the army facing the Tallahatchie, where the Confederates were strongly entrenched, having destroyed the railway bridge over the river. Grant, however, sent his cavalry up stream and secured a crossing higher up. Thereupon *Van Dorn* evacuated his position and the Union troops advanced to beyond Oxford, where Grant called a halt to repair the railway and reorganize his line of supply.

Important changes had now been made in the Confederate higher command. Disappointed by *Van Dorn*'s defeat at Corinth, on 14 October *Jefferson Davis* had placed *John Clifford Pemberton* in command of the troops under *Van Dorn* and *Price* in the Mississippi area, and on 24 November he made *Joseph Eggleston Johnston* Commander-in-Chief in the western theatre, with his headquarters at Chattanooga (Tenn).

Towards the end of November Grant, with his headquarters at Oxford, was preparing to continue his southward advance, when he at last received from Halleck a directive which completely disrupted his plans. This new order instructed him that:

The enemy must be turned by a movement down the river from Memphis as soon as sufficient force can be collected.

Grant was also informed that he would shortly receive reinforcements amounting to 20,000 men. This order, which was actually inspired by Lincoln, meant that Grant must abandon his intention of defeating *Pemberton*'s field army before attempting to reduce Vicksburg. Instead of making his main thrust down the railway, he must now remain on the defensive there and commit the bulk of his troops to the hazardous scheme of endeavouring to penetrate the almost impassable network of forest and bayous which covered Vicksburg from the north. On 5 December Halleck sent Grant a further order directing him

3. Acting for Hurlbut, who had been wounded at Pocahontas in October.

not to attempt to hold the country south of the Tallahatchie, but to collect 25,000 troops at Memphis by the 20th for the Vicksburg expedition. This new plan meant splitting Grant's force into two halves, each of which would be inferior in numbers to *Pemberton*'s army, which could operate on interior lines, based on Vicksburg.

Grant decided to place the Vicksburg task force under the command of Sherman, whom he considered the most reliable and experienced of his subordinates. Accordingly, on 8 December from Oxford he sent Sherman the following order:

> You will proceed, with as little delay as possible, to Memphis, Tennessee, taking with you one division of your present command. On your arrival at Memphis you will assume command of all the troops there, and that portion of General Curtis's forces at present east of the Mississippi River, and organize them into brigades and divisions in your own army. As soon as possible move with them down the river to the vicinity of Vicksburg, and with the co-operation of the gunboat fleet under command of Flag-Officer Porter proceed to the reduction of that place in such manner as circumstances, and your own judgment, may dictate.... Inform me at the earliest practicable day of the time when you will embark, and such plans as may then be matured. I will hold the forces here in readiness to co-operate with you in such manner as the movements of the enemy may make necessary.
>
> Leave the District of Memphis in the command of an efficient officer, and with a garrison of four regiments of infantry, the siege guns, and whatever cavalry may be there.
>
> U. S. Grant, Major-General[4]

This was a model of what an operational directive should be, leaving the detailed planning of a difficult manœuvre to the soldier and sailor on the spot.

Halleck's order to attack Vicksburg by the river route from Memphis had been inspired by Lincoln himself. The President had always been in favour of amphibious operations on the Mississippi, to follow up Grant's successful river-borne expeditions up the Tennessee and the Cumberland. Since Farragut's running the gauntlet of the New Orleans batteries at the end of April, the Union navy had made two efforts to approach Vicksburg from the south. Farragut had steamed up the Mississippi with his gunboats in the latter half of May, and had actually got within gunshot of Vicksburg, but he had insufficient troops with him to effect a landing. Farragut made a second effort on 28 June, when his gunboats successfully passed the Confederate batteries at Vicksburg, and got in touch with Flag-Officer Davis's squadron operating down stream from Memphis. Farragut even sent a reconnaissance up the Yazoo River, where the Confederates were building a powerful armoured gunboat provided with a ram, but again could effect nothing owing to the lack of troops; he therefore withdrew down stream at the end of July, but his squadron effected a permanent occupation at Baton Rouge (La). Like the unsupported bombardment of

4. *Grant*, I, 429.

the Dardanelles forts by the Royal Navy half a century later, these isolated attempts merely alerted the defenders, and the 'Queen City of the Bluff' was soon converted into a formidable fortress.

Meanwhile, behind Grant's back, a curious intrigue was started in Washington at the highest level. John Alexander McClernand, one of Grant's divisional commanders, had served under him at Belmont, Fort Donelson and Shiloh, though he had never displayed any conspicuous ability. He was a politician without any military training, and Grant had never trusted him, always preferring to have Sherman in the front line at critical moments. Before the battle of Corinth, Grant had given McClernand leave of absence to go to Washington, where he contacted the Secretary of War, Edwin M. Stanton, to whom he made adverse criticisms both of McClellan's strategy in the east and of Grant's in the west. Stanton took him to Lincoln, who was anxious to appease the influential Democratic congressman from Illinois. McClernand told the President that the West Point generals were mismanaging the war by their clumsy, red-tape methods, and suggested that he himself, if given an independent command, could capture Vicksburg by an *attaque brusquée* based on Memphis. Lincoln was impressed by his bombastic oratory and gave him authority to raise an independent task force of volunteers which he was to levy from the Governors of Illinois, Indiana and Iowa. Grant was not informed of this curious arrangement, but got wind of it from a newspaper report, and had it confirmed by his naval colleague at Memphis. When Halleck heard about McClernand's appointment, he realized its absurdity, and insisted that McClernand should remain subordinate to Grant.

On 18 December Grant received an order from Halleck to organize his army into four corps, so he appointed to these commands his four senior divisional commanders: McClernand (XIII), Sherman (XV), Hurlbut (XVI) and McPherson (XVII). At the same time Halleck informed Grant that the President wished McClernand to be put in command of the expedition to reduce Vicksburg.

Grant's extended line of rail communication had now become vulnerable to enemy raids. On 15 December the Confederate cavalry leader under *Bragg's* command, *Nathan B. Forrest*, crossed the Tennessee River and raided Humboldt, north of Jackson (Tenn), destroying the track, a number of bridges and a supply depot. On 20 December a worse disaster occurred. *Van Dorn*, at the head of 3,500 cavalry, attacked Grant's advanced base at Holly Springs. The local commander was the same Colonel R. C. Murphy who, three months earlier, had basely evacuated Iuka without a fight. With his garrison of 1,500 men Murphy now repeated his miserable performance and abandoned to the enemy one and a half million dollars' worth of military stores. These were burnt by *Van Dorn*, who also destroyed many miles of track and telegraph line. Murphy was tried by court martial and dismissed the service, and Grant had cause to regret his leniency on the previous occasion; one of his faults was that he was too tolerant of inefficient subordinates; in this respect he was a

Wavell, not a Montgomery. The loss of his advanced depot of ammunition, rations and forage was a serious blow to Grant's plans. In consequence, on 23 December he withdrew his headquarters from Oxford to Holly Springs and formed a new advanced base at Grand Junction.

On being informed by Halleck that the President wished the Vicksburg expedition to be commanded by McClernand, Grant sent a telegram to that officer, who was still haranguing his constituents at Springfield (Ill). Owing, however, to *Van Dorn* having cut the railway and telegraph line, the telegram never reached him, so that, much to Grant's satisfaction, Sherman was left to command the expedition as already arranged.

Sherman reached Memphis on 12 December and planned his operation in conjunction with Flag-Officer David Dixon Porter, who on 15 October had taken over command of the Mississippi Flotilla from Charles Henry Davis. Porter was now given the rank of Acting Rear-Admiral; his flagship was the 'Benton', the powerful armoured gunboat, mounting 16 guns, which had been inspected by Anthony Trollope at Cairo during the previous February.[5] Sherman's force of 16,000 men embarked on 20 December and steamed down stream, escorted by Porter's gunboats. The distance from Memphis to Vicksburg is only 200 miles as the crow flies, but 400 miles by river owing to the tortuous meanders of the Mississippi, so that it took the transports five days to reach Milliken's Bend, a great loop of the river 15 miles north-west of Vicksburg. On the way, at Helena (Ark), Sherman picked up a reinforcement of 9,000 men. His force now consisted of four divisions, under Andrew Jackson Smith, Morgan Lewis Smith, George Washington Morgan and Frederick Steele.

On 23 December Admiral Porter, ahead of Sherman's transports, steamed up the tributary Yazoo River with the 'Benton', 'Tyler', 'Lexington' and some auxiliary vessels. After three days' incessant labour, under musketry fire from the banks, the flotilla worked up to a point within range of the enemy's heavy batteries at Haynes's Bluff, 11 miles north of Vicksburg. The 'Benton' sustained the fire of the shore batteries for two hours without being much damaged, but her commander, Lieutenant-Commander W. Gwin, was mortally wounded. This naval demonstration served little purpose, but it effectively alerted the Confederate garrison. *Pemberton* had as early as the 21st received intelligence of the start of Sherman's expedition, and had immediately sent two additional brigades to reinforce *Martin Luther Smith* in Vicksburg, so that by 27 December the fortress was held by 12,000 men. *Pemberton* himself withdrew behind the Yalobusha River to Grenada, and *President Davis* reinforced him with another division of 10,000 men from *Bragg*'s command.

Having reached Milliken's Bend on Christmas Day, Sherman landed two brigades on the right bank to destroy the railway running west to Shreveport

5. See page 15.

(La), Vicksburg's main link with the west. This was a good thing to do, but it involved an unfortunate waste of time, for the river was now rising rapidly as a result of the winter rains.

Eight miles above Vicksburg the Mississippi is joined by the Yazoo River, which for most of the way between Memphis and Vicksburg follows a parallel course; it is in fact an old bed of the main river. Just east of the Yazoo River, and parallel to it, runs a continuous escarpment, 100 to 200 feet high, which forms the eastern boundary of the Mississippi flood-plain. This escarpment of low clay cliffs extends southward from Memphis to Port Hudson (La) for a distance of 300 miles. Vicksburg itself is built on a promontory of this escarpment which, just north of the town, is known as the Walnut Hills or Chickasaw Bluffs. The formidable line of the Chickasaw Bluffs was now Sherman's tactical objective, but in order to reach it his troops would have to cross the swampy jungle of the flood-plain, intersected by a maze of stagnant bayous on either side of the serpentine bends of the Yazoo River.

On 26 December, preceded by the gunboats, Sherman's transports steamed eight miles up the Yazoo River. That afternoon three of his divisions (Morgan Smith, Morgan and Steele) landed on the left bank at a point six miles north of Vicksburg. Each division sent forward a brigade to clear paths through the swampy undergrowth, but progress was slow, as the tracks were blocked by abatis, which had to be removed under close rifle fire from the enemy outposts. On the following day A. J. Smith's division landed on their right, and on the 28th all four divisions deployed for the attack, but there was a dense fog which caused some units to lose their direction.

The Confederates, meanwhile, had occupied a forward defensive line at the foot of the Chickasaw Bluffs, where the ground was more open. This line was four miles long and could not be turned, for its right rested on the broad Chickasaw Bayou and its left on the bank of the Mississippi, just above Vicksburg. It was held by two brigades in front and one in reserve, some 10,000 men, with 34 guns. In front of the line lay a chain of flooded bayous, some of them 100 feet wide and 15 feet deep. Behind this forward line, the main defensive position, strongly entrenched, ran along the crest of the bluffs.

Sherman's attack was launched on the morning of 29 December. His troops moved forward with the greatest courage, but the physical obstacles were too much for them. Pontoon bridges had to be built under close-range rifle fire and canister shot. The attack was repulsed with 1,776 casualties, while the Confederates lost only 207. That night it rained very hard, and Sherman halted the operations. In consultation with Admiral Porter he then decided to switch the attack to Haynes's Bluff, 11 miles north of Vicksburg, to be launched with 10,000 men at daylight on 1 January. But a thick fog came on and the river continued to rise, so that the land almost disappeared from sight under the flood, rendering navigation through the tortuous channels impossible. Porter reported to Sherman that the attack on Haynes's Bluff must be called off, so on the night of the 1/2 January he re-embarked his troops and moved down the Yazoo to its confluence with the Mississippi. There he was met by McClernand, who had just arrived from Washington and Illinois after an absence of four months. As senior ranking officer, and armed with Presidential authority, McClernand now assumed command of Sherman's force, which he styled the 'Army of the Mississippi'.

Sherman's frontal assault on the Chickasaw Bluffs had proved a complete failure. It was an operation which he should never have attempted, but he had been induced to do so by two misapprehensions. Firstly, he thought that Grant was simultaneously attacking *Pemberton* by the overland route, and would prevent the latter from sending reinforcements to Vicksburg. But the telegraph from Memphis to Holly Springs had been cut, and Sherman did not know that Grant had been forbidden by Halleck to advance south of the Tallahatchie. Secondly, Sherman had been informed that Nathaniel Banks was leading an expedition up the Mississippi from New Orleans to attack Vicksburg from the south, but Banks had not got farther than Baton Rouge. Grant has summarized Sherman's failure as follows:

> The waters were high so that the bottoms were generally overflowed, leaving only narrow causeways of dry land between points of debarkation and the high bluffs. These were fortified and defended at all points. The rebel position was impregnable against any force that could be brought against its front. Sherman could not use one-fourth of his force. His efforts to capture the city or the high ground north of it were necessarily unavailing.[6]

On taking over command of Sherman's force at Milliken's Bend, McClernand reorganized it into two corps under Morgan and Sherman respectively. Sherman now suggested to McClernand an expedition up the Arkansas River, a right-bank tributary of the Mississippi, in order to capture Fort Hindman, a Confederate stronghold at Arkansas Post, about 40 miles up the river. Sherman had heard from an escaped prisoner-of-war that this fort was only weakly held. McClernand agreed, rather reluctantly, and decided to lead the expedition in person with his whole army. Escorted by Admiral Porter with seven gunboats, the force, consisting of 33,000 men and 40 guns, steamed up the Arkansas River, and on 9 January disembarked on the left bank about three miles below Fort Hindman, which the gunboats bombarded and damaged severely. After two days' fighting the fort surrendered, 4,791 prisoners and 17 guns being handed over. The Confederates only lost 140 killed and wounded, but the Union casualties amounted to 1,061.

Elated by this success, McClernand now proposed to Sherman and Porter that they should proceed 80 miles further up the river in order to capture Little

6. *Grant*, I, 437.

Rock, the State capital of Arkansas, where a Confederate force was concentrated. Sherman and Porter were horrified at this dispersal of force, when their real objective was Vicksburg. On hearing of McClernand's proposal, Grant telegraphed to Halleck for instructions. Halleck authorized him to relieve McClernand of his command, whereupon Grant ordered McClernand to return with his expedition at once to the Mississippi. McClernand sulkily obeyed and Grant, who had meanwhile established his headquarters at Memphis, went down to meet him on 17 January at the mouth of the Arkansas River. Grant has recorded his own feelings as follows:

> It was here made evident to me that both the army and navy were so distrustful of McClernand's fitness to command that, while they would do all they could to insure success, this distrust was an element of weakness. It would have been criminal to send troops under these circumstances into such danger. By this time I had received authority to relieve McClernand, or to assign any person else to the command of the river expedition, or to assume command in person. I felt great embarrassment about McClernand. He was the senior major-general after myself within the department. It would not do, with his rank and ambition, to assign a junior over him. Nothing was left, therefore, but to assume the command myself.[7]

Grant then returned to Memphis to reorganize his army for the next move against Vicksburg. On 29 January he went down river to Milliken's Bend, where XIII and XV Corps were now assembled. There on the 30th he personally took over command. McClernand still stuck his toes in, and as a final blast wrote a personal letter to Lincoln, in which he complained: 'My success here is gall and wormwood to the clique of West Pointers who have been persecuting me for months.' Grant was always willing to turn the other cheek:

> General McClernand took exception in a most characteristic way – for him. His correspondence with me on the subject was more in the nature of a reprimand than a protest. It was highly insubordinate, but I overlooked it, as I believed, for the good of the service.[8]

With this irritating thorn in his flesh, the long-suffering Commander-in-Chief now set himself to devise a new plan for the capture of Vicksburg.

7. *Grant*, I, 440.
8. *ibid.*, I, 441.

XV

The Vicksburg Campaign
February–July 1863

(See Map 20 at end of book)

After Sherman's failure at Chickasaw Bluffs, Grant was confirmed in his view that Vicksburg could not be attacked from the north or west, since the physical obstacle of the Mississippi flood-plain rendered impracticable any military operations from that direction. The fortress could only therefore be approached from the *terra firma* lying to the east. That, of course, had been Grant's original strategic plan – to move southward along the Mississippi Central Railroad from Grand Junction to Grenada and Jackson (Miss), and then to turn westward on Vicksburg, after cutting its communications with the east and south. But he had been diverted from this line of approach by Lincoln's insistence that he should follow the river artery through Memphis, so that the bulk of his army was now concentrated on the west bank of the Mississippi just opposite Vicksburg. In order to transfer it to the east bank, he would have to retreat to Memphis, more than 200 miles to the north, and then repair hundreds of miles of railway track which the enemy had destroyed. This solution had to be ruled out for political as well as military reasons, as Grant has explained:

> At this time the North had become very much discouraged. Many strong Union men believed that the war must prove a failure. The elections of 1862 had gone against the party which was for the prosecution of the war to save the Union. . . . Voluntary enlistments had ceased . . . and the draft had been resorted to to fill up our ranks. It was my judgment at the time that to make a backward movement, as long as that from Vicksburg to Memphis, would be interpreted . . . as a defeat. . . . There was nothing left to be done but to *go forward to a decisive victory*.[1]

This shows that Grant possessed sound political sense as well as strategic ability. He then proceeded to consider the military tasks confronting him:

> The problem then became, how to secure a landing on high ground east of the Mississippi without an apparent retreat. Then commenced a series of experiments to

1. *Grant*, I, 443.

15 Union gunboats under Admiral Porter steaming down the Mississippi under fire from the Vicksburg batteries, night of 16 April 1863

16 Grant with his favourite bay charger 'Cincinnati'

consume time, and to divert the attention of the enemy, of my troops and of the public generally. I, myself, never felt great confidence that any of the experiments resorted to would prove successful. Nevertheless I was always prepared to take advantage of them in case they did.[2]

We need not examine these 'experiments' in detail, as none of them proved practicable. They consisted in four engineering projects designed to link up the various tributaries and bayous on either side of the Mississippi and Yazoo Rivers so as to provide a continuous waterway by which troops could by-pass the Vicksburg channel and gain the firm ground east of the river. At all events they served the purpose of keeping the troops actively employed and also of mystifying the enemy as to Grant's intentions. The winter of 1862–63 was phenomenal for the amount of rainfall and high water in the Mississippi Valley, and Grant realized that at least two months must elapse before he could take the field.

Grant's military rivals and political detractors did not fail to seize on the pretext of this apparent inaction to denigrate his qualities as a commander. As he records:

Visitors to the camps went home with dismal stories to relate; Northern papers came back to the soldiers with these stories exaggerated. Because I would not divulge my ultimate plans to visitors, they pronounced me idle, incompetent and unfit to command men in an emergency, and clamored for my removal. They were not to be satisfied, many of them, with my simple removal, but named who my successor should be. McClernand, Frémont, Hunter and McClellan were all mentioned in this connection.[3]

But he was not entirely without supporters on the highest level:

With all the pressure brought to bear upon them, both President Lincoln and General Halleck stood by me to the end of the campaign. I had never met Mr. Lincoln, but his support was constant.[4]

It certainly was; to an adviser who suggested replacing Grant, he said: 'I rather like the man; I think we'll try him a little longer.'

At last, towards the end of March, the floods began to subside, and Grant proceeded to execute the great chain of operations which he had planned. In order to maintain secrecy, he did not even disclose his plan beforehand to his staff; the only person with whom he discussed it was Admiral Porter, whose cooperation was essential and was readily accorded. The essence of Grant's plan was to cross the Mississippi *below* Vicksburg, and attack the fortress from the east, after destroying the Confederate field forces in that area. This meant that Porter's flotilla must first destroy the Confederate armoured vessels which patrolled the river south of Vicksburg, as far down stream as Port Hudson; to

2. *Grant*, I, 446.
3. *ibid.*, I, 458.
4. *ibid.*, I, 460.

do this, Porter's gunboats must run the gauntlet of the Confederate heavy batteries, both at Vicksburg and at Grand Gulf, 25 miles farther south. The U.S. Navy had already made several attempts to do so; on 2 February the 'Queen of the West', of Porter's flotilla, successfully passed the Vicksburg batteries, followed on the 12th by the 'Indianola', but both vessels were later disabled and captured. On 14 March Admiral Farragut, coming up the river from New Orleans, got past the Port Hudson batteries with two vessels and destroyed the Confederate gunboats.

Grant had now collected from river ports as far away as St. Louis and Chicago a fleet of yawls and barges for the transportation of his army's supplies and ammunition, which would have to run the gauntlet of the Vicksburg batteries by night. The troops could not march along the right bank of the Mississippi, where they would be seen by the enemy, so they had to make a circuitous détour through the wooded swamps. Grant intended to make for a landing place called Hard Times, 28 miles below Vicksburg,[5] where he would cross to a landing on the left bank at Grand Gulf. This was commanded by an enemy battery which would have to be silenced by Porter's gunboats. Three corps were now concentrated near Duckport on Milliken's Bend, McClernand (XIII), Sherman (XV) and McPherson (XVII). Hurlbut's XVI Corps was left behind to hold Memphis and secure the lines of communication.

On 29 March the southward advance began, McClernand in the lead, followed by McPherson. Sherman was ordered to move up the Yazoo River and make a feint attack on Haynes's Bluff, north of Vicksburg, in order to mislead the enemy. The progress of the main body was slow, as the country was still water-logged; many streams and bayous had to be bridged, and timber had to be felled to build corduroy roads. On 6 April McClernand's corps reached New Carthage, 27 miles down stream from Vicksburg. The ground was so sodden that the troops could not be accompanied by their ammunition and supply trains, so Grant now called on Admiral Porter to run the Vicksburg batteries. On the night of 16 April the Admiral in his flagship 'Benton', with five other gunboats, passed the batteries successfully, escorting three transports towing barges. The gunboats were under fire for two hours and were hit many times, but only one of the transports was sunk. The enemy illuminated the river by lighting bonfires along the left bank. Grant watched the exciting spectacle from the deck of a transport.

Meanwhile, Grant had devised another project to mystify and mislead the enemy. Remembering ruefully the successful Confederate cavalry raid which had destroyed his advanced base at Holly Springs four months earlier, he took a leaf out of *Van Dorn*'s book and organized a still more effective counter-raid. On 17 April Colonel Benjamin Henry Grierson, at the head of three cavalry regiments numbering 1,700 men, made a dash southward from Grand Junction

5. As the crow flies, but 48 miles by river.

through the State of Mississippi, by-passing Vicksburg and Jackson. Grierson's raid covered 600 miles, cutting railway and telegraph lines and effectually isolating Jackson, the State capital, from the north, east and south. Finally, on 2 May, Grierson safely reached Baton Rouge (La), where he joined Banks's army which was slowly advancing from the south. Grierson's raid effectively disrupted the Confederate communications and diverted their attention from the river crossing which Grant was preparing.

It now became necessary to run another convoy down the river to transport all the supplies and ammunition for three corps, which could not be conveyed overland owing to the swampy tracks. This was accomplished on the night of 22 April, when five steamers got through, more or less disabled, only one being sunk. Half the barges made the passage with their precious freight. Sherman's xv Corps, after making its feint attack on Haynes's Bluff, had followed the other two, but progress was necessarily slow. Below New Carthage the ground was more swampy than ever, and the troops had to follow the circuitous meanders formed by the former beds of the river. The map distance between Duckport and Hard Times landing was only 28 miles, but the marching distance which the troops had to follow was 64. It was not until 28 April that the two leading corps were assembled with their stores at Hard Times.

On 27 April Grant issued the following operation order to McClernand, whose corps was to lead the crossing:

> Commence immediately the embarkation of your corps, or so much of it as there is transportation for. Have put aboard the artillery and every article authorized in orders limiting baggage, except the men, and hold them in readiness, with their places assigned, to be moved at a moment's warning.
>
> All the troops you may have, except those ordered to remain behind, send to a point nearly opposite Grand Gulf, where you see, by special orders of this date, General McPherson is ordered to send one division.
>
> The plan of the attack will be for the navy to attack and silence all the batteries commanding the river. Your corps will be on the river, ready to run to and debark on the nearest eligible land below the promontory first brought to view passing down the river. Once on shore, have each commander instructed beforehand to form his men the best the ground will admit of, and take possession of the most commanding points, but avoid separating your command so that it cannot support itself. The first object is to get a foothold where our troops can maintain themselves until such time as preparations can be made and troops collected for a forward movement.
>
> Admiral Porter has proposed to place his boats in the position indicated to you a few days ago, and to bring over with them such troops as may be below the city after the guns of the enemy are silenced. . . .
>
> If not already directed, require your men to keep three days' rations in their haversacks, not to be touched until a movement commences.[6]

Considering that no large-scale maps of the country were available, this operation order was as clear as could be expected, while leaving all matters of detail

6. *Grant*, I, 474–5.

to the local commander. It is somewhat reminiscent of Napoleon's order to his corps commanders on the eve of the battle of Jena.

At 8 a.m. on 29 April Porter opened fire on the Grand Gulf batteries and kept up his bombardment for five hours without silencing a single enemy gun, as the shore batteries were sited too high on the bluff to be hit by the gunboats. At 1.30 p.m. the fleet withdrew after suffering 74 casualties among the crews. Grant then learnt from a local negro that at Bruinsburg, nine miles farther down the river, there was a good landing place with a road leading to Port Gibson, 12 miles inland. Here the two leading corps crossed unopposed on the following day. Grant had hoped that a rapid advance would cut off the Confederate brigade holding Grand Gulf, but McClernand was slow in moving off and the chance was missed. On 1 May McClernand's advance was held up four miles west of Port Gibson by a Confederate force of 8,500 men sent out from Vicksburg. McPherson came up on the left and outflanked the enemy, who withdrew after suffering 1,650 casualties, the Union troops losing 850. On the following day the Confederates evacuated their strong position at Grand Gulf, which Grant occupied on 3 May and established there his advanced base. Sherman's corps had now reached the right bank and was ordered to cross to Grand Gulf.

Grant had previously been told by Halleck that he should not advance on Vicksburg until he had joined forces with Banks, who with a corps of 15,000 had reached Baton Rouge, 180 miles down the river. On 2 May Grant heard from Banks that he would not be able to move until the 10th. This placed Grant in a seriously exposed position. He now had three of his corps, 41,000 men, on the left bank of the Mississippi, with a very precarious line of communications, confronted by *Pemberton*'s army in and around Vicksburg, amounting to 32,000, with a detachment of 1,000 holding the important railway junction at Jackson, 45 miles east of Vicksburg. And now *J. E. Johnston*, the Confederate Commander-in-Chief in the west, was hastening south-westwards with 16,000 men to support *Pemberton*. The latter had two divisions holding a strong covering line along the Big Black River, a left-bank tributary of the Mississippi, which ran in a deep valley ten miles to the east and south of Vicksburg.

Grant was now in a similar position to that which confronted Bonaparte in 1796, when he found himself between the Austrian and Sardinian armies in the foothills of Piedmont; he must defeat each of his opponents separately before they could unite. But, if Grant moved north to attack *Johnston*, he would expose his tenuous line of communications with Grand Gulf to be cut by *Pemberton*. He then took the boldest decision made in the Civil War – he abandoned entirely his line of supply. Every wagon that had been ferried across the river was loaded up with ammunition, giving two wagons to each regiment, and five days' rations were issued to the troops, who were told to live on the country after these had been consumed.

Grant's first objective was to strike north and cut the Vicksburg–Jackson railway, so as to interpose himself between *Pemberton* and *Johnston*. The advance started on 7 May, with his three corps abreast: McClernand on the left, moving parallel to the Big Black River, to cut the railway at Edward's Station, 16 miles east of Vicksburg; Sherman in the centre, directed on Raymond, and then to push on to Jackson; on the right McPherson was also directed on Raymond and Jackson. On 12 May McPherson encountered a force of 5,000 Confederates at Raymond and drove them back to Jackson. Leaving small detachments to threaten *Pemberton* on the line of the Big Black River, Grant moved XIII and XV Corps eastward to support McPherson at Jackson, as he knew that *Johnston* was due to arrive there. On the following day *Johnston* reached Jackson, but with only 6,000 men and too late. McClernand had already reached Clinton, nine miles west of Jackson, so the railway was cut. On the 14th McPherson attacked and overwhelmed *Johnston*'s force, taking 800 prisoners and all his guns. *Johnston* thereupon withdrew to Canton, 30 miles to the north. McPherson intercepted a copy of an order from *Johnston* telling *Pemberton* to move forward and meet him at Clinton. The latter crossed the Big Black River, hoping to cut Grant's supply line, and with 18,000 men occupied a strong position at Champion's Hill, just south of the railway. Grant, leaving Sherman to destroy the bridges, railway lines and stores at Jackson, turned west with the corps of McClernand and McPherson, 29,000 in all, and on 16 May attacked *Pemberton*'s position at Champion's Hill. After a six hours' battle the Confederates were routed, losing 1,400 killed and wounded, 2,500 prisoners and all their guns. The Union casualties were 2,441.

After his defeat at Champion's Hill, *Pemberton* withdrew the shattered remains of his army to the lines of Vicksburg, leaving a rearguard of 5,000 men to hold the bridge over the Big Black River, from which they were soon driven by the advance of McClernand's corps, but the burning of the bridges caused some delay, and temporary bridges had to be constructed, some with pontoons made of cotton bales, to allow the three corps to cross.

During the battle of Champion's Hill, Grant ordered Sherman, who had been left behind to destroy the railway at Jackson, to rejoin the army. Sherman was now ordered to cross the Big Black River at Bridgeport, six miles farther up stream, and from there to push on to Haynes's Bluff in order to prevent *Pemberton* attempting to join *Johnston*.

On 17 May, while Grant was watching his troops drive the enemy rearguard across the Big Black River, an incident occurred which Grant describes as follows:

An officer from Banks's staff came up and presented me with a letter from General Halleck, dated the 11th of May. It had been sent by the way of New Orleans to Banks to be forwarded to me. It ordered me to return to Grand Gulf and to cooperate from there with Banks against Port Hudson, and then to return with our combined forces to besiege Vicksburg. I told the officer that the order came too late, and that Halleck would not give it now if he knew our position. The bearer of the dispatch insisted that

I ought to obey the order, and was giving arguments to support his position when I heard great cheering to the right of our line and, looking in that direction, saw Lawler [a brigade commander] in his shirt sleeves leading a charge upon the enemy. I immediately mounted my horse and rode in the direction of the charge, and saw no more of the officer who delivered the dispatch.[7]

On the 18th the whole army crossed the Big Black River and closed in on Vicksburg. Grant joined Sherman and rode with him at the head of his column till they reached Haynes's Bluff, the north flank of the Vicksburg defences. They captured the outworks there with little resistance, and Sherman looked down at the scene of his defeat five months earlier.

Less than three weeks had elapsed since Grant ferried his army across the Mississippi. At the cost of less than 4,500 casualties he had defeated two armies in five battles, capturing nearly 100 guns and putting out of action 10,000 of the enemy. It matched the achievement of Bonaparte, 67 years earlier, when he crushed alternately the armies of Beaulieu and Colli. The Vicksburg campaign ensured Grant a place in the galaxy of the Great Captains.

When *Johnston* heard of *Pemberton*'s defeat at Champion's Hill on the 16th, he sent him an order to evacuate Vicksburg and march north-eastward to join him at Brownsville. But it was now too late, for Sherman had cut that escape route. There was nothing for *Pemberton* to do but to await his fate. On the 19th Grant drew his net tighter round the entrenched lines of Vicksburg. Sherman held the northern face, with McPherson and McClernand confronting the eastern face. Hoping to storm the fortress by an *attaque brusquée*, Grant ordered an assault that very afternoon, but it failed completely. Grant had not realized how quickly defeated troops can recover their morale when protected by stout breastworks and supported by well emplaced artillery. Undeterred by this failure, he ordered a second and more carefully prepared attack to be launched two days later, as he knew that *Johnston* was assembling a large army in his rear, only 50 miles away. This also was a complete failure. Grant describes it as follows:

The attack was ordered to commence on all parts of the line at 10 o'clock a.m. on the 22nd with a furious cannonade from every battery in position. All the corps commanders set their time by mine so that all might open the engagement at the same minute. The attack was gallant, and portions of each of the three corps succeeded in getting up to the very parapets of the enemy and in planting their battle flags upon them; but at no place were we able to enter.... This last attack only served to increase our casualties without giving any benefit whatever.[8]

In the first attack the Union troops had suffered 942 casualties, and in the second 3,199, which was a useless sacrifice of life. In spite of his experience at Fort Donelson, Grant was really a novice at siege operations. Instead of making

7. *Grant*, I, 524-6.
8. *ibid.*, I, 531.

a wild rush all along a five-mile front, he should have carefully reconnoitred the enemy lines, selected one key point to attack and, after making feint attacks elsewhere, he should then have launched an overwhelming concentration on that key point to effect a penetration. Grant now settled down to a regular siege of Vicksburg, and asked Halleck to send him reinforcements, as the 35,000 men at his disposal were insufficient both to invest the fortress and to keep a reserve in hand to ward off *Johnston*.

Vicksburg was protected on the north and east by a continuous line of entrenchments, seven miles in length, with both flanks resting on the bluffs, 200 feet high, overlooking the Mississippi. The ground was much intersected by wooded gullies. To hold this perimeter, *Pemberton* had four divisions, numbering 30,000 men, well supplied with heavy artillery. Grant's only siege guns were six 32-pounders, but he borrowed some large-calibre naval guns from Admiral Porter, and the next few weeks were employed in digging in and emplacing the siege batteries. The opposing trenches were nowhere more than 600 yards apart, in many places much less.

Grant's strained relations with his senior corps commander, McClernand, now came to a head. On 30 May McClernand had issued to his corps a laudatory order of the day, extolling their achievements and belittling the efforts of the other corps. Grant describes the incident as follows:

> On the 17th [June] I received a letter from General Sherman and one on the 18th from General McPherson, saying that their respective commands had complained to them of a fulsome, congratulatory order published by General McClernand to the 13th corps, which did great injustice to the other troops engaged in the campaign. This order had been sent North and published, and now papers containing it had reached our camps. The order had not been heard of by me, and certainly not by troops outside of McClernand's command until brought in this way. I at once wrote to McClernand, directing him to send me a copy of this order. He did so, and I at once relieved him from the command of the 13th army corps and ordered him back to Springfield, Illinois. The publication of his order in the press was in violation of War Department orders and also of mine.[9]

Grant had at last learnt to be tough with his erring subordinates. He replaced McClernand by Edward Ord, the senior divisional commander in Hurlbut's corps. Curiously enough, Marshal Bernadotte had committed an identical misdemeanour after the battle of Wagram (July 1809), and Napoleon had sent him back to Paris in disgrace.

About the middle of June Halleck sent Grant three more divisions, bringing the investing force up to 71,000, and by the end of the month he had 220 guns in action, mainly field-pieces. Two mines were exploded under the enemy trenches, on 25 June and 1 July, but they failed to make a breach wide enough for a storming party. On 1 July Grant ordered preparations to be made for a final assault on the 6th. *Pemberton*, however, realized that further resistance was hopeless, as he had heard nothing more from *Johnston*. After consulting

9. *Grant*, I, 546.

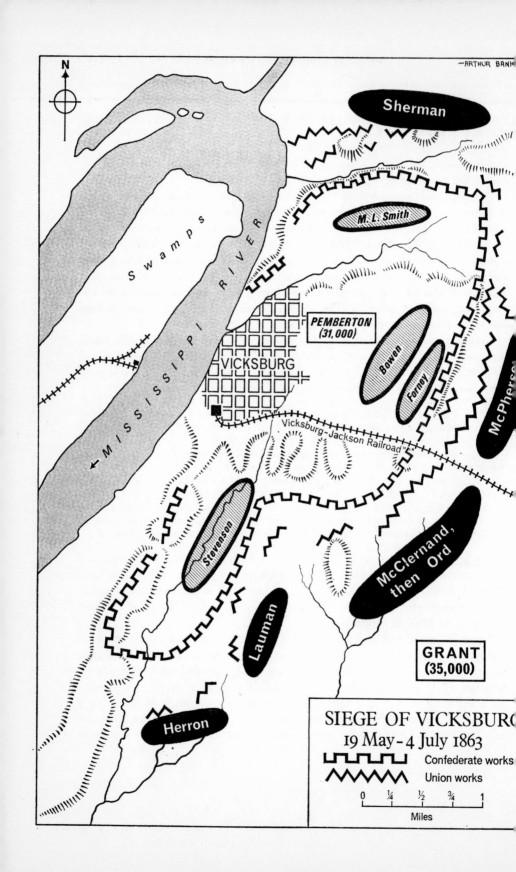

SIEGE OF VICKSBURG
19 May – 4 July 1863

Confederate works

Union works

0   ¼   ½   ¾   1

Miles

his four divisional commanders, he sent the senior of them, *John S. Bowen*, on the morning of 3 July with a flag of truce to Grant's headquarters, asking for an armistice to arrange terms for capitulation. Grant replied with his usual formula of 'unconditional surrender of the city and garrison'. *Bowen* then asked if Grant would meet *Pemberton* for a personal talk, to which Grant consented. The two commanders met that afternoon between the lines. They were already acquainted, having served together in the same division during the Mexican War. After some hard bargaining, it was agreed that the garrison would march out and lay down their arms on condition that each individual would sign a written parole not to serve again during the war. They would then be free to return home, each officer being allowed to retain his sword and one horse, and his personal baggage. Thirty horse-drawn wagons would be permitted to carry rations and cooking utensils for the troops.

These fairly generous terms were actually of considerable advantage to Grant, who otherwise would have had to detach a large proportion of his troops to guard and escort 30,000 prisoners of war, and employ all his steamers to transport them up the river. That afternoon he despatched one of his A.D.C.s with the following message to Halleck:

The enemy surrendered this morning. The only terms allowed is their parole as prisoners of war. This I regard as a great advantage to us at this moment. It saves, probably, several days in the capture, and leaves troops and transports ready for immediate service. Sherman, with a large force, moves immediately on *Johnston*, to drive him from the State.

At Vicksburg, 31,600 Confederate troops surrendered, with 172 cannon and 60,000 muskets. Here again a Napoleonic echo strikes one: at Ulm on 20 October 1805, General Mack, with 33,000 Austrians and 60 guns, surrendered to the Emperor.

The fall of Vicksburg was the turning point of the Civil War. Five days later Port Hudson surrendered to Nathaniel Banks, so that the entire river, from its source to the Gulf of Mexico, was now under Union control, thus isolating the western States of Arkansas, Louisiana and Texas. The Confederacy had received a mortal blow, although its agony was to continue for 20 months longer. Coincidentally, the surrender of Vicksburg took place on 4 July, the date sacred to the Union as the anniversary of its liberation from an overseas domination.[10] By a still more remarkable coincidence, the Confederacy sustained on the same day another deadly stroke in Meade's defeat of *Lee* in the hard-fought battle of Gettysburg (Pa), which forced the invading Confederate army to retreat to Virginia.

10. The Declaration of Independence was a resolution passed by the Continental Congress on 2 July, 1776. John Adams, one of its sponsors, held that that date should be adopted as the country's National Day, but the final vote of the Congress was not registered until the 4th (see *The Americans*, Daniel J. Boorstin, 1966).

As soon as Lincoln heard of the capture of Vicksburg, he promoted Grant to be Major-General in the Regular Army, which gave him higher seniority in the Army List, as he had previously only held the rank of Major-General of Volunteers, to which he had been promoted after the capture of Fort Donelson. At the same time Lincoln wrote Grant a magnanimous congratulatory letter, in which he paid a graceful compliment to Grant's strategic perception:

My dear General:

I do not remember that you and I ever met personally. I write this now as a grateful acknowledgment for the almost inestimable service you have done the country. I wish to say a word further. When you first reached the vicinity of Vicksburg, I thought you should do what you finally did – march the troops across the neck, run the batteries with the transports, and thus go below; and I never had any faith, except a general hope that you knew better than I, that the Yazoo Pass expedition and the like could succeed. When you got below and took Port Gibson, Grand Gulf, and vicinity, I thought you should go down the river and join General Banks; and when you turned northward, east of the Big Black, I feared it was a mistake. I now wish to make the personal acknowledgment that you were right and I was wrong.

Lincoln himself was no mean strategist, although he committed several serious errors. Fortunately he had found in Grant an abler exponent of the art of war, and he was big-minded enough to recognize it.

XVI

Chattanooga
October–November 1863

After the fall of Vicksburg, Grant sent Sherman with 50,000 men eastward to drive the last Confederate forces from the State of Mississippi. On 11 July Sherman reached the outskirts of Jackson, where *Joseph Johnston* had concentrated a force of 31,000. After the Confederate position had been shelled, *Johnston* evacuated the town during the night of the 16th/17th, and retired to the east, eluding Sherman's pursuit.

Grant now felt strongly that he should exploit his Vicksburg success by advancing southward to capture Mobile (Ala), the only seaport on the Gulf of Mexico remaining in Confederate hands. Had he been allowed to carry out this perfectly feasible operation, he would have tightened the Union stranglehold on the Confederate economy and possibly shortened the war by a year. Grant proposed this strategic manœuvre to Halleck, but it was turned down in Washington, as Lincoln had other political preoccupations. The French Emperor, Napoleon III, after his military successes in Italy, had extended his imperial ambitions to a French occupation of Mexico, where 30,000 French troops had been landed. Lincoln feared that the ambitious Emperor might recognize the Confederate States as belligerents, or even intervene on their behalf, and he therefore wanted to concentrate troops in west Louisiana and east Texas in order to watch the Rio Grande frontier. Consequently, Grant was ordered to send his XIII Corps under Ord to reinforce Banks's XIX Corps at New Orleans to form the 'Army of the Gulf'. While conferring there with Banks in August, Grant, who had been given a vicious horse to ride at a review, was badly thrown and suffered very severe injuries,[1] much worse than

---

1. A different version of the cause of Grant's accident has been given by William Buel Franklin, who was on parade at this review, having on 20 August taken over command of XIX Corps from Banks. Many years later Franklin told Mark Twain that on this occasion he saw Grant, who was drunk, fall off his horse. There is no other corroboration of this story. Franklin knew Grant well, having been one of his class-mates at West Point. If this

those which he had sustained in his riding accident during the battle of Shiloh. This misadventure laid him low for several weeks at Vicksburg. On 23 September he received a telegram from Halleck ordering him to send at once all available forces from Memphis eastward by rail towards Chattanooga, where Rosecrans, commanding the Army of the Cumberland, was in serious trouble. We must therefore now briefly review the course of operations in that area.

After Vicksburg, the most important military objective for the Union armies in the western theatre was the railway junction of Chattanooga on the upper Tennessee River, covering a main gateway through the western ranges of the Alleghenies. It will be remembered that Buell had failed to reach this objective during the late summer of 1862, despite all the reinforcements which he had received from Grant's army, and Chattanooga remained firmly in Confederate hands. After the battle of Corinth, Lincoln had replaced the dilatory Buell by Grant's subordinate, the rather insubordinate Rosecrans, who was given the urgent task of capturing Chattanooga with an army of 50,000 at his disposal.

In the advance from his headquarters at Nashville (Tenn) towards Chattanooga, Rosecrans was mainly restricted to overland transport, as in the autumn the Cumberland River was not navigable above Nashville, and on the Tennessee only small vessels could ascend above Florence (Ala), 180 miles below Chattanooga. His communications therefore were largely dependent on the railway from Louisville through Bowling Green and Nashville, which was subject to constant raids by the Confederate cavalry. *Bragg*, now the Confederate commander in the western theatre, had concentrated an army of 38,000 at Murfreesboro, 32 miles south-east of Nashville. But Rosecrans was even more deliberate in his movements than Buell had been, and made no move southward until 26 December 1862. He encountered *Bragg* in a strong position on Stones River on 30 December and, after a hard-fought three-day battle, the Confederates withdrew to the south-west, each side having suffered about 12,000 casualties. As usual, Rosecrans made no effort to pursue the enemy.

Throughout the spring of 1863 Halleck constantly prodded Rosecrans to continue his advance on Chattanooga, but the latter still hesitated and did not move until 26 June. Rosecrans had now 65,000 men, opposed to *Bragg*'s 62,000, and the latter withdrew to a position covering Chattanooga. The Union advance, however, was so slow that no effective action took place until 20 August. Rosecrans then made a clever move to his right and crossed the Tennessee River 50 miles below Chattanooga, thus forcing *Bragg* to evacuate the town, but the Confederates took up a strong position a few miles further back, behind the Chickamauga Creek, a left-bank tributary of the Tennessee. Severe fighting took place between 10 and 20 September, and the Union troops were badly repulsed. Although he had displayed some strategic ability in his advance,

---

was the cause of Grant's accident, it was a lesson which he took to heart, for there is no later authenticated record of his intemperance (cf. *Mark Twain's Letters*, II, 457).

Rosecrans proved a poor tactical leader in the field. As a result of his faulty handling of the battle the Union troops suffered a serious defeat, and were only saved from complete disaster by the heroic stand made by one of his corps commanders, George Henry Thomas, who was afterwards known as the 'Rock of Chickamauga'. The battle fought on 19/20 September was one of the most hardly contested of the whole war, the Union casualties amounting to 16,170 while the Confederates lost 18,454.

As a result of the battle of Chickamauga Creek, the Army of the Cumberland was driven back nine miles into the town of Chattanooga itself. Here again Rosecrans made a fatal tactical blunder, for he withdrew the covering detachment which held the northern spur of Lookout Mountain, a precipitous cliff towering 630 feet above the river and two miles south of the town. This feature, 2,392 feet above the sea, commanded every approach to the town by river, road or railway. *Bragg* at once occupied Lookout Mountain, and also Missionary Ridge, a separate feature running north and south, three miles east of the town and 500 feet above the level of the river. Rosecrans and his army of 45,000 now faced disaster, as their communications were in peril and they were already reduced to half rations.

To meet this emergency, Lincoln's first step was to move Joseph Hooker, with two corps from the Army of the Potomac, to reinforce Rosecrans at Chattanooga. Hooker was not the most brilliant officer in the Union army. He had been commissioned from West Point six years before Grant and had served with distinction in the Mexican War, but had resigned his Commission in 1853. As a Brigadier in the Army of the Potomac he had earned the nickname of 'Fighting Joe', but was unfitted to command any formation higher than a division. At the battle of Chancellorsville, five months earlier, he had been thoroughly beaten by *Lee* and *Jackson*. Hooker, with XI and XII Corps, numbering 23,000, after making a circuitous journey by rail through Pennsylvania, Ohio and Kentucky, reached Stevenson (Ala) on the Tennessee River on 3 October. On arrival his two corps were combined to form XX Corps, and under orders from Rosecrans he moved up to Bridgeport, 47 miles below Chattanooga, and prepared to cross the river.

In accordance with Lincoln's orders received on 23 September, Grant had at once sent off Sherman's XV Corps of four divisions to reinforce Rosecrans, and he also moved McPherson's XVII Corps eastwards. But these troops had over 300 miles to travel on a single and much damaged railway track, and could not reach Chattanooga before several weeks. Lincoln now realized that, to avoid a major disaster, a radical change of command was essential. On 3 October he decided to entrust Grant with the chief command of all the Union forces between the Mississippi and the Alleghenies. Grant was then at Vicksburg, still crippled by his riding accident. He did not receive the telegram until the 10th, but immediately answered the call. Travelling by steamer up the Mississippi, he reached Cairo on the 17th and took train for Louisville (Ky), where he had been ordered to report. There he was met by Edwin McMasters Stanton, the Secretary of War, who confirmed his appointment to command the 'Military Division of the Mississippi', which embraced the Armies of the Tennessee, the Cumberland and the Ohio. Stanton gave him the choice of either Rosecrans or Thomas to command the Army of the Cumberland. Grant chose Thomas without hesitation, and Rosecrans was sent to the rear to command the Department of Missouri. Sherman, now on his way eastward, was given command of the Army of the Tennessee; Ambrose Everett Burnside, further east at Knoxville, was commanding the Army of the Ohio.

Rosecrans indeed had proved quite unequal to the occasion. The War Department representative at his headquarters had reported to Washington on 16 October:

> Nothing can prevent the retreat of the army from this place within a fortnight.... General Rosecrans seems to be insensible to the impending danger, and dawdles with trifles in a manner which can scarcely be imagined.... All this precious time is lost because our dazed and mazy commander cannot perceive the catastrophe that is close upon us, nor fix his mind upon means of preventing it. I never saw anything which seemed so lamentable and hopeless.

Grant certainly had his work cut out to avoid the impending catastrophe. His first telegram to Thomas was: 'Hold Chattanooga at all hazards; I will be there as soon as possible.' Thomas replied: 'We will hold the town till we starve.' They had already nearly reached that point. Grant with his staff left Louisville by train on 21 October via Nashville and Stevenson, reaching railhead at Bridgeport the following day. Bridgeport was on the right bank of the Tennessee River and 47 miles down stream from Chattanooga, so Grant had to undergo a long and arduous ride over roads knee-deep in mud. He still had to walk on crutches, so he had to be carried across places where it was not safe to ride.

Grant reached Thomas's headquarters at Chattanooga a little before dark on 23 October. The first problem to be solved was a logistic one, namely to organize a secure supply line to Chattanooga from railhead at Bridgeport. Grant found that Thomas, on taking over from Rosecrans, had already evolved a plan which resulted from suggestions made to him on the 19th by his Chief Engineer, Brigadier-General William Farrar Smith. Grant had known Smith at West Point, when the latter was a cadet, two years his junior, and he at once recognized the merits of Smith's plan, which he adopted. This involved the construction of two pontoon bridges, one at Brown's Ferry, 1½ miles west of Chattanooga, and the other 12 miles down stream at Kelly's Ferry. Provided that a covering force were stationed in Lookout Valley, these bridges would enable reinforcements and supplies to be conveyed from Bridgeport to Chattanooga by a wagon-road out of range of the Confederate artillery on Lookout Mountain. On the following day Grant ordered Hooker's corps to cross the

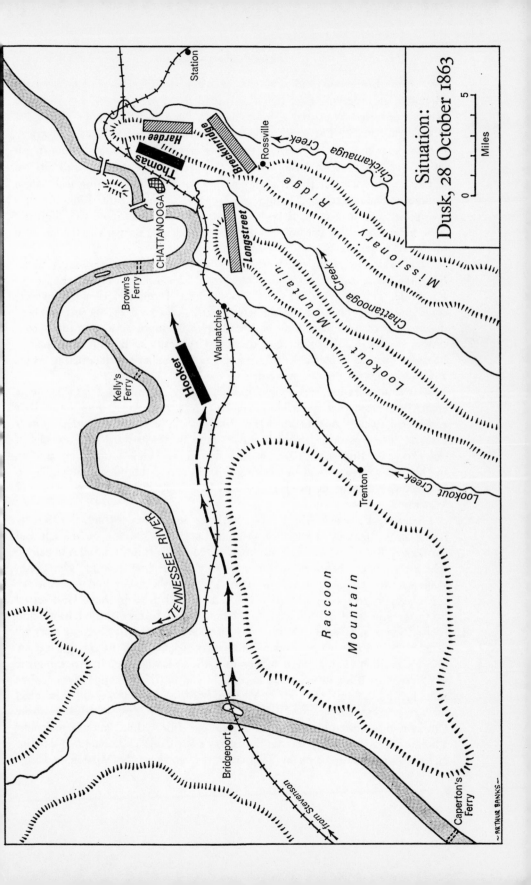

Situation:
Dusk, 28 October 1863

Miles
0   5

~ARTHUR BANKS~

river from Bridgeport and occupy a position in the valley facing Lookout Mountain in order to cover the wagon-road to Brown's Ferry. On the 28th Hooker occupied Wauhatchie in Lookout Valley, and that night repulsed a Confederate attack. The army's supply line was now secure. It was known by the troops as the 'cracker line', as they now received their biscuit ration regularly. Within a week of Grant's arrival, his army was restored to full rations.

The establishment of the 'cracker line' was quite an engineering feat, as the Tennessee River between Chattanooga and Kelly's Ferry runs through a narrow gorge, 300 to 400 yards wide, and the current is so rapid that steamers have to be hauled up stream by winch. The bridge at Brown's Ferry involved the use of 60 pontoons.

Grant was now being constantly urged by Lincoln to do something to relieve the pressure on Burnside, who with 25,000 men was blockaded in Knoxville, 113 miles to the north-east in East Tennessee. Grant, however, could undertake no offensive operation until the arrival of Sherman, whose divisions were now hastening eastward from Memphis under arduous conditions, as the Confederates had destroyed the railway in numerous places. Sherman eventually reached Bridgeport on 13 November and reported to Grant at Chattanooga on the following day.

Meanwhile Grant's opponent, *Braxton Bragg*, committed a fatal strategic error. Influenced perhaps by his President, *Jefferson Davis*, who a few days earlier had visited Lookout Mountain, *Bragg* on 3 November despatched *James Longstreet*'s corps of 20,000 men and 80 guns north-eastward to Knoxville in order to crush Burnside's Army of the Ohio. Thus, while Grant was building up his army, *Bragg* was weakening his. It was a blunder comparable to Napoleon's when he despatched Grouchy in pursuit of Blücher on the eve of Waterloo.

Tactically, however, *Bragg*'s position was immensely strong. Firmly entrenched on the crest of the high ground, Lookout Mountain on the left and Missionary Ridge on the right, his line formed a re-entrant, ten miles in extent, which completely hemmed in Grant's army in the low ground below him, while Grant's troops had an unfordable river in their rear and a precarious line of supply to their railhead, which ran parallel to their front. Undeterred by these physical disadvantages, Grant determined to take the offensive, and evolved his plan of attack. With *Longstreet*'s departure and Sherman's arrival he now had a distinct numerical superiority, 60,000 men to *Bragg*'s 33,000. *Bragg*'s position, too, though topographically so favourable, had one logistic weakness, for all his supplies had to come by rail to Chickamauga Station, four miles behind the northern spur of Missionary Ridge. This was also the railhead for *Longstreet*'s corps, now moving on Knoxville. Grant decided to make Chickamauga Station his main tactical objective. His outline plan was to mount a holding attack with Hooker on the enemy's left flank on Lookout Mountain, and another holding attack by Thomas in the centre on the Missionary Ridge position. *Bragg* would thus be induced to weaken his right flank at Tunnel Hill, the northern extremity of Missionary Ridge. Meanwhile Sherman's xv Corps would cross to the right bank of the Tennessee by the pontoon bridge at Brown's Ferry, and would be hidden in a concealed camp two miles north of Chattanooga. During the night Sherman's troops would recross the river in ferry-boats at the point, up stream of Chattanooga, where the river is joined by Chickamauga Creek. Sherman would then with three divisions deliver the main assault on Tunnel Hill and press on to Chickamauga Station. It was a clever plan and it eventually succeeded, though not exactly as Grant had intended.

The Union preliminary attack was launched at 2 p.m. on 23 November. Thomas's two corps, Gordon Granger's iv Corps and John McCauley Palmer's xiv Corps, moved out from their trenches as if in drill order and captured the Confederate picket line, which occupied a lower crest in front of Missionary Ridge. The new line was entrenched during the night and reinforced with artillery. This attack on the enemy centre induced *Bragg* to transfer a division from his left flank to reinforce Missionary Ridge. This enabled Hooker, who had been reinforced with one of Sherman's divisions, to attack and capture Lookout Mountain on the 24th after a stiff engagement, which Hooker fancifully called 'the battle above the clouds'. In fact the weather was so bad that the mountain-top was shrouded in mist.

On the left flank, however, Sherman's progress had not been so rapid as Grant had expected, for he had encountered unforeseen delays. Having got two of his divisions across the river at Brown's Ferry, a sudden rise of the river destroyed the pontoon bridge, so that his third division was unable to cross. Grant therefore had to reinforce him with one of Thomas's divisions. During the night of the 23rd/24th Sherman's two divisions crossed the river in 116 boats, each carrying 30 men. The Confederate pickets on the left bank were overrun and a bridgehead established. Under the supervision of Grant's Chief Engineer, Brigadier-General W. F. Smith, a pontoon bridge, 450 yards long, was constructed immediately after daylight and Sherman's artillery and cavalry crossed over. At midday he launched his divisions to attack Tunnel Hill, and by sunset had reached and occupied the crest, but found to his dismay that this was only a subsidiary ridge; the main ridge of Tunnel Hill still faced him across a steep ravine.

During the day *Bragg* realized that the *Schwerpunkt* of Grant's attack was directed on the right flank at Tunnel Hill. He therefore withdrew the troops holding Lookout Mountain and transferred them to his right on Missionary Ridge, leaving a screen of troops to hold the line of the Chattanooga Creek. He held the main crest of Missionary Ridge with three divisions of *Breckinridge*'s corps, while *Hardee* with three divisions was moved northward to defend Tunnel Hill. Grant ordered Sherman to renew his attack on Tunnel Hill at daybreak on the 25th.

The morning of 25 November dawned clear and frosty after the rain and mist of the previous day. Certain gains had been made, but the battle had not gone as Grant had planned it. Indeed the main advance had been made by Hooker on the right, where Grant had only intended a demonstration, and Sherman's principal assault on the left had been held up. *Bragg* had realized that this was the danger spot and was sending every available man from his left and centre to reinforce *Hardee* at Tunnel Hill. The critical moment had now come. Grant was directing the battle from Thomas's command post at Orchard Knob, below the centre of Missionary Ridge. This was in the new forward line which Thomas's men had gained on the 23rd, and was now held by four divisions, two of Gordon Granger's IV Corps and two of Palmer's XIV Corps, commanded respectively by Richard Johnson, Philip Sheridan, Thomas John Wood and Absalom Baird. From here Grant had a good view of the whole battlefield. He had ordered Hooker to swing to his left and roll up the enemy resistance on Missionary Ridge, but Hooker's move northward was held up, as the Confederates had destroyed the bridges over the Chattanooga Creek. Grant now decided that he must relieve the pressure on Sherman by making a strong demonstration against Missionary Ridge to prevent *Bragg* from detaching more troops to Tunnel Hill. For this he intended to use Thomas's four divisions, numbering 20,000 bayonets. Facing them on the ridge and strongly entrenched were *Breckinridge*'s 13,000 infantry and 2,000 gunners. At 3.30 p.m. the signal for the forward move was given by six guns fired in rapid succession from Orchard Knob. Thomas's four divisions advanced up the slope, preceded by two lines of skirmishers. The attack overran the forward Confederate line, capturing a thousand of the defenders, but there they were halted by a hail of musketry and grape shot from the strongly entrenched main position. The issue hung in the balance; had they retreated, Grant's army would have been split in two and driven into the Tennessee River. However, the whole Union line, without orders but obeying an instinctive urge to advance, continued their assault up the steep slope and carried the main Confederate position. From Orchard Knob Grant, Thomas and Granger watched this astonishing spectacle with apprehension; if the attack were repulsed, the battle would be lost. 'Who ordered those men up the ridge?' snapped Grant. Thomas denied having issued any order to advance beyond the forward enemy line. Granger added: 'They are going without orders; when those fellows get started, all hell can't stop them.'

There was no need to worry. In spite of heavy casualties the four Union divisions pressed forward to the crest and carried the main Confederate position. A panic seized *Breckinridge*'s men and they streamed down the rear slope in confusion. Meanwhile Hooker had succeeded in crossing the Chattanooga Creek and rolled up the defenders from the south. *Hardee*'s corps on Tunnel Hill, seeing its retreat threatened, also abandoned the field. The pursuit was continued for two days and Grant detached Sherman's corps north-eastward

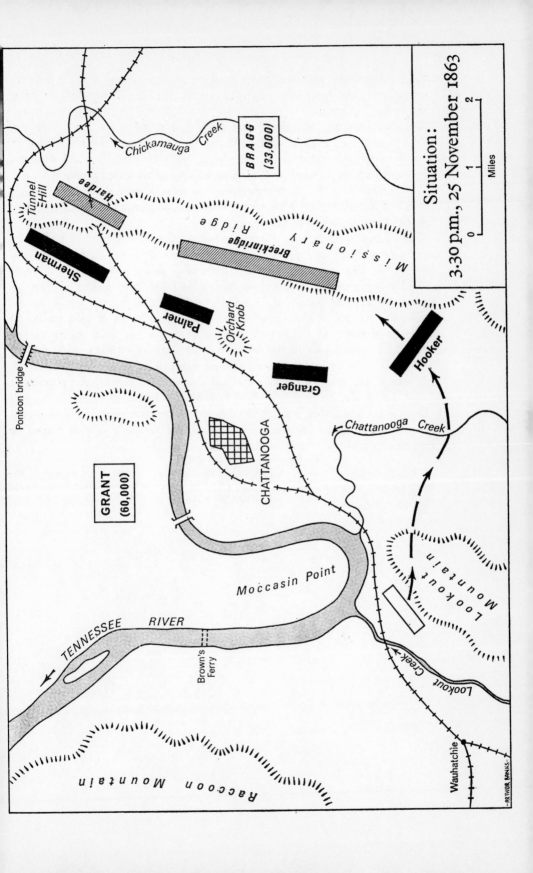

Situation:
3.30 p.m., 25 November 1863

Miles
0   1   2

BRAGG
(33,000)

Chickamauga Creek

Hardee

Tunnel Hill

Sherman

Breckinridge

Missionary Ridge

Palmer

Orchard Knob

Hooker

Granger

Chattanooga Creek

CHATTANOOGA

Pontoon bridge

GRANT
(60,000)

Moccasin Point

Lookout Mountain

TENNESSEE RIVER

Brown's Ferry

Lookout Creek

Wauhatchie

Raccoon Mountain

ARTHUR BANKS

to relieve Burnside, who was being hard pressed by *Longstreet* at Knoxville. Sherman reached Knoxville on 6 December, forcing *Longstreet* to retire through the mountains.

The casualties on both sides were fairly heavy, 5,815 for the Union and 6,687 admitted by the Confederates. But the greater part of the admitted Confederate loss was reported as 4,146 prisoners,[2] so that their killed and wounded only numbered 2,541, whereas the Union killed and wounded numbered 5,465. The difference was due to the fact that the former were defending strongly entrenched positions and had every advantage of ground. The Union army captured 40 guns and more than 7,000 rifles.

Chattanooga was perhaps Grant's greatest tactical victory. He had taken over command of an army which was not only defeated, demoralized and starving, but also occupied a tactically impossible position. Yet within a month he had reorganized it, restored its morale and led it to victory. When his original battle plan miscarried, he quickly reacted to each fresh situation, and successfully controlled the action of his troops on a front of nine miles. As the result of two and a half years' campaigning he had now grown to full stature as a commander in the field. By his successive victories at Vicksburg and Chattanooga he had destroyed the two main nerve centres of Confederate resistance in the western theatre. He had also at last liberated the population of east Tennessee, an objective close to Lincoln's heart.

During its December session the United States Congress in Washington resolved that 'a medal be struck for General Grant, and a vote of thanks be given to him and the officers of his army'.

2. The figure reported by the Confederate staff, but Grant asserts in his account of the battle that 'we captured 6,142 prisoners', which is more probably correct. This would increase the total Confederate casualties to 8,683 (*Grant*, II, 95).

PART III

ACHIEVEMENT

XVII

Supreme Command
March–April 1864

After his striking victory at Chattanooga, Grant withdrew his headquarters to Nashville, where he was more centrally placed and had better communications. Thomas was left at Chattanooga, while Sherman watched *Longstreet* in the Alleghenies. Grant would now have liked to execute his previous project of advancing south to Mobile on the Gulf and also south-east to occupy Atlanta (Ga), which would have cut the main supply artery of *Lee*'s Army of Northern Virginia, the largest Confederate Army now in the field. In his Memoirs he has recorded his plan as follows:

> I expected to retain the command I then had, and prepared myself for the campaign against Atlanta. I also had great hopes of having a campaign made against Mobile from the Gulf. I expected after Atlanta fell to occupy that place permanently, and to cut off *Lee*'s army from the West by way of the [rail]road running through Augusta to Atlanta and thence south-west.[1]

But this ambitious plan was not approved in Washington, so Grant occupied himself by inspecting in turn his widely dispersed troops. Towards the end of December he went to Knoxville, where the Army of the Ohio was commanded by John Gray Foster, who had replaced Ambrose Burnside, now demoted to command a corps in the eastern theatre. The weather turned intensely cold, the thermometer falling to zero Fahrenheit, which discouraged further military operations.

Early in January Grant decided to send Sherman west to Memphis and Vicksburg with the object of clearing the Confederates out of Mississippi, where *Leonidas Polk* had concentrated two infantry divisions and a large force of cavalry at Meridian, an important railway junction which would make a good starting-place for an advance on either Mobile or Atlanta. On 3 February Sherman, with two columns under McPherson and Hurlbut, advanced through

1. *Grant*, II, 100.

Jackson, occupied Meridian on the 14th and destroyed the railway, the enemy retreating into Alabama. In conjunction with Sherman's advance Grant ordered Thomas to move south on Dalton (Ga), where he was confronted by the main Confederate army in the west, now commanded by *Joseph Johnston*, who had replaced *Bragg* after the battle of Chattanooga. On 3 March, however, an entirely new situation arose, for Grant was ordered by Lincoln to report to Washington and assume supreme command of all the Union armies.

Lincoln had at last grasped the basic necessity for unity of command. Previously, he had been distracted between divergent strategic aims with a plethora of military commanders in two geographically distinct theatres of war. Disappointed by incompetent professionals like McClellan and Halleck, he had for a time tried both to govern the country and to command its armies in person which, besides being too great a strain, was beyond his competence. Now at last, after three years of war, he had found the ideal Commander-in-Chief, one who had proved himself in the field by winning battles, and who also possessed common sense and a balanced mind; above all, one who would not attempt to override political principles with military demands, for Grant was firmly imbued with the doctrine that strategy must be the servant and not the dictator of policy. Between these two men of humble origin, the great statesman and the good soldier, there was formed at once a bond of mutual confidence and respect, which would at last break the deadlock of the Civil War.

On 8 March the new Commander-in-Chief, accompanied by his eldest son Fred, a teen-ager, arrived at Washington and booked a room at Willard's Hotel. That evening the President gave a reception at the White House in his honour and greeted him cordially. They had never met before; the lanky six-foot-four President towered above the stocky five-foot-eight General. On the following day Grant reported at the Executive Mansion, where Lincoln in the presence of the Cabinet formally handed to him his commission as Lieutenant-General in the U.S. Army, which gave him senior rank to every other serving officer.[2] Halleck, the previous General-in-Chief, was relegated to the newly created post of Chief of Staff in the War Department, an appointment for which his purely administrative abilities were better suited.

Grant had already decided that Sherman would succeed him in command of the 'Military Division of the Mississippi', that is, the area between the Mississippi and the Alleghenies, and that his other favourite subordinate, McPherson, would replace Sherman in command of the Army of the Tennessee, McPherson's xv Corps being taken over by John Alexander Logan. Thomas was left in command of the Army of the Cumberland, and John McAllister Schofield had previously been promoted to command the Army of the Ohio at Knoxville. These appointments were all confirmed by the President.

2. Grant was the first officer to be promoted to Lieutenant-General in the U.S. Army since Washington. Winfield Scott only held the rank of Brevet Lieutenant-General.

17 *Field Telegraph battery wagon in Wilderness battle, 1864*

18 *Railway bridge over Potomac River repaired by Union engineers*

19   *General* Robert E. Lee (*1807–1870*)

20   *Major-General W. T. Sherman*
(1820–1891)

The command structure in Washington appeared to Grant to be top-heavy and cumbersome; Halleck and Stanton, the Secretary of War, were dealing directly with 19 separate commanders, and Grant determined to simplify the chain of command.

Grant has described in his Memoirs his first private conversation with the President:

> In my first interview with Mr. Lincoln alone he stated to me that he had never professed to be a military man or to know how campaigns should be conducted, and never wanted to interfere in them: but that procrastination on the part of commanders, and the pressure from the people at the North and Congress, *which was always with him,* forced him into issuing his series of 'Military Orders'.... All he wanted or had ever wanted was some one who would take the responsibility and act, and call on him for all the assistance needed, pledging himself to use all the power of the Government in rendering such assistance. Assuring him that I would do the best I could with the means at hand, and avoid as far as possible annoying him or the War Department, our first interview ended.[3]

Grant had originally intended to exercise his command from some central place in the western theatre, but he now decided that his headquarters must be in Virginia, so as to be in close touch both with the Government in Washington and with the headquarters of the Army of the Potomac, which was now facing *Lee's* army on the banks of the Rapidan. On the day after his interview with the President, therefore, he paid a visit to General Meade's headquarters at Brandy Station, 50 miles from Washington, on the Orange and Alexandria Railroad. George Gordon Meade, whom Grant had not met since the Mexican War, was nearly seven years his senior in age. He had graduated from West Point eight years before Grant, but, having no military ambition, he resigned his commission in the following year to become a civil engineer. Six years later, however, he obtained a commission in the Corps of Topographical Engineers, in which he was serving as a Captain on the outbreak of war in 1861. His fighting record had been good, though not brilliant; he had commanded a brigade in the Seven Days' Battle in June 1862, a division at Fredericksburg six months later, and a corps at Chancellorsville in May 1863. Three days before the victory of Gettysburg he had replaced the incompetent Hooker in command of the Army of the Potomac, but incurred Lincoln's censure by his failure to exploit that success. He was slow and methodical; not a thruster. Grant describes his interview with Meade as follows:

> Meade evidently thought that I might want to make still one more change not yet ordered. He said to me that I might want an officer who had served with me in the West, mentioning Sherman specially, to take his place. If so, he begged me not to hesitate about making the change.... For himself, he would serve to the best of his ability wherever placed. I assured him that I had no thought of substituting any one for him. As to Sherman, he could not be spared from the West.[4]

3. *Grant,* II, 122.
4. *ibid.,* II, 117.

As soon as he had returned to Washington from his visit to Meade, Grant set off to Nashville for a conference with Sherman to discuss future plans in the western theatre. Grant's intention was that Sherman should advance southward from Chattanooga and destroy *Joseph Johnston*'s army which was concentrated near Dalton (Ga); he would then press on to occupy Atlanta. Meanwhile, Banks, who had a separate force of 40,000 men in Louisiana, would capture Mobile and then swing east to support Sherman in Georgia. Unfortunately, in January Halleck had dispatched Banks's force on an expedition up the Red River, a right-bank tributary of the Mississippi, with the object of occupying Shreveport (La), a perfectly futile dispersal of force which served no strategic purpose. Banks had already progressed so far that it was now too late to recall him.

On returning to Washington, Grant's next step was to effect a complete reorganization of the Union cavalry, which hitherto had not been properly handled in tactical cooperation with the other arms, but was dispersed in independent brigades, which were mainly employed in guarding lines of communication or in raiding enemy territory. Now, for the first time in the history of the U.S. Army, Grant created a Cavalry Corps. In command of it, to the consternation of the War Department, he placed a young infantryman, Philip Henry Sheridan, 33 years old, who had displayed conspicuous qualities as a leader while commanding an infantry division of IV Corps in the storming of Missionary Ridge at the battle of Chattanooga. The Cavalry Corps, some 12,000 strong, consisted of three cavalry divisions, each of two or three cavalry brigades. Each division had two batteries of horse artillery, with two more batteries in corps reserve.

With considerable magnanimity, Grant now urged the Secretary of War to reinstate his old colleague and rival at Shiloh, Don Carlos Buell, who had been removed from command of the Army of the Cumberland after *Bragg*'s invasion of Kentucky in 1862. As a result, Buell was offered a command in Sherman's army, but declined it, as he was senior to Sherman as a Major-General. As Grant rather bitterly remarked: 'The worst excuse a soldier can make for declining service is that he once ranked the commander he is ordered to report to.'

The eastern theatre of war, to which Grant had now been called, was very different geographically from the Mississippi Basin in which he had previously been operating. The river system of Tidewater Virginia, instead of offering arteries for the invasion of Confederate territory, presented a series of formidable transverse barriers: the Rappahannock with its tributary the Rapidan; the Mattapony; the Pamunkey with its tributaries, the North and South Anna; and finally the great James River, which expanded to a broad estuary some miles south of Richmond. These rivers formed a succession of strong defensive lines behind which *Lee*'s army was securely entrenched. It is true that they all debouched into Chesapeake Bay, where the supremacy of the Union navy afforded an opportunity for amphibious operations to turn the enemy's eastern flank, but in practice such operations would be difficult to carry out, and the enemy would be acting on interior lines. The country between the rivers was in those days heavily timbered; the roads were narrow and very bad; the soil was a heavy clay which, until the end of April, made the movement of troops and transport extremely arduous. It was largely due to these geographical factors, coupled with the defensive power of the rifle, that throughout three years the Army of Northern Virginia, although far inferior numerically, had been able to withstand the repeated assaults of the Army of the Potomac.

It may be that at first Grant did not fully appreciate the enormous odds against offensive operations in such terrain. He may have imagined that a little more drive and more forceful leadership would suffice to break the Confederate resistance. He probably underestimated the sacrifice of human life that would be entailed in order to achieve victory. On the other hand, he did realize the determination of the Southerners to fight to the bitter end in defence of their State liberties, which meant that their armies must be crushed decisively, both in the east and in the west. This involved a war of attrition. But Grant's vision extended farther than a mere attrition of the enemy's man-power; he intended also to cut off the Confederate armies from their material resources. By the beginning of 1864 the food supplies of Virginia had been exhausted, and *Lee*'s army was now entirely dependent on supplies from Alabama, Georgia and the Carolinas. Richmond, the capital, possessed the only gun factory in the South; but there was also a steel rolling-mill at Atlanta (Ga); there were powder mills at Raleigh (N.C.) and Augusta (Ga), and there were factories for the manufacture of small-arms and small-arms ammunition at Fayetteville and Asheville (N.C.), Charleston (S.C.), and at Augusta and Savannah (Ga). Augusta and Atlanta were the main railway junctions by which supplies could reach the front. Grant's strategic plan therefore envisaged an offensive operation by all the Union armies on a front which stretched from the Mississippi to Chesapeake Bay, a distance of 800 miles. While Meade's army in the east held and wore down the Army of Northern Virginia under *Lee*, Sherman's Army of the Mississippi would pivot on Chattanooga, crush *Joseph Johnston*'s army and wheel south-eastward through Atlanta, thus severing the Confederate forces from their souces of supply. It was a conception of colossal scope; in fact it was the 'Schlieffen Plan' multiplied by four, so far as distances were involved. The plan succeeded eventually, but not until 12 months later.

Schlieffen's last will and testament to the German General Staff had been 'make my right wing strong'. Because they failed to make the decisive right wing strong enough, the Germans in September 1914 lost the battle of the Marne. Similarly, Grant was forced by political circumstances to make his left wing and centre stronger than his right, so that Sherman was not given that preponderance of strength which would have enabled him to crush *John-*

ston's army west of the Alleghenies and swing south-eastward into Georgia. *Lee* had already twice crossed the Potomac to invade Union territory and threaten Washington, once in September 1862 and again in June 1863. Lincoln could not afford to let this happen a third time, especially in the year of the Presidential election. The bulk of the Union armies had therefore perforce to be concentrated in the eastern theatre. Owing to Banks's force (40,000) having already been diverted to an extraneous operation in Louisiana, Sherman was left with only 100,000 to deal with *Johnston*'s 71,000.

In the eastern theatre, apart from the large number of troops tied up in the Washington defences and in guarding the lines of communication, Grant had available some 185,000 fighting men. These again, owing to political considerations, had to be split up between several separate commands. The bulk of them, some 100,000, made up Meade's Army of the Potomac in central Virginia, which was facing *Lee*'s Army of Northern Virginia (64,000) on the Rapidan. On Meade's left flank was Butler's Army of the James (33,000) at Fortress Monroe on Chesapeake Bay. Covering Meade's right flank was the Army of West Virginia (32,000) under Franz Sigel, which guarded the strategic corridor of the Shenandoah Valley and also protected the important Baltimore and Ohio Railroad. In general reserve in Maryland, besides the troops allotted to the Washington defences, was Ambrose Burnside's IX Corps (20,000).

Grant was far from happy about the abilities of his subordinate commanders, particularly in the eastern theatre. They were a poor lot, but many of them had to be retained for political reasons. Meade was not a brilliant soldier, but he was popular with the troops, though not with his officers, and after all he was the victor of Gettysburg. A far worse case was Benjamin Franklin Butler, who commanded the left wing of the armies. Butler was an astute politician and lawyer, but without any military ability. In April 1862, when Admiral Farragut was responsible for the capture of New Orleans, Butler had been in command of the occupying troops, but his treatment of the civilian population had aroused general condemnation. At a later stage Grant was compelled to remove him from command of the Army of the James, but he had to be retained until after the Presidential election in November owing to the political influence which he wielded. Another political friend of Lincoln was Ambrose Everett Burnside, who had been removed from command of the Army of the Potomac after the ineptitude which he had displayed at Fredericksburg in December 1862. He was now commanding IX Corps, which formed the reserve to Meade's army, and should have formed part of it, but Burnside, who ranked senior to Meade, refused to serve under him, so had to be left independent. He too had to be removed later. Grant's other independent subordinate, Franz Sigel, also lacked military ability, in spite of his early training as a Lieutenant in the Grand Ducal army of Baden. After taking part in the 1848 Revolution, he had emigrated to America and exercised considerable influence over the large community of German settlers in St. Louis (Mo), whom he had encouraged to enlist in the cause of the Union. His appointment had been made to capture the German vote. Within a fortnight of the opening of the 1864 campaign he suffered a serious reverse and Grant relieved him of his command. Banks, commanding the Army of the Gulf in Louisiana, also owed his appointment to political reasons, and had to be removed later for incompetence.

Apart from the handicap of being saddled with incompetent subordinates whom he could not dismiss until they committed gross blunders in the field, Grant had to consider other political factors in planning his next campaign. In view of the enormous advantages possessed by the Union in manpower and material resources, a Fabian form of strategy might have proved cheaper in human lives, for the Confederate economy could have been completely strangulated by the pressure of naval blockade combined with control of the Mississippi. But this would need time, and the time factor might well favour the South. The Presidential election impending in November made it essential to convince the electorate than an early Northern victory was assured. Otherwise, war weariness, already prevalent, might bring about a reaction in favour of a peace settlement at the price of dissolving the Union, which was very far from Lincoln's aim. The lapse of time might also favour the Confederacy in another way. Owing to the close blockade of the Southern ports by the Union navy, the export of raw cotton had now almost ceased, and the textile mills of Lancashire were in consequence at a standstill. Economic pressure might therefore induce the British Government to intervene on behalf of the South by insisting on a negotiated settlement. For all these reasons, and it required no prompting from Lincoln to endorse them, Grant realized that he must strike the enemy vigorously as soon as the state of the ground made military operations practicable.

After his conference with Sherman in the western theatre Grant returned to the east, and on 26 March established his general headquarters at Culpeper Court House, six miles further south down the Orange and Alexandria Railroad from Meade's army headquarters at Brandy Station. Grant had thus interposed his command post between Meade's headquarters and the front line. In locating his headquarters so far forward, Grant committed a serious error which, strangely enough, has escaped comment by any of his military critics. Grant was not so much breathing down Meade's neck as breathing down his shirt-front. Culpeper Court House was six miles further forward than Meade's headquarters and only six miles distant from the front line on the Rapidan. Indeed it was only 17 miles away from *Lee*'s army headquarters near Orange Court House. The establishment of his general headquarters so far forward indicated that he had little confidence in Meade's tactical ability; besides, it deprived Grant of that wider perspective of the whole theatre of operations which was essential for the conduct of war on such a wide front. His general headquarters would have been more suitably located 33 miles further back at Manassas Junction, or even 57 miles further back at Alexandria, where he would have been in closer touch with the President and the War Department in Washington, as well as with Butler and Sigel. Grant's proximity to Meade's headquarters in fact resulted in his interfering too much with the tactical operations of Meade's army, and led to a steady deterioration in the relations between the two commanders.

A further disadvantage of his headquarters being located so far forward was the danger to Grant's personal security; indeed it nearly led to his capture before the campaign started. On 30 April the Commander-in-Chief had gone to Washington for a final conference with the President. During his return journey to Culpeper in a special train without any escort, a large cloud of dust was seen to the east as the train approached Warrenton Junction, 23 miles north of Culpeper. When Grant's party reached the junction they heard that a large body of Confederate cavalry had just passed through on a raid behind the Union lines. It was a narrow escape.

As soon as he had settled down at Culpeper, Grant thought out his plan for the 1864 campaign, which he then outlined in separate directives to his five army commanders. On 4 April his instructions to Sherman were as follows:

It is my design, if the enemy keep quiet and allow me to take the initiative in the spring campaign, to work all parts of the army together, and somewhat towards a common centre.... I have sent orders to Banks, by private messenger, to finish up his present expedition to Shreveport with all dispatch; ... to abandon all of Texas, except the Rio Grande ... and to collect from his command not less than 25,000 men. To this I will add 5,000 men from Missouri. With this force he is to commence operations against Mobile as soon as he can.... You I propose to move against *Johnston*'s army, to break it up and to get into the interior of the enemy's country as far as you can, inflicting all the damage you can against their war resources.

I do not propose to lay down for you a plan of campaign, but simply lay down the work it is desirable to have done, and leave you free to execute it in your own way. Submit to me, however, as early as you can, your plan of operations.

To Meade he wrote five days later:

For information and as instruction to govern your preparations for the coming campaign, the following is communicated confidentially for your own perusal alone.

So far as practicable all the armies are to move together, and towards one common centre. Banks has been instructed ... to move on Mobile.... Sherman will move at the same time you do, or two or three days in advance, *Jo. Johnston*'s army being his objective point, and the heart of Georgia his ultimate aim. If successful he will secure the line from Chattanooga to Mobile with the aid of Banks.

Sigel cannot spare troops from his army to reinforce either of the great armies, but he can aid them by moving directly to his front. This he has been directed to do.... Butler will seize City Point, and operate against Richmond from the south side of the river. His movement will be simultaneous with yours.

Lee's army will be your objective point. Wherever *Lee* goes, there you will go also.[5]

5. This last sentence is quoted verbally from a directive which Lincoln had given to Hooker a year earlier.

Meade's directive goes on to discuss two alternative tactical plans, whether his attack should be aimed at *Lee*'s right flank or his left; this would be decided later after further discussion. Butler and Meade were later given orders to commence their forward move on 4 May, Sherman to move a day later.

These two directives are models of the instructions which a Commander-in-Chief should issue to his Army Commanders. The enemy's main armies were the principal objectives given, not merely the occupation of geographical points. Each commander was given an outline of the other commanders' operational roles, so that intelligent cooperation between them was assured. Each commander was left to work out his own tactical dispositions and administrative arrangements, knowing the general intentions of his Commander-in-Chief. This was the principle followed in all Grant's directives to his subordinates. As he had remarked to an officer of his staff before the battle of Chattanooga,

When I have sufficient confidence in a general to leave him in command of an army, I have enough confidence in him to leave his plans to himself.

Grant invariably made this his practice when dealing with Sherman, whom he trusted implicitly, but less so in the case of Meade who did not inspire him with the same confidence. That was doubtless the reason for the establishment of his headquarters at Culpeper.

Grant's headquarters was in fact a forward tactical command post, consisting of only about a dozen officers. He now had 533,000 troops under his command, but the detailed administration of this vast array was handled by Halleck and Stanton at Washington, which left Grant free to concentrate his attention on the tactical operations in the east. Besides his trusted Chief of Staff, Brigadier-General John Rawlins, the civilian lawyer who had been his *fidus Achates* since he rejoined the army at Galena, Illinois, on the outbreak of war, his staff comprised two Military Secretaries, four Assistant-Adjutant-Generals, one Assistant Quartermaster and five Aides-de-Camp. Four of the A.D.C.s were Regular Lieutenant-Colonels and West Point graduates. They were employed as liaison officers and to carry important orders. One of the A.A.G.s, Captain Ely Samuel Parker, a capable lawyer and engineer, was a full-blooded American-Indian of the Seneca tribe.[6]

By the end of April the dirt roads of Virginia were drying up and becoming passable for military transport vehicles. Grant decided to set in motion his five armies simultaneously in the first week of May. The essence of his plan was that these armies would make a concentric advance directed on Atlanta and Richmond, each army pinning down the enemy forces on its immediate front, so that the Confederates would have no chance of switching their troops

6. Son of the Seneca chief, he was a pre-war friend of Grant at Galena (Ill). He was officially refused a commission on the outbreak of war on account of his race.

from one theatre to another as they had done so successfully in the previous campaigns. Never before had the Union forces all marched to battle in unison, under a single controlling hand and with one concentrated purpose. It was a grandiose plan, but strategically it had its flaws. As already pointed out, the main *Schwerpunkt* of the offensive was to be directed on Atlanta, in order to tear out the enemy's vitals. But Sherman's army, which was to deliver that blow, was weaker than the forces retained on the left wing opposite Richmond, owing to the need to protect the Union capital. Sherman would also have to force his way through the foothills of the Allegheny Range where the defenders would have the advantages of the terrain in their favour.

Another defect in the scheme was that all the armies were strung out in a more or less continuous line from Chattanooga to Chesapeake Bay, a front of over 500 miles. No reserve army was kept in hand to exploit a gap and pour through in an 'expanding torrent'. The eastern theatre did have a local reserve in Burnside's IX Corps, but this was earmarked as a reinforcement for Meade's army, and indeed was already fully committed in guarding his line of communications along the Orange and Alexandria Railroad. There was also Sheridan's newly formed Cavalry Corps of over 12,000 men, but this too was tied to the support of Meade's army.

It would be unfair to criticize Grant for these strategic flaws in his plan of campaign. They were mainly beyond his control, being dictated by prior political requirements. Grant had intended that Sherman's drive on Atlanta would be supported by a turning movement on the part of Banks from the Mississippi Valley, but this never took place owing to Banks having been sent by Halleck to Louisiana on another task, and being now beyond recall. Banks indeed was soon to suffer a severe reverse, and took no further part in the campaign. In the time at his disposal – less than two months from the date of his appointment to supreme command – it was impossible for Grant to effect a more sweeping reorganization of the available formations. He had, in fact, within the space of seven weeks, from a chaotic medley produced a coordinated group of armies imbued with a coherent strategic purpose.

Having outlined his grand strategy for the forthcoming campaign, Grant had to decide on his detailed plan for the eastern theatre where he intended to direct operations personally. Here he was faced with several alternatives. First of all, he had the opportunity of profiting by the naval supremacy of the Union to move part of the Army of the Potomac by sea to some point southeast of Richmond, thus turning *Lee*'s right flank. This project at first sight looked attractive, but Grant rejected it for several reasons. A large force could not be moved in secrecy, and *Lee*, who was operating on interior lines, could have dispatched sufficient troops to repel a hostile landing, while remaining secure behind his fortified position at Richmond. Furthermore, as Grant has pointed out,

If the Army of the Potomac had been moved bodily to the James River by water, *Lee* could have moved a part of his forces back to Richmond, called *Beauregard* from the south to reinforce it, and with the balance moved on Washington.[7]

The governing *political* factor in any strategic plan was that a sufficiently large Union force must always be interposed between *Lee*'s army and Washington. The ruling *military* principle was that *Lee*'s field army must be destroyed, preferably in the open. Merely to drive him into the strong fortress of Richmond and engage in protracted siege operations was not the answer.

The next point to be decided was whether to turn *Lee*'s left flank or his right. The Confederate army, 63,000 strong, was now strongly entrenched on a front of 12 miles behind the upper Rapidan River; its left (west) flank covered the important Orange and Alexandria Railroad, while its right (east) flank rested on Mine Run, a right-bank tributary of the Rapidan. On *Lee*'s right flank, between Mine Run and Fredericksburg, and south of the Rapidan, stretched an extensive jungly tract of country, 15 miles long and 10 miles in depth, known as 'The Wilderness'. This tract of country formed a formidable military obstacle, which had already caused the Army of the Potomac serious trouble in the Chancellorsville campaign of the previous summer. The original forest here had been cut down to supply fuel for smelting iron ore, giving rise to a thick undergrowth of small saplings, 15 to 20 feet high, which restricted vision generally to less than a hundred yards. It was an area more suitable for guerrilla warfare than for the movement of large troop formations. Except in a few clearings, artillery could only operate at point-blank range.

Lee's position south of the Rapidan possessed another topographical advantage. Behind his front line rose a steep hog's-back ridge named Clark Mountain, rising to a height of 1,082 feet above the sea. This afforded *Lee* a series of splendid observation posts from which he could scan the whole Virginian plain to the north and west, similar to Wellington's look-out post on Monte Socorro which dominated the country north and east of the Lines of Torres Vedras.

Grant had now to decide whether to turn *Lee*'s left flank, which would cut him off from Gordonsville and his communications with Atlanta and the south-west, or to turn his right so as to sever his link with Richmond. Grant chose the latter course; according to his own Memoirs this was for purely logistic reasons:

I was not entirely decided as to whether I should move the Army of the Potomac by the right flank of the enemy, or by his left. Each plan presented advantages. If by his right – my left – the Potomac, Chesapeake Bay and tributaries would furnish us an easy line over which to bring all supplies to within easy hauling distance of every position the army could occupy from the Rapidan to the James River. But *Lee* could, if he chose, detach or move his whole army north on a line rather interior to the one I would have to take in following. A movement by his left – our right – would obviate this; but all

7. *Grant*, ii, 141.

that was done would have to be done with the supplies and ammunition we started with. All idea of adopting this latter plan was abandoned when the limited quantity of supplies possible to take with us was considered.[8]

Apart from the logistic aspect, Grant felt that from the strategic point of view he must choose the eastern approach in order to coordinate his advance on land with Butler's move by sea to the mouth of the James River. As he wrote to Halleck on 29 April:

> My own notions about our line of march are entirely made up, but as circumstances beyond my control may change them, I will only state that my effort will be to bring Butler's and Meade's forces together.

Strategically and logistically, Grant made the right choice, but from the tactical point of view his decision was to prove an extremely expensive one, for it resulted in the Army of the Potomac being led to slaughter in the labyrinthine thickets of the Wilderness.

Before describing the operations of the 1864 campaign it will be convenient to tabulate here the order of battle of the opposing sides in the eastern theatre.

UNION FORCES

ARMY OF THE JAMES (Benjamin Franklin Butler)
x Corps (Quincy Adams Gillmore) ⎫
xviii Corps (William Farrar Smith) ⎭   33,000

ARMY OF THE POTOMAC (George Gordon Meade)

ii Corps (Winfield Scott Hancock)	27,000
v Corps (Gouverneur Kemble Warren)	24,000
vi Corps (John Sedgwick)	23,000
ix Corps (Ambrose Everett Burnside)[9]	20,000
Cavalry Corps (Philip Henry Sheridan)	12,000
Artillery and Engineers	14,000

ARMY OF WEST VIRGINIA (Franz Sigel)
viii Corps (Edward Otho Cresap Ord) ⎫
Mixed force (George Crook)   ⎭   32,000

                                            185,000

CONFEDERATE FORCES

ARMY OF NORTHERN VIRGINIA (*Robert Edward Lee*)

i Corps (*James Longstreet*)	11,000
ii Corps (*Richard Stoddert Ewell*)	17,000
iii Corps (*Ambrose Powell Hill*)	22,000

8. *Grant*, ii, 134–7.
9. Burnside's corps was not under Meade's orders, but directly under Grant, until 24 May.

| Cavalry (*James Ewell Brown Stuart*) | 9,000 |
| Artillery and Engineers | 5,000 |

SHENANDOAH VALLEY FORCE (*John Cabell Breckin-ridge*)   12,000

RICHMOND GARRISON   6,000

RESERVE IN NORTH CAROLINA
(*Pierre Gustave Toutant Beauregard*)   15,000

                                                     97,000

Thus Grant's forces in the eastern theatre outnumbered *Lee*'s by two to one. Formations on both sides were similarly organized, each corps, either infantry or cavalry, having three divisions[10] and an artillery brigade. Each infantry division consisted of three infantry brigades, each of five or six regiments. In the Army of the Potomac each artillery brigade had eight to ten batteries, each of six guns. The total number of guns in that army was 316. *Lee*'s Army of Northern Virginia had a total of 274 guns; Confederate batteries had only four guns apiece owing to shortage of equipment.

In the western theatre Sherman had been given *carte blanche* to plan his own campaign for the destruction of *Johnston*'s army. In the centre Sigel was to advance up the Shenandoah Valley from Winchester to Staunton in order to cut the East Tennessee–Virginia railway, in cooperation with another column under Crook in the Alleghenies. On the Union left flank Butler was to embark his two corps at Fortress Monroe and land at Bermuda Hundred, on the right bank of the James River, 16 miles south-east of Richmond and 10 miles north-east of Petersburg. Butler was then to move on Richmond in cooperation with Meade's army.

'D Day' for all the Union armies was fixed for 4 May; the two great protagonists, Grant and *Lee*, were now to cross swords for the first time in mortal combat.

10. Burnside's ix Corps had a fourth division consisting of coloured troops.

Executive Mansion
Washington, April 30. 1864

Lieutenant General Grant,

Not expecting to see you again before the Spring campaign opens, I wish to express, in this way, my entire satisfaction with what you have done up to this time, so far as I understand it. The particulars of your plans I neither know, or seek to know. You are vigilant and self-reliant; and, pleased with this, I wish not to obtrude any constraints or restraints upon you. While I am very anxious that any great disaster, or the capture of our men in great numbers, shall be avoided, I know these points are less likely to escape your attention than they would be mine—. If there is anything wanting which is within my power to give, do not fail, to let me know it. And now with a brave Army, and a just cause, may God sustain you,

Yours very truly
A. Lincoln.

President Lincoln's final directive to Grant before the opening of the 1864 campaign

XVIII

The Wilderness Campaign
4–19 May 1864

On the evening of 3 May Grant summoned the eight senior officers on his staff to a final conference in his headquarter office at Culpeper Court House. He gave them an outline of his plan for the campaign and said:

> I expect to send you to the critical points of the lines to keep me promptly advised of what is taking place, and in cases of great emergency, when new dispositions have to be made on the instant, or it becomes suddenly necessary to reinforce one command by sending to its aid troops from another, and there is not time to communicate with head-quarters, I want you to explain my views to commanders, and urge immediate action, looking to cooperation, without waiting for specific orders from me.[1]

Thus Grant intended to keep the tactical control of every battle in his own hands through the medium of his own personal staff, thereby short-circuiting the commander and staff of the Army of the Potomac. This was not quite the function to be expected of the Generalissimo of five Union armies operating on a front of over 500 miles, but in the circumstances it was justified. *Lee*, when acting on the defensive, had hitherto defeated each successive commander of the Army of the Potomac, including Meade. Grant was not going to risk any repetition of these failures. He was now going to challenge *Lee* on the very same battlefield where *Lee* and *Stonewall Jackson* had so decisively beaten 'Fighting Joe' Hooker exactly twelve months previously. Meade was a better commander than Hooker, but in times of stress he tended to become nervous and irascible; he was known to his staff as 'the Snapping-Turtle'. Grant was certainly right to retain tactical control of the operations in his own hands, and he was a big enough man to assume the entire responsibility for failure or defeat.

Nor did the Generalissimo lose his grip on the other armies under his command. The field telegraph, employed now for the first time in the history

1. *Porter*, 38.

145

of warfare, had revolutionized the system of battlefield communications. Grant himself has described the functioning of his signal corps:

> Nothing could be more complete than the organization and discipline of this body of brave and intelligent men. Insulated wires – insulated so that they would transmit messages in a storm, on the ground or under water – were wound upon reels, making about 200 pounds weight of wire to each reel. Two men and one mule were detailed to each reel. The pack-saddle on which this was carried was provided with a rack ... so that the reel, with its wire, would revolve freely. There was a wagon, supplied with a telegraph operator, battery and telegraph instruments for each division, each corps, each army and my headquarters. ... The mules thus loaded were assigned to brigades, and always kept with the command they were allotted to. ... Thus, in a few minutes longer time than it took a mule to walk the length of its coil, telegraphic communication would be effected between all the headquarters of the army.[2]

By means of this novel communication system Grant not only maintained touch with every infantry brigade on his immediate front, but was also continuously linked with the President and the administrative services in Washington, as well as with Sherman, Sigel and Banks.

The operations of the Army of the Potomac were timed to start at midnight of 3/4 May. Preceded by two of Sheridan's cavalry divisions, the troops moved eastward in two columns down the left bank of the Rapidan. The Union cavalry seized two crossing-places, six miles apart, at Germanna Ford and Ely's Ford, driving away the Confederate pickets. At each crossing-place the engineers rapidly constructed a double pontoon bridge without meeting any hostile opposition. At 6 a.m. the infantry began to cross in two columns, Warren's v Corps followed by Sedgwick's vi Corps at Germanna Ford, and Hancock's ii Corps at Ely's Ford. After crossing the river, the columns plunged into the dense thickets of the Wilderness and headed south-east.

Grant's intention was to outflank *Lee* and march by Spottsylvania Court House to Guiney's Station on the Richmond–Fredericksburg Railroad, 20 miles to the south-east. By doing so he would interpose his army between *Lee* and Richmond, and force *Lee* to fight him in the open. By that time Grant hoped to have joined forces with Butler's army, which was then landing on the south bank of the James River within striking distance of Richmond. Grant's army combined with Butler's would number 150,000, while *Lee*'s mobile force only numbered 64,000, so it should have been easy to crush *Lee* and capture the Confederate capital. It was a sound strategic conception, but it was doomed to failure, firstly owing to the unsuitability of the Wilderness as a battlefield, and secondly because of the tactical ineptitude of Benjamin Butler.

Grant's manœuvre would doubtless have been successful had he pressed on swiftly from the Rapidan bridges to Spottsylvania, only ten miles to the south-east and clear of the Wilderness. Instead of that he ordered his troops to halt a few miles south of the river and bivouac for the night, in order to await the

2. *Grant*, ii, 205–7.

crossing of his supply trains. This was quite unnecessary, for each of his men carried 50 rounds of ammunition and three days' rations in his haversack. The Army of the Potomac was now enmeshed in the Wilderness thickets, exactly where *Lee* was anxious to engage it.

About noon on 4 May Grant and Meade with their staffs crossed the Rapidan at Germanna Ford behind Warren's v Corps. Grant established his temporary headquarters in a deserted house on the south bank of the river and dispatched an urgent order to Burnside's ix Corps, which was guarding the railway at Warrenton Junction, 30 miles in rear, to make a forced march through the night, cross the Rapidan at Germanna Ford, and close up in support of the Army of the Potomac. The rest of the army settled down for the night in its bivouacs, Warren (v) in front at Old Wilderness Tavern, Sedgwick (vi) between him and the river, and Hancock (ii), who had marched from Ely's Ford on a parallel track, six miles farther east at Chancellorsville. The leading troops entrenched and sent out reconnaissance patrols. The Union cavalry scouted to the south-east and encountered elements of the Confederate cavalry near Todd's Tavern.

Meanwhile *Lee* had not remained inactive. Early on the 4th his look-out posts on Clark Mountain reported the movement of the Union columns towards the lower Rapidan, and he at once ordered his three corps to march eastward. Two parallel roads led eastward from Orange Court House through the Wilderness to Fredericksburg. The most northerly was a macadamized road known as the Orange Turnpike; south of it was a corduroy road of felled timber, known as the Orange Plank Road. *Ewell* (ii), holding the right sector of his front, was to march by Locust Grove and follow the Orange Turnpike to the Old Wilderness Tavern. A march of 14 miles would bring him in contact with Warren's corps. *A. P. Hill* (iii), holding the left sector, was to march by New Verdierville and the Orange Plank Road to Parker's Store, a distance of 20 miles. *Longstreet* (i), who was in reserve at Gordonsville, seven miles south of Orange Court House, had much further to march. He was ordered to follow *Hill* along the Orange Plank Road, but actually took the more southerly Catharpin Road, which gave him a march of at least 28 miles, and his pace was somewhat leisurely. *Lee*, in fact, was in no particular hurry, as he wanted to get the whole of Grant's army, with all its supply trains, entangled in the Wilderness before attacking him, so he ordered *Ewell* not to engage the enemy until *Hill* and *Longstreet* had come up abreast of him. *Lee*'s cavalry corps, under *J. E. B. Stuart*, was unfortunately 30 miles away to the east in the Rappahannock Valley south of Fredericksburg, where it had been sent owing to the shortage of forage supplies. It was therefore not able to delay the Union troops while crossing the Rapidan, nor could it operate effectively with *Lee*'s infantry columns. *Lee* has been criticized for keeping *Longstreet* so far back. but he was well placed there had Grant's plan been to turn *Lee*'s left flank instead of his right. On the evening of the 4th *Ewell* had reached a point on the

Orange Turnpike four miles east of Mine Run, where he bivouacked for the night to await the arrival of the other two corps.

Thanks to his efficient telegraphic communications, on the night of the 4th Grant received news that the forces of Sherman, Sigel and Butler had all moved off according to plan. Grant then ordered Meade to continue the advance on the following morning, Warren (v) was to move to Parker's Store, preceded by James Wilson's cavalry division and followed by Sedgwick (vi). Hancock (ii) was to close to his right, keeping touch with Warren, and if the enemy were encountered to move up on Warren's left.

Burnside's ix Corps made a rapid forced march during the night and crossed the Rapidan early on 5 May. At dawn Meade moved his headquarters up to Old Wilderness Tavern, Grant waiting behind to see Burnside on arrival. At 9 a.m. he received a message from Meade to say that an enemy column was approaching along the Orange Turnpike, and that he was deploying Warren's and Sedgwick's corps westward to engage it. Grant at once moved up to Old Wilderness Tavern and established his headquarters close to Meade's, without waiting for Burnside.

Heavy fighting now took place in the thick woods astride the Orange Turnpike, two miles west of the Wilderness Tavern, between the troops of Warren and *Ewell*. As Warren was being hard pressed, Meade brought two of Sedgwick's divisions up to extend his right, sending the third division round to fill the gap on Warren's left. About midday *Hill's* iii Corps had passed Parker's Store on the Orange Plank Road and was threatening to turn Warren's left, so Hancock (ii), who had spent the night at Chancellorsville, was brought round to counter him. Furious fighting now took place along a front of four miles astride the Turnpike and Plank Roads. The Union superiority in rifled artillery was of little use, for very few batteries could be brought into action owing to the thick undergrowth, and they had to fire at point-blank range. As Grant said:

> This arm was in such abundance that the fourth of it could not be used to advantage in such a country as we were destined to pass through. The surplus was much in the way, taking up as it did so much of the narrow and bad roads.[3]

No worse ground could have been chosen for the tactical cooperation of the three arms, and vision was so restricted that the higher commanders could do little to control the action. One of Grant's staff officers described the terrain as follows:

> The outlook was limited in all directions by the almost impenetrable forest with its interlacing trees and tangled undergrowth. The ground upon which the battle was fought was intersected in every direction by winding rivulets, rugged ravines, and ridges of mineral rock. Many excavations had been made in opening iron-ore beds, leaving pits bordered by ridges of earth. Trees had been felled in a number of places to furnish fuel

3. *Grant*, ii, 181.

and supply sawmills. The locality is well described by its name. It was a wilderness in the most forbidding sense of the word.[4]

And one of Hancock's brigade commanders, Alexander Stewart Webb, has thus described the battlefield from his point of view:

As for the Wilderness, it was uneven, with woods, thickets, and ravines right and left. Tangled thickets of pine, scrub-oak, and cedar prevented our seeing the enemy, and prevented any one in command of a large force from determining accurately the position of the troops he was ordering to and fro. The appalling rattle of the musketry, the yells of the enemy, and the cheers of our own men were constantly in our ears. At times, our lines while firing could not see the array of the enemy, not fifty yards distant. After the battle was fairly begun, both sides were protected by log or earth breastworks.[5]

Lee now came up the Orange Plank Road to *Hill*'s command post east of Parker's Store and took charge of the Confederate attack. As *Longstreet* was still several miles from the battlefield, *Lee* halted *Hill*'s advance, which gave Hancock (II) the opportunity to reach and consolidate his position along Brock Road, an important track leading south-east from Old Wilderness Tavern to Spottsylvania. The Union now had three corps in line against the Confederate two, but numbers counted for little as they could not be effectively deployed in the thick woods, but merely blocked the narrow trails. There was hardly any possibility of manœuvre, and the Union commanders had only very inaccurate maps; movements had to be directed by compass bearings, which led to much confusion. The Confederates were on the whole better woodsmen, besides being familiar with the country. Fighting was fierce and frequently hand to hand, so that heavy casualties were incurred by both sides. When night fell at 8 p.m. the battle had reached a deadlock, and the troops on both sides threw up breastworks of logs and earth, more or less on the line of their original collision, and lay down under arms within close range of each other.

That evening Grant felt confident of success. Burnside's IX Corps was now approaching Wilderness Tavern from Germanna Ford, and would be able to attack on the following day, in spite of its long forced march from Warrenton. Grant knew that *Lee* still had *Longstreet*'s I Corps in reserve, and he was anxious to attack at dawn next day before *Longstreet*'s arrival. He ordered Meade to launch his attack at 4.30 a.m. and Burnside (who was not under Meade's command) to move southward to fill the gap in the centre between Warren and Hancock. Meade objected strongly to the early start, as his units had got much intermingled in the wood fighting, and required some hours of daylight to reorganize. Grant relented slightly, ordering the Union attack to be launched at 5 a.m. on 6 May.

Grant had since noon personally directed the operations, so far as he could

4. *Porter*, 49–50.
5. *Battles and Leaders*, IV, 154.

in the confused fighting and difficult terrain. As his command post and Meade's were close together near Wilderness Tavern, he normally issued orders through Meade, though he sometimes gave verbal orders directly to Warren; Burnside, of course, was not under Meade's command at all, which must have been rather exasperating for the nominal commander of the Army of the Potomac.

Having issued his orders for the next day, Grant retired to his tent before 11 p.m., remarking to his staff:

> We shall have a busy day tomorrow, and I think we had better get all the sleep we can tonight. I am a firm believer in the restorative qualities of sleep, and always like to get at least seven hours of it, though I have often been compelled to put up with much less.[6]

At 4.30 a.m. on the 6th – the zero hour which Grant had originally ordered – *Ewell* launched an unexpected attack on Sedgwick's corps, driving back one of the Union brigades, but the situation was quickly restored. Then at 5 a.m. the main Union attack started, but only by Hancock's corps and the left division of Warren's. Burnside's corps, which Grant had intended to take part in the attack, had lost their way in the woods and his leading division did not reinforce Hancock's right until 8 a.m.; the other two divisions arrived much later. Hancock's attack was at first successful. *Hill*'s troops opposing him were very tired, and were driven back for a mile down the Orange Plank Road, where *Lee* had spent the night close to *Hill*'s command post. He had sent an urgent order to *Longstreet* to march all night and deploy on *Hill*'s right. About 6 a.m. the head of *Longstreet*'s column arrived, just in the nick of time to save the Confederate right wing from disaster. *Lee* on his famous grey horse 'Traveller' was trying in person to rally *Hill*'s exhausted and broken troops, when *Longstreet*'s Texan brigade came up at the double. *Lee* led these fresh troops forward in a spirited counter-attack. Hancock's troops, taken by surprise, were driven back with heavy loss. By 11 a.m. both sides were fought out for the time being. *Longstreet* now discovered that the sunken cutting of an unfinished railway offered a covered approach by which he could outflank the Union left. An attack was then made by four brigades along this route in conjunction with a drive by *Longstreet* up the Plank Road. This was initially successful, but Hancock managed to rally his men behind the breastworks they had built along the Brock Road. While *Longstreet* was leading this advance, some of his own troops who had lost direction fired at his party, and he fell, severely wounded. This mishap occurred within a mile of the spot where *Stonewall Jackson* had been shot by his own men a year previously. *Lee* then took tactical command of the Confederate right wing until *Longstreet*'s replacement by *Richard Heron Anderson*, the senior divisional commander in *Hill*'s corps.

On the Union right the battle had reached a complete deadlock, neither

6. *Porter*, 54.

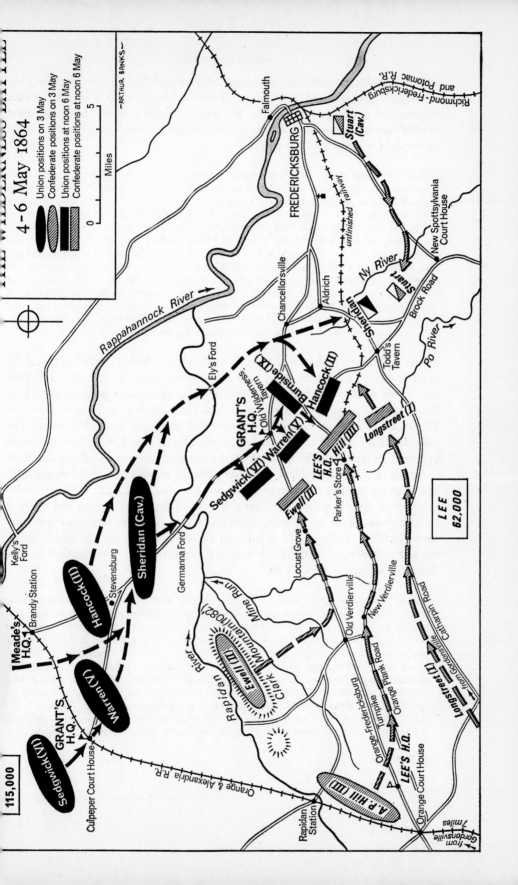

THE WILDERNESS BATTLE

4–6 May 1864

Union positions on 3 May
Confederate positions on 3 May
Union positions at noon 6 May
Confederate positions at noon 6 May

Miles
0   5

~ARTHUR BANKS~

115,000

LEE
62,000

Meade's H.Q.
GRANT'S H.Q.
Sedgwick (VI)
Warren (V)
Hancock (II)
Sheridan (Cav.)
Kelly's Ford
Brandy Station
Culpeper Court House
Stevensburg
Rappahannock River
Germanna Ford
Ely's Ford
Chancellorsville
Aldrich
Falmouth
FREDERICKSBURG
Stuart (Cav.)
New Spottsylvania Court House
Ny River
Sheridan
Stuart
Brock Road
Todd's Tavern
Po River
Old Wilderness Tavern
GRANT'S H.Q.
Sedgwick (VI)
Warren (V)
Burnside (IX)
Hancock (II)
LEE'S H.Q.
Hill (III)
Longstreet (I)
Ewell (II)
Parker's Store
Locust Grove
Mine Run
Mount Pisgah (1082)
Clark
Ewell (II)
Rapidan River
Rapidan Station
Orange & Alexandria R.R.
from Gordonsville
Orange Court House
A.P. Hill (III)
New Verdierville
Old Verdierville
Orange Plank Road
Orange-Fredericksburg Turnpike
Catharpin Road
LEE'S H.Q.
Longstreet (I)
from Gordonsville
7 miles
unfinished railway
Richmond - Fredericksburg and Potomac R.R.

side being able to gain any advantage. Grant and Meade moved their joint command post forward to a house south of the Orange Turnpike, three-quarters of a mile south-west of Wilderness Tavern and a mere half-mile behind the breastworks of Warren's corps. One of Grant's staff has recorded an incident which now took place:

> Warren's troops were driven back on a portion of his line in front of general head-quarters, stragglers were making their way to the rear, the enemy's shells were beginning to fall on the knoll where General Grant was seated on the stump of a tree, and it looked for a while as if the tide of battle would sweep over that point of the field. He rose slowly to his feet, and stood for a time watching the scene, and mingling the smoke of his cigar with the smoke of battle, without making any comments. His horse was in charge of an orderly just behind the hill, but he evidently had no thought of mounting. An officer ventured to remark to him, 'General, wouldn't it be prudent to move headquarters to the other side of the Germanna road till the result of the present attack is known?' The general replied very quietly, between the puffs of his cigar, 'It strikes me it would be better to order up some artillery and defend the present location.' Thereupon a battery was brought up, and every preparation made for defense. The enemy, however, was checked before he reached the knoll.[7]

Heavy fighting now broke out on the left wing, where Hancock, behind his breastworks on the Brock Road, was bearing the brunt of the battle. Burnside had at last managed to bring his three divisions into action north of the Plank Road, thus plugging the gap which had been created on Warren's left by Hancock's retirement. At 4 p.m. *Lee* renewed his attack on the Union left. His men stormed forward and succeeded in planting their battle-flags on the Union breastworks lining the Brock Road, but a counter-attack restored the situation.

At 6 p.m. *Lee* made a last desperate effort to storm the Union breastworks, this time by turning their right flank north of the Turnpike. One of *Ewell*'s brigades made a surprise attack on the right of Sedgwick's corps and drove it back in disorder for half a mile, capturing 600 prisoners and two brigade commanders. This nearly caused a panic in the Union lines, but the Confederates too lost cohesion, and the attack was not pressed home. The incident is thus described by one of Grant's staff:

> Aides came galloping in from the right, laboring under intense excitement, talking wildly, and giving the most exaggerated reports of the engagement. Some declared that a large force had broken and scattered Sedgwick's entire corps. Others insisted that the enemy had turned our right completely, and captured the wagon-train. It was asserted at one time that both Sedgwick and Wright had been captured. Such tales of disaster would have been enough to inspire serious apprehension. . . . But it was in just such sudden emergencies that General Grant was always at his best. Without the change of a muscle of his face, or the slightest alteration in the tones of his voice, he quietly interrogated the officers who brought the reports. . . . Reinforcements were hurried to the point attacked, and preparations made for Sedgwick's corps to take up a new line, with the front and right thrown back. General Grant soon walked over to his own camp,

7. *Porter*, 59.

seated himself on a stool in front of his tent, lighted a fresh cigar, and there continued to receive further advices from the right.[8]

Another General (Meade?) then came up and exclaimed excitedly:

'This is a crisis that cannot be looked upon too seriously. I know *Lee*'s methods well by past experience; he will throw his whole army between us and the Rapidan, and cut us off completely from our communications.' The general rose to his feet, took his cigar out of his mouth, turned to the officer, and replied, with a degree of animation which he seldom manifested: 'Oh, I am heartily tired of hearing about what *Lee* is going to do. . . . Go back to your command, and try to think what we are going to do ourselves, instead of what *Lee* is going to do.'[9]

These incidents, told by a staff officer who was present at the time, afford striking evidence of Grant's imperturbability in moments of extreme crisis. The stubborn and bitter conflict had continued without a lull for two consecutive days. Now, as night closed in at the end of the second day there might have been an excuse for frayed nerves. Every officer and man had been under arms since 4 a.m. that morning. Perhaps it was the 20 cigars that Grant smoked that day that steadied his nerves; his breakfast had consisted of a strong cup of coffee and a cucumber dipped in vinegar. Anyway, it was fortunate for the Union that the Wilderness battle was controlled by the 'unflappable' Grant, and not by the excitable Meade.

The fall of night brought the two-day battle to an end. Grant himself has vividly described the aspect of the battlefield towards the end of the struggle:

The ground fought over had varied in width, but averaged three-quarters of a mile. The killed, and many of the wounded, of both armies, lay within this belt where it was impossible to reach them. The woods were set on fire by the bursting shells, and the conflagration raged. The wounded who had not strength to move themselves were either suffocated or burned to death. Finally the fire communicated with our breastworks in places. Being constructed of wood, they burned with great fury.[10]

Thus came to an end the Wilderness battle, in which the casualties had been heavier than in any previous action of the Civil War, with the exception of Gettysburg.[11] The Union losses in the two-day battle were 17,666, of which 2,246 were killed. The Confederate loss was smaller, although they had been attacking continuously, and amounted to 11,400. But *Lee* could ill afford such a loss, while Grant could call on a far greater reserve of manpower.

From the tactical point of view, the Wilderness battle was a draw, but strategically it ended in Grant's favour, for he had succeeded in outflanking *Lee* in the attempt to get between him and his base at Richmond. Grant might have gained a decisive victory had he handled Sheridan's Cavalry Corps with

8. *Porter*, 68–70.
9. *ibid.*
10. *Grant*, II, 200–1.
11. The Gettysburg casualties were: Union, 23,049; Confederates, 28,063.

more imagination. The three cavalry divisions rendered little assistance in the battle, being mainly engaged in skirmishing with the Confederate cavalry on Grant's left flank. One cavalry division should have been sufficient to carry out local protection and reconnaissance duties; the other two could have made a feint movement against *Lee*'s left flank by threatening Gordonsville, just as Allenby did with his cavalry in the battle of Gaza in October 1918. *Lee* would have been left in uncertainty as to which direction Grant would take, and would then have been forced to leave *Longstreet*'s corps at Gordonsville. With only two corps available he could not have attacked Grant's four corps in the Wilderness, and Grant would have had a clear run to Richmond, thus cutting *Lee* off from his base. The Confederate cavalry too were of little use to *Lee*, for they were too far separated from their infantry. Had Grant pushed on rapidly to Spottsylvania through the Wilderness on the evening of 4 May, without waiting for his supply-train to come up, or sent his cavalry ahead, he would have beaten *Lee* in the race for Richmond, and would have been able to fight him with superior numbers in more open country. By letting himself be caught in the Wilderness, where the tactical conditions favoured the Confederates, he narrowly escaped defeat.

On the morning of 7 May neither side was anxious to renew the fight. The morning mist, mingled with the smoke from the smouldering forest fires, obscured the landscape, but reconnaissances showed that the Confederates had withdrawn from their forward breastworks. Grant, who had risen at dawn, decided to push on to Richmond, and at 6.30 a.m. issued orders for the army to march to Spottsylvania Court House, ten miles to the south-east, as soon as it was dark. Hancock's II Corps was to hold the present front line while Warren's V Corps moved off down the Brock Road. Sedgwick's VI Corps, followed by Burnside (IX), was to march by a parallel track from Chancellorsville.

During the afternoon Grant received a dispatch from Washington, informing him that Butler had successfully disembarked his army on the right bank of the James River, and that Sherman was advancing south into Georgia and expected to encounter *Johnston* that day.

Preceded by the cavalry divisions, the Army of the Potomac moved off at 8.30 p.m. as soon as it was dark. *Lee* was quick to notice the Union move. At first he thought that Grant was retiring on Fredericksburg, and ordered I Corps, now commanded by *Anderson*, to move to Spottsylvania in order to get between Grant and Richmond. He was to give his troops another night's rest and move the next morning. As, however, the forest was still burning, *Anderson* decided not to bivouac there, but pushed on directly to Spottsylvania, which he reached before dawn, driving out one of Sheridan's cavalry divisions, which was just arriving. Thus, by a curious chance, *Lee* forestalled Grant in the move on Spottsylvania; as Grant remarked, 'Accident often decides the fate of battle.' This particular accident was unfortunate, for, instead of cutting *Lee* off from Richmond, Grant's direct road to that objective was now blocked.

However, *Lee*'s army, not Richmond, was Grant's main objective, so he now prepared to give battle to *Lee* at Spottsylvania.

Another incident had contributed to Grant's losing the race for Spottsylvania. Sheridan's cavalry had been skirmishing with *Stuart*'s cavalry throughout the afternoon of the 7th in the neighbourhood of Todd's Tavern, and Sheridan had ordered Wesley Merritt's division to move to Spottsylvania to support James Wilson's division in seizing it. Meade, however, issued contrary orders to Merritt, who was thus unable to support Wilson in holding Spottsylvania before *Anderson*'s arrival. On the morning of the 8th Sheridan went to Meade's headquarters in a fury and accused him of giving counter-orders to his divisions; an acrimonious dispute broke out, as Meade also lost his temper and accused Sheridan of blocking the advance of the infantry with his cavalry divisions. Sheridan insisted that the only way to beat *Stuart* was to keep his own divisions concentrated and attack him. Meade at once went over to Grant's tent and reported what Sheridan had said. Grant only remarked coolly: 'Did Sheridan say that? Well, he generally knows what he is talking about. Let him start right out and do it.' He then issued orders to Sheridan to take his Cavalry Corps on a long-distance raid to Richmond. Sheridan was to 'cut loose from the Army of the Potomac, pass round the left of *Lee*'s army and attack his cavalry.' Sheridan was then to destroy the railways between *Lee* and Richmond and push on to join Butler's army on the James River, where he was to replenish his supplies and make his way back. Sheridan lost no time. The following morning at 6 a.m. he started off with 10,000 troopers and no transport. Each man carried on the saddle three days' rations and a half-day's ration of forage. Heading south, he crossed the North and South Anna Rivers on 10 and 11 May and destroyed a section of the Virginia Central Railroad, releasing several hundred Union prisoners. He then pushed on to Yellow Tavern, six miles north of Richmond, spreading consternation in the Confederate capital. There he was caught up by the Confederate Cavalry Corps of 4,500 men under *Stuart*, who had set off in hot pursuit. In the ensuing engagement *Stuart* and one of his brigade commanders were killed. Sheridan continued on his way, crossed the Chickahominy River 12 miles east of Richmond and then crossed the James on the 14th and joined Butler's army. After resting and refitting there for three days he rejoined Grant on 24 May at Chesterfield Station, north of the North Anna, after a ride of 180 miles. During his fortnight's expedition his losses were 625 men and 300 horses.

Sheridan's Richmond raid was an adventurous foray but it had little strategic effect. The absence of the Cavalry Corps seriously hampered the operations of the Army of the Potomac, which was left without its mounted arm for reconnaissance duties. In the fighting round Spottsylvania Sheridan's men, armed as they were with Sharp's breech-loading carbines and Spencer magazine carbines, would have been an invaluable adjunct had they been used as mobile mounted infantry. Grant had in fact sent Sheridan off for two reasons: firstly, to remove him from Meade's command, as the two were no longer on speaking terms; secondly, to act as a link with Butler's Army of the James, which Grant imagined to be then closing in on Richmond from the south-east. Unfortunately, however, Butler's part of the campaign had been a complete failure.

The Army of the James numbered 36,000 men and consisted of x Corps, under Quincy Adams Gillmore, and xviii Corps under William Farrar Smith. On 5 May the whole force had landed without opposition on the right bank of the James River at City Point and Bermuda Hundred, nine miles north-east of Petersburg. If Butler had marched directly on Petersburg he could have entered it unopposed, thus cutting the main communication line between Richmond and the south. Unfortunately, Grant's directive of 2 April instructed Butler 'that Richmond is to be your objective, and that there is to be cooperation between your force and the Army of the Potomac.' Grant would have been better advised to tell Butler to seize Petersburg first and then to march north on Richmond. That would have shortened the war and saved a large number of Union casualties.

After landing unopposed on 5 May at City Point and Bermuda Hundred, Butler set his troops to work on entrenching a defensive line, 3½ miles long, across the isthmus between the James River and its right-bank tributary the Appomattox. In spite of the advice of his corps commanders to seize Petersburg at once, Butler sat still for a week, and then on 12 May started an advance northward towards Richmond.

Meanwhile *Beauregard*, who commanded all the Confederate troops south of the James and the Appomattox, had succeeded in concentrating 30,000 men at Drewry's Bluff, an exceedingly strong sector of the outer Richmond defences, eight miles south of Richmond, on the right bank of the James. President *Davis* and his Chief of Staff, *Braxton Bragg*, arrived from Richmond at Drewry's Bluff on 14 May for a consultation with *Beauregard*, who was given a reinforcement from the Richmond garrison. Butler's troops were ordered to assault the Confederate position at Drewry's Bluff at dawn on 16 May. There was a dense fog that morning and the attack made little progress. *Beauregard*'s troops counter-attacked strongly and split the two Union corps apart. Butler then ordered a retreat to their fortified position on the isthmus, where *Beauregard* effectively bottled them up for the rest of the campaign. The Union casualties were 6,215, the Confederates losing 3,449.

From the story of Butler's fiasco with the Army of the James we can now return to the operations of the Army of the Potomac in the Wilderness. Throughout the 8 May Grant's infantry, in two columns, but deprived of the services of their cavalry, advanced south-eastward towards Spottsylvania, which was now unfortunately occupied by the whole of *Lee*'s army. The country here was rather more open than the thick Wilderness forest, and *Lee* had already entrenched his troops in a strong defensive position which crowned the high ground between the Po and Ny Rivers, uniting lower down to form the

Mattapony. This position effectively barred the Brock Road leading to Richmond, and Grant could not outflank it without exposing his own vulnerable line of communications back through Fredericksburg.

Lee was an experienced engineer officer, and also a master of defensive tactics. The position which he had fortified was an L-shaped salient with the angle pointing approximately north. The left sector, 2½ miles long, faced north-west and its left flank was covered by the unfordable Po River, 50 feet wide. This sector was occupied by *Anderson*'s 1 Corps. The right sector, two miles long and facing east, ran along the ridge separating the valleys of the Po and the Ny. It was held by III Corps, now commanded by *Jubal Anderson Early*, in replacement of *Hill*, who had reported sick after the Wilderness battle. The right flank of this sector was half a mile south of Spottsylvania Court House. The apex of the salient was strongly fortified with a semi-circular redoubt, which became the focus for the fiercest combats in the ensuing battles. This sector was held by *Ewell*'s II Corps and was later known as the 'Mule Shoe' or 'Bloody Angle'.

The Confederate trenches were well concealed by trees and undergrowth, and an advanced line of skirmishers harassed the reconnaissance patrols which Grant sent forward during 9 May to ascertain the extent of the enemy position. While carrying out a reconnaissance, John Sedgwick, commanding Grant's VI Corps, was shot dead by an enemy sniper. He was replaced by Horatio Gouverneur Wright, who had been a cadet with Grant at West Point.

On the morning of 10 May Grant deployed his four corps facing the Confederate position. Hancock (II) was ordered to move south along the right bank of the Po River to fix *Lee*'s left, while Burnside (IX) was sent eastward by the Fredericksburg–Spottsylvania road to feel for the right flank. Warren (V) and Wright (VI) deployed in the centre, opposite the north-western face of the salient held by *Ewell* (II) and *Anderson* (I). Hancock moved south, as ordered, and succeeded in getting one of his divisions across the Po, round *Anderson*'s left flank, but Grant, rather unfortunately, recalled him, as he had decided to make a frontal attack on *Anderson*'s sector further north with II, V and VI Corps, timed to start at 5 p.m. In the early afternoon Warren (V) reported to Meade that he saw a good chance of making an immediate attack on his front. He was allowed to do so, and led his men to the assault at 4 p.m., but the Union attack was driven back with heavy losses. After this failure, Wright (VI) launched an attack with 12 regiments against the west face of the 'Mule Shoe', which over-ran the Confederate trenches and 1,200 prisoners were captured, but as the attack was unsupported the Union troops were forced to withdraw after dark. On the eastern sector, Burnside had dug in half a mile in front of *Early*'s position.

On the following day no fighting took place. Grant evacuated his wounded, replenished ammunition and prepared new plans for another attack on 12 May. As soon at he had eaten breakfast he wrote to Halleck:

We have now ended the 6th day of very hard fighting. The result up to this time is much in our favor. But our losses have been heavy as well as those of the enemy. We have lost to this time eleven General Officers killed, wounded and missing, and probably twenty thousand men. I think the loss of the enemy must be greater – we having taken over four thousand prisoners in battle, whilst he has taken from us but few except stragglers. I am now sending back to Belle Plaine all my wagons for a fresh supply of provisions and ammunition, and propose to fight it out on this line if it takes all Summer.[12]

Grant's figures, of course, cover the Wilderness battle and the fighting at Spottsylvania on 9 and 10 May. The plan for the 12th was for a concentrated attack by three corps on the apex of the salient. Hancock (II) in the centre, with Wright (VI) on his right and Burnside (IX) on his left were to launch a concentric attack at dawn on the 'Mule Shoe' held by *Ewell*. Further west Warren (V) was to be ready to exploit success.

The 12 May dawned with rain and fog. The concentric attack by the three corps successfully overran the 'Mule Shoe', capturing 20 guns and 2,800 prisoners, including a divisional commander, *Edward Johnson*. But the men of all three corps now got hopelessly mixed up and cohesion was lost. *Ewell*'s troops rallied behind a reserve trench which had been built across the base of the salient, and at 6 a.m. a Confederate counter-attack drove the attackers back. Meade then ordered Warren (V) to attack *Anderson*'s sector, but this also failed with heavy loss. Savage fighting continued throughout the day and the following night, during which *Ewell* completely evacuated the 'Mule Shoe', now deservedly known as the 'Bloody Angle', and consolidated the reserve trench in rear of it. The only result of the three days' fighting, except for very heavy Union casualties, was the flattening out of the apex of the salient.

During the 13th the two exhausted armies licked their wounds, and Grant decided on an entirely new plan, all his attacks on the north-west sector of *Lee*'s position having failed. The wide Po River protected the enemy's left (west) flank, so Grant planned to move V and VI Corps round to the east side and attempt to turn *Lee*'s right, which rested on Spottsylvania Court House. This meant a very arduous night march for Warren's and Wright's corps across trackless wooded country, intersected by many small creeks. The units had to find their way in pouring rain and fog, so that they did not reach their assembly areas until long after dawn on the 14th; which was zero hour, and the attack had to be cancelled. *Lee* at once discovered the change in Grant's dispositions and quickly reacted. He moved *Anderson*'s I Corps across from the left flank to the east sector, thus prolonging *Early*'s line for two miles to the south of Spottsylvania Court House, his right flank protected by the Po River. Grant thus missed his chance of turning *Lee*'s right flank.

12. *Grant*, II, 226. The word 'propose' in the second last line is so written in Grant's MS letter, but in his Memoirs it is printed 'purpose'.

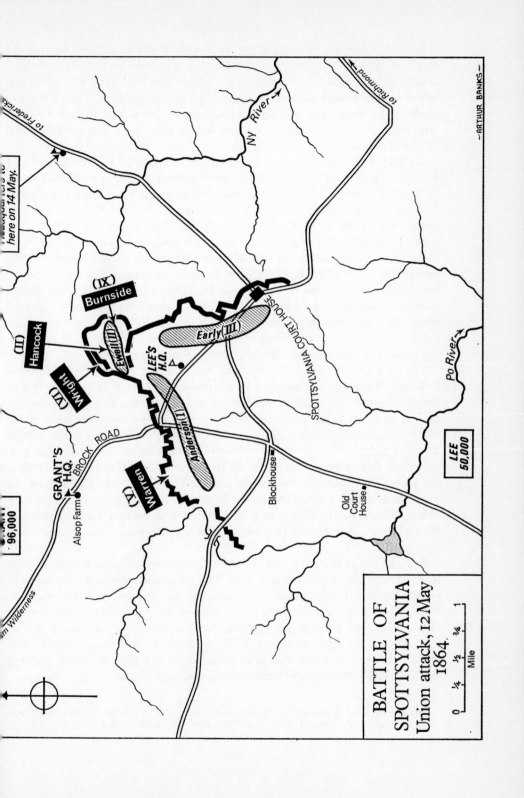

BATTLE OF
SPOTTSYLVANIA
Union attack, 12 May
1864.

0 ¼ ½ ¾ 1
Mile

~ARTHUR BANKS~

to Richmond

Ny River

to Fredericks

Headquarters to
here on 14 May.

(IX)
Burnside

Hancock (II)

Early (III)

Ewell (II)

LEE'S
H.Q.

Wright (VI)

Anderson (I)

SPOTTSYLVANIA COURT HOUSE

Po River

GRANT'S
H.Q.

BROCK ROAD

Warren (V)

Alsop Farm

Blockhouse

Old Court
House

96,000

LEE
50,000

m Wilderness

Instead, therefore, of attacking *Anderson*'s newly established line, Grant switched Wright's corps again to the north, and at dawn on the 18th attempted another frontal attack on *Ewell*'s corps, which now held *Lee*'s left sector, and which Grant thought must be decimated by constant fighting. The assault was made by the three corps of Wright, Hancock and Burnside. Although delivered with great energy and courage, it crumpled up with heavy losses. Grant called off the action at 10 a.m.

On that day Grant again revised his plans. Having at last recognized that *Lee*'s strong position could not be stormed without incurring exorbitant losses, he decided to try and lure *Lee* out into the open. He accordingly reorganized his forces. Hancock (ii) was pulled back into reserve and Burnside (ix) was transferred to the south flank on the left of Warren (v) and Wright (vi). Grant's intention was to send Hancock south towards Richmond in the hope that *Lee* would pursue him. He would have done better to have resorted to this manoeuvre at an earlier stage. Grant had rightly set himself the task of destroying *Lee*'s field army, but he had not yet learnt the lesson that the most gallant assaults cannot succeed against steady infantry, strongly entrenched and armed with rifled weapons. Meanwhile *Lee* had pushed *Ewell*'s corps forward on Grant's right to carry out a reconnaissance in force with the object of ascertaining Grant's intentions, and some desultory fighting took place.

The ten days' struggle at Spottsylvania had proved a grievous disappointment to Grant. The casualties incurred by his troops had been even heavier than in the Wilderness battle; they had lost 18,399 in carrying out frontal assaults against well-entrenched positions, while the Confederate casualties were of the order of 10,000. A more accurate estimate cannot be made owing to the sketchy way in which the Confederate records were kept during the last year of the war.

In these first encounters between the two great protagonists *Lee* had certainly out-generalled Grant. He had fought a pitched battle with the Union leader in a terrain which was most unfavourable to the Northern troops; he had then induced Grant to attack him in a well chosen and strongly fortified position. He had in fact repeated the tactics with which Wellington defeated Massena in Portugal.

One can also criticize the way in which Grant exercised tactical control of his four corps in the Spottsylvania battles. His battlefront was over five miles in extent, yet he at first established his command post at Alsop farm-house on the Brock Road, little over one mile to the *west* of the 'Mule Shoe' salient, where the heaviest fighting took place. From there he could not adequately control the action on the other sectors of the front, where tactical success might more easily have been achieved. A case in point occurred during the heavy fighting on 10 May. To quote from Grant's own account:

Burnside on the left had got up to within a few hundred yards of Spottsylvania Court House, completely turning *Lee*'s right. He was not aware of the advantage he had gained, and I, being with the troops where the heavy fighting was, did not know of it at the time. He had gained his position with but little fighting, and almost without loss. Burnside's position now separated him widely from Wright's corps, the corps nearest to him. At night he was ordered to join on to this. This brought him back about a mile, and lost to us an important advantage. I attach no blame to Burnside for this, but I do to myself for not having had a staff officer with him to report to me his position.[13]

Actually, Grant *had* sent one of his most efficient aides, Lieutenant-Colonel Horace Porter, to accompany Burnside throughout that day, although Grant seems to have forgotten that fact when he wrote his Memoirs. Porter tells us exactly what happened:

I had ridden with General Burnside to the front to watch the movement. The advance soon reached a point within a quarter of a mile of Spottsylvania, and completely turned the right of the enemy's line. . . . I had sent two bulletins to General Grant describing the situation on the left, but the orderly who carried one of the despatches never arrived, having probably been killed, and the other did not reach the general till quite late, as he was riding among the troops in front of the center of the line, and it was difficult to find him. I started for headquarters that evening, but owing to the intense darkness, the condition of the roads, and the difficulty of finding the way, did not arrive till long after midnight.[14]

Had Grant established his command post further back, or had an efficient report centre been more centrally sited, advantage might have been taken of this heaven-sent opportunity of turning *Lee*'s right flank on the first day of the battle. A similar chance of turning *Lee*'s left flank occurred on the same day, when Hancock (II) managed to get a whole division round *Anderson*'s entrenchments, but was recalled as Grant was intent on smashing in the apex of *Lee*'s salient.

Grant appears to have soon realized the unsuitable location of his headquarters, for on the morning of the 14th Porter tells us:

It had been decided to move headquarters a little nearer to the center of the lines, . . . farther east to a position on some high ground three quarters of a mile north of the Ny River, and near the Fredericksburg and Spottsylvania Court-house road.[15]

This was a far more central position from which to control the battle, and it was a pity it was not chosen earlier.

13. *Grant*, II, 225.
14. *Porter*, 95.
15. *ibid.*, 117.

XIX

Grant's Advance on Richmond
20–31 May 1864

Grant's strategic plan for the 1864 campaign had envisaged a three-pronged advance southwards through Virginia in order to crush *Lee*'s field army; the main central thrust across the Rapidan by the Army of the Potomac was to be supported by a left hook by Butler's Army of the James closing in on Richmond from the south-east, and a right hook by Sigel's Army of West Virginia, which was to advance up the Shenandoah Valley to Staunton and Lynchburg with the objective of cutting the East Tennessee and Virginia Railroad, *Lee*'s main link with the west. We have seen how Butler's effort against Richmond had been a complete failure, and the bulk of *Beauregard*'s troops opposing him were now being transferred to reinforce *Lee*.

Unfortunately, Sigel's operations in the Shenandoah Valley had been no more successful. On 1 May he advanced up the North Fork of the Shenandoah from Martinsburg to Winchester with a force of 6,500 men and 28 guns. On his right flank he was supported by another column of 6,000 infantry under George Crook and a cavalry division of 2,000 under William Woods Averell, who advanced through the Alleghenies. On 10 May Sigel reached Woodstock south of Strasburg; four days later he was engaged at New Market, 70 miles south of Martinsburg, by a Confederate division, 5,000 strong, under *Breckinridge*, and suffered a severe reverse, losing 831 men and five guns. The Confederate casualties numbered 577. Sigel thereupon withdrew to Strasburg; Crook's column on his right also failed to make much progress. A fortnight later Sigel was removed from his command and replaced by David Hunter, an undistinguished officer, 62 years old, who had graduated from West Point in the same year that Grant was born. His appointment to command was due to political rather than to military reasons.

Both of the supporting flank offensives having failed miserably, the operations in the eastern theatre were reduced to Grant's pursuit of *Lee* towards Richmond with the Army of the Potomac. However, before continuing to follow events in that main theatre, we must take a glance at the western one, in which Grant's trusted subordinate, Sherman, was acting independently of the Generalissimo's immediate control.

Sherman had been given a free hand by Grant, but also a very definite objective, namely, to destroy *Joseph Johnston*'s army. But the country in which he had to operate was even more favourable for defensive tactics than Virginia, with its parallel river lines. The Alleghenies presented to the attacker a series of steep parallel ridges, each of which offered the Southern commander a good defensive position. Grant's original idea had been that Banks, closing in from the extreme right with an army of 40,000, would turn the west flank of these successive defensive lines, thus forcing *Johnston* to fall back on Atlanta. Banks, however, having been defeated and dispersed in Louisiana a month earlier, this flank pressure never materialized, and Sherman was forced to rely on his own efforts to attain his objective.

Sherman began his advance from Chattanooga on 5 May, having at his disposal 100,000 men and 254 guns. These were organized in three armies: on the right, the Army of the Tennessee under McPherson (25,000); in the centre, Thomas with the Army of the Cumberland (60,000); on the left, the Army of the Ohio under Schofield (14,000). The topographical conditions favoured a turning movement from the west, in order to cut *Johnston*'s railway communication from Dalton to Atlanta, so Sherman should have kept his strongest army (Thomas's) on the right flank instead of McPherson's. Keeping the weaker army on the right flank may have been forced on him by logistic considerations, but it seriously prejudiced his operations during the advance.

To begin with, *Johnston* had only two corps, under *John Bell Hood* and *William Joseph Hardee*, numbering 60,000 men and 144 guns, but on 11 May he was joined by a third corps under *Leonidas Polk* (20,000).

Johnston's first defensive position was a particularly strong one, on a long rocky ridge covering the railway station at Dalton. Sherman ordered McPherson to advance and occupy a position which threatened to turn the Confederate left flank. McPherson did so, but *Johnston* reinforced his left with three divisions, and McPherson, rather timidly, withdrew; a great opportunity was thus missed. McPherson's withdrawal may have been due to Sherman's orders not having made his intention sufficiently clear. The campaign continued indecisively for the next two months, with Sherman constantly threatening *Johnston*'s left flank, and *Johnston* adroitly extricating himself and falling back. The Confederates indeed were playing for time, as they did not want to incur a decisive defeat before the Presidential election in the North in the autumn. This Fabian strategy continued until 27 June, when Sherman made an unnecessary frontal attack on a strong Confederate position at Kenesaw Mountain, 20 miles northwest of Atlanta, which was repulsed with a Union loss of 2,500 men. President *Davis*, however, was disappointed with the continued withdrawal of *Johnston*, who had meanwhile been reinforced, and three weeks later replaced him by one of his corps commanders, *John Bell Hood*.

Although Sherman possessed considerable strategic ability, he had many failings as a tactician. At Shiloh he had committed unpardonable blunders which seriously prejudiced the Union chances of success in that battle; at Chickasaw Bluffs, north of Vicksburg, he suffered a severe tactical reverse; when allotted the decisive role at Chattanooga he failed to reach his objective. He was, however, a straightforward and loyal subordinate, besides being brimful of energy and offensive spirit, and he had won Grant's complete confidence. His Atlanta campaign might have produced speedier and more decisive results had it been under Grant's continuous direction. For instance, he might have been told to make more effective use of his four cavalry divisions. It would appear that Grant placed too much faith in Sherman, while having too little confidence in Meade, so that, instead of performing the functions of a Generalissimo, he merely acted as the superior commander of the Army of the Potomac. We can now return to the operations of that army.

As described in the preceding chapter, Grant's repeated frontal assaults on *Lee*'s strongly entrenched position at Spottsylvania had only produced heavy casualties, so, rather late in the day, he made an attempt to lure *Lee* out of his trenches and fight him in the open. After the failure of his last assault on 18 May, he issued the following directive to Meade:

> Before daylight tomorrow morning I propose to draw Hancock and Burnside from the position they now hold, and put Burnside to the left of Wright. Wright and Burnside should then force their way up as close to the enemy as they can get without a general engagement, or with a general engagement if the enemy will come out of their works to fight, and intrench. Hancock should march and take up a position as if in support of the two left corps. Tomorrow night, at twelve or one o'clock, he will be moved southeast with all his force and as much cavalry as can be given to him, to get as far towards Richmond on the line of the Fredericksburg Railroad as he can make, fighting the enemy in whatever force he can find him. If the enemy make a general move to meet this, they will be followed by the other three corps of the army, and attacked, if possible, before time is given to intrench.[1]

This manœuvre was carried out, and on 20 May Hancock (II) reached Guiney's Station on the Richmond and Fredericksburg Railroad and then followed it south towards Richmond. On the next day he was followed by Warren (v) and Wright (vi), Burnside (ix) being left to hold *Lee*. Grant had thus divided his forces to give *Lee* an opportunity of striking, but the Confederate commander was too old a bird to be caught with this kind of chaff, and slipped away by the Telegraph Road to a strong position which had been previously entrenched on the south bank of the North Anna River, 20 miles further south.

On 18 May, when Grant had decided to move from Spottsylvania, he advanced his supply base from Belle Plaine on the Potomac to Port Royal on the

---

1. *Grant*, II, 242.

Rappahannock estuary, thus profiting by the command of the sea and tidal waters possessed by the Union navy. He also sent back a proportion of his artillery, which he found merely encumbered the roads and slowed down his movements. Even with this precaution, however, the Union advance was not a rapid one. Grant's directive to Meade had not stressed the need for any urgency, and Meade's staff had not told Warren and Wright which roads they were to follow. Burnside had been ordered to cross the Po River and follow the Telegraph Road southwards, but he had found that road blocked by the enemy, so turned east and followed the other corps, which caused some confusion and delay. *Lee's* army, therefore, having a shorter road to travel, was firmly established behind the North Anna by the evening of 22 May. Grant was also handicapped by being short of cavalry, as Sheridan had not yet returned from his Richmond raid.

Lee meanwhile had received a useful reinforcement of 8,500 men, withdrawn from the forces of *Beauregard* south of Richmond and of *Breckinridge* in the Shenandoah Valley, after the defeat of Butler and Sigel. Thus Grant's attempt to manœuvre *Lee* into the open, and to get between him and Richmond, had completely failed. He had been unable to slip round *Lee's* flank in the Wilderness, he had then failed to anticipate him at Spottsylvania, and had now been beaten a third time in the race for Richmond. The Confederate commander was a master of defensive tactics and had a marvellous eye for ground. He had again established his position as a right-angled salient, five miles in length, the central apex, held by *Anderson* (I), being entrenched on the steep right bank of the North Anna. The right sector, which rested on the railway at Hanover Junction, was held by *Ewell* (II) and flanked by marshy ground. The left wing under *A. P. Hill* (III) was bent back westward and rested on a tributary stream, the Little River.

The Union army came up on the following day, and Grant deployed his four corps in the endeavour to outflank the enemy position. Hancock (II) drove *Ewell's* outposts from the railway bridge over the river and pressed them back to their main position covering Hanover Junction. Burnside (IX) came up on Hancock's right, but was unable to make any impression on *Anderson's* strongly entrenched position on the south bank of the river. Warren (V) and Wright (VI) crossed the North Anna farther up stream, but were checked by Hill's entrenchments on the west flank. Grant's troops were now awkwardly placed, as three of his corps had crossed the river, while most of Burnside's was still on the north bank. *Lee*, on the other hand, could rapidly reinforce any sector of his front. Had he not been a sick man at the time, he might have counter-attacked with success the separated Union corps.

After a careful reconnaissance of *Lee's* position, Grant came to the conclusion that it was too strong to be assaulted, so he planned to slip round *Lee's* right flank once more by moving down the Pamunkey River (formed by the junction of the North and South Annas) to try again to manœuvre him into the open.

Sheridan returned on the 24th from his bold but rather futile raid, and Grant sent one of his cavalry divisions round to the west to give *Lee* the impression that his left flank was being threatened. On the 26th he wrote to Halleck describing the situation and his future intentions:

> The relative position of the two armies is now as follows: *Lee*'s right rests on a swamp east of the Richmond and Fredericksburg road and south of the North Anna, his centre on the river at Ox Ford, and his left at Little River with the crossings of Little River guarded as far up as we have gone. Hancock with his corps and one division of the ix Corps crossed at Chesterfield Ford and covers the right wing of *Lee*'s army. One division of the ix Corps is on the north bank of the Anna at Ox Ford. . . . The v and vi Corps with one division of the ix Corps run from the south bank of the Anna from a short distance above Ox Ford to Little River. . . . To make a direct attack from either wing would cause a slaughter of our men that even success would not justify. To turn the enemy by his right, between the two Annas, is impossible on account of the swamp upon which his right rests. To turn him by the left leaves Little River, New Found River and South Anna River, all of them streams presenting considerable obstacles to the movement of our army, to be crossed. I have determined therefore to turn the enemy's right by crossing at or near Hanover Town. This crosses all three streams at once, and leaves us still where we can draw supplies.[2]

Grant then described how his side-slip to the left would be carried out and added, rather optimistically:

> *Lee*'s army is really whipped. The prisoners we now take show it, and the action of his army shows it unmistakably. A battle with them out of intrenchments cannot be had. Our men feel that they have gained the *morale* over the enemy, and attack him with confidence. I may be mistaken, but I feel that our success over *Lee*'s army is already assured. . . .
>
> Even if a crossing is not effected at Hanover Town it will probably be necessary for us to move on down the Pamunkey until a crossing is effected. I think it advisable therefore to change our base of supplies from Port Royal to the White House. I wish you would direct this change at once, and also direct Smith to put the railroad bridge there in condition for crossing troops and artillery and leave men to hold it.

White House was a port on the lower Pamunkey River, only 25 miles east of Richmond. At West Point,[3] some miles farther down stream, the Pamunkey and the Mattapony unite to form the broad estuary of the York River, so the Union navy could now guarantee Grant a secure advanced base within 25 miles of the enemy's capital. White House was also connected to the capital by the Richmond and York River Railroad, which crossed the Pamunkey by an important bridge and continued eastward from White House to West Point at the head of the York estuary. The Smith referred to above was William Farrar Smith, commanding xviii Corps in Butler's Army of the James. Grant had

2. *Grant*, ii, 252–3.

3. West Point (Va), not to be confused with West Point (N.Y.), the seat of the United States Military Academy.

already, through Halleck, ordered Smith's corps to be transferred from Butler's army to the Army of the Potomac. Smith's XVIII Corps disembarked at White House from City Point on 30/31 May, bringing Grant's strength up to five corps, numbering 108,000 men.

It was now evident that the Civil War was to be fought to a finish in the eastern theatre; Grant and *Lee* were pitted against each other as the two great protagonists of their respective sides; they were locked in a death-struggle which was to be prolonged for another ten months. The troops on both sides were now veterans toughened by three years of warfare, but Grant's army had a considerable numerical superiority over his opponent's, and a far greater reserve of manpower to support it; the Union army had also certain advantages in equipment, for its cavalry were armed with breech-loading magazine carbines, while the Confederate cavalry had only muzzle-loaders. The strategy of the campaign was increasingly influenced by political considerations. With the impending Presidential election and the growing war-weariness in the Northern States, Grant was anxious to press matters to a quick conclusion; hence his urge to maintain the offensive and to keep on attacking at all costs. *Lee*, on the other hand, was playing for time, in spite of the steady drain on the material and economic resources of the Confederacy. President *Davis*'s Government still hoped for foreign intervention, or alternatively that the peace party in the North would offer some mutually acceptable terms which would grant independence to their 'erring sister States' in the South.

The increased fire-power of the newly adopted rifle had given the defence an enormous advantage over the attacker. The Virginian lowland, in which the main campaign was now being fought, offered a succession of admirable defensive positions, protected by numerous unfordable rivers and marshy creeks. *Lee* himself was a master of field fortification and defensive tactics; by holding carefully prepared positions, economizing his forces and acting on interior lines, he felt that he had a fair chance of prolonging the military struggle until the political situation might dawn more brightly.

On the other hand, *Lee* did not rely solely on a passive defence. In the thickets of the Wilderness, where the fighting was largely hand to hand and superior numbers availed little, the Confederate attacks had inflicted heavy casualties on the less mobile Union troops. At Spottsylvania every trench taken had been recovered by Confederate counter-attacks. It is true that a great chance had been missed on the North Anna, for *Hill* might have successfully counterattacked the corps of Warren and Wright as they were crossing the river. But during the whole of 24 May *Lee* was confined to his tent with a crippling attack of diarrhœa, and the opportunity was allowed to slip; *Lee* later reprimanded *Hill* for his negligence.

Grant had profited by the experience of the Wilderness and Spottsylvania, and wisely refrained from assaulting *Lee*'s strong position on the North Anna. His manœuvre round *Lee*'s right flank was skilfully planned and executed. It was an extremely delicate operation, first to extricate the v and vi Corps from south of the river without attracting the enemy's notice, and then to move his whole army round *Lee*'s flank without inviting a counter-stroke. Grant's directive to Meade, written from his command post at Quarle's Mill, on the left bank of the North Anna, on the afternoon of 25 May, was as follows:

> Direct Generals Warren and Wright to withdraw all their teams and artillery, not in position, to the north side of the river tomorrow. Send that belonging to General Wright's corps as far on the road to Hanover Town as it can go, without attracting attention to the fact. Send with it Wright's best division, or division under his ablest commander. Have their places filled up in the line so if possible the enemy will not notice their withdrawal. Send the cavalry tomorrow afternoon, or as much of it as you may deem necessary, to watch and seize, if they can, Littlepage's Bridge and Taylor's Ford, and to remain on one or other side of the river at these points until the infantry and artillery all pass. As soon as it is dark tomorrow night start the division which you withdraw first from Wright's corps to make a forced march to Hanover Town, taking with them no teams to impede their march.... As soon as the troops reach Hanover Town they should get possession of all the crossings they can in that neighbourhood. I think it would be well to make a heavy cavalry demonstration on the enemy's left, tomorrow afternoon, also.[4]

This manœuvre was greatly facilitated by the return of Sheridan on the 24th from his Richmond raid. James Harrison Wilson's cavalry division was sent to make a feint attack on *Lee*'s left (west) flank to cover the Union withdrawal round the other flank. The diversion was successfully carried out and left *Lee* uncertain of Grant's intentions. Although Wilson's early training had been that of a topographical surveyor, he proved to be an outstanding cavalry leader. The rest of the Cavalry Corps preceded the infantry down the Pamunkey Valley to Hanover Town,[5] 25 miles down stream, where Grant planned to make his main crossing. There they formed a bridgehead, under cover of which two pontoon bridges were constructed.

The Union withdrawal was successfully carried out during the night of the 26th, and by noon on the 27th the leading divisions reached Hanover Town, 16 miles north-east of Richmond. They wheeled to their right and crossed the Pamunkey at Hanover Town and the fords above it. They then deployed for the advance on Richmond, vi and ii Corps on the right, with ix and v on the left. On the 29th, however, when only ten miles from Richmond, they were confronted by *Lee*'s army on the upper Totopotomoy[6] Creek. Despite Wilson's demonstration, *Lee* had discovered on the morning of the 27th that the Union troops had 'folded their tents and silently stolen away'. He soon divined Grant's intentions, and at once set off to intercept him. The Confederates, being on interior lines, had only 20 miles to march from Hanover Junction, while the

4. *Grant*, ii, 254–5.
5. Hanover Town, on the Pamunkey River, is 17 miles south-east of Hanover Junction.
6. Named after an Indian chief at the time of the first English settlement of Virginia in the seventeenth century.

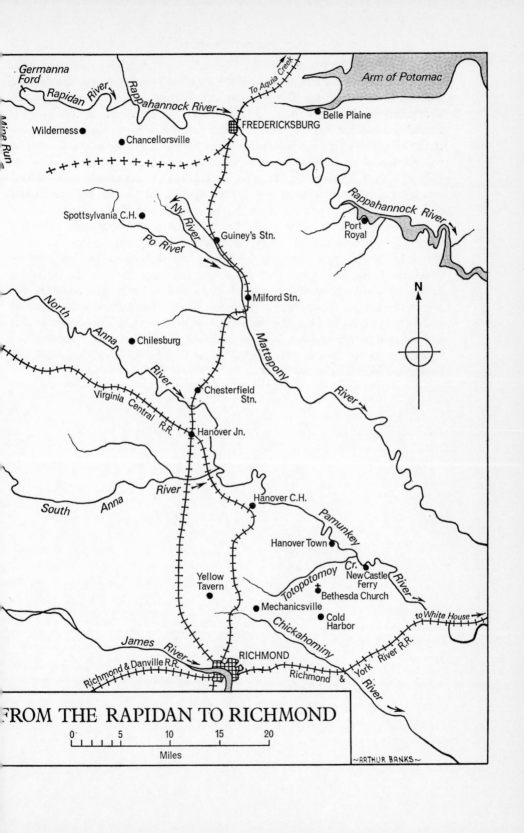

FROM THE RAPIDAN TO RICHMOND

0 5 10 15 20
Miles

~ARTHUR BANKS~

Union troops on the left bank of the Pamunkey had to make a more circuitous journey of 30 miles. Thus they found the Confederates already established on a ten-mile front behind the Totopotomoy Creek, their right flank resting on the Chickahominy River south of Cold Harbor, and their left on the Virginia Central Railroad at Atlee's Station. Grant had therefore once more been forestalled. Desultory fighting took place, but Grant decided not to attack until he was reinforced by Smith's XVIII Corps, which was due to disembark at White House on the following day. On 31 May *Anderson*'s 1 Corps made a determined attack on Sheridan's troopers, who had occupied Cold Harbor, but was driven back by the rapid fire of their seven-shooter magazine carbines.

Grant had again failed to bring *Lee* to battle in the open, and the Confederates were now strongly entrenched between the Union troops and Richmond. In the scrappy fighting on the North Anna River and the Totopotomoy Creek the Union troops had incurred nearly 4,000 casualties, the Confederates having only lost approximately half of that number. From now onwards, the war in the eastern theatre was to become one of static attrition rather than of mobile manœuvre. In the first month of Grant's offensive in Virginia his armies had suffered over 60,000 casualties, and the butcher's bill was still to mount up. Politicians in the North were beginning to wonder whether they were not paying too high a price for victory.

XX

The Killing at Cold Harbor
1–3 June 1864

The battle of Cold Harbor is the most controversial one that Grant ever fought; it is certainly the one which has aroused the severest criticism of his conduct as a commander. We need only quote one adverse comment, made by a senior Union officer:

> In the opinion of a majority of its survivors, the battle of Cold Harbor should never have been fought. There was no military reason to justify it. It was the dreary, dismal, bloody, ineffective close of the Lieutenant-General's first campaign with the Army of the Potomac, and corresponded in all its essential features with what had preceded it.[1]

This is an unduly harsh condemnation. In retrospect, Grant himself wrote of the battle:

> I have always regretted that the last assault at Cold Harbor was ever made. I might say the same thing of the assault of the 22nd of May, 1863, at Vicksburg. At Cold Harbor no advantage whatever was gained to compensate for the heavy loss we sustained. Indeed, the advantages, other than those of relative losses, were on the Confederate side.[2]

No commander, after a failure, has cried *'mea culpa!'* so candidly. Before analysing the operations at Cold Harbor, we must consider the conditions under which they were undertaken.

As indicated in the preceding chapter, Grant was under strong political pressure to force the pace of the campaign in order to gain a decisive victory which might bring about the enemy's collapse before the Presidential election in the autumn. The expenses of the war were costing the Union nearly four million dollars a day, and commercial circles in New York were criticizing Lincoln's policy of pursuing the war *coûte que coûte*. Besides this, the opinion

1. *Battles and Leaders*, IV, 213. The writer of this scathing criticism was Lieut.-Colonel Martin Thomas McMahon, Chief of Staff of VI Corps throughout the 1864 campaign.
2. *Grant*, II, 276.

was prevalent that the longer the war continued, the greater likelihood there was of France and Britain, though for different reasons, recognizing the Confederacy and giving it material assistance.

Apart from these economic and political considerations, the malarial summer season was now approaching, when troops engaged in the low-lying swamps of Tidewater Virginia were bound to suffer serious casualties from sickness as the summer wore on; the losses thus incurred might well be heavier than those sustained in battle. The Confederate troops, being more acclimatized to such conditions, would suffer less.

We must remember that Grant was grossly mistaken about the state of morale of his enemy. He reckoned that *Lee*'s army was 'really whipped' and incapable of standing up to Union troops in the open field. The two armies were now facing each other only a few miles outside the perimeter of the fixed fortifications of Richmond; Grant was anxious to launch an *attaque brusquée* before the enemy could dig in and entrench securely on the line of the Chickahominy River, or fall back within the Richmond perimeter. He was therefore determined to deliver a crushing blow as soon as he was reinforced by the arrival of Smith's xviii Corps from the Army of the James at City Point. These factors sufficiently explain Grant's reasons for an immediate attack on *Lee*'s army in the first days of June; they do not excuse the mistakes which occurred in the execution of his plan.

Lee, having forestalled Grant in his move on Richmond, had occupied and hastily entrenched a line, seven miles in length, running north-west to the Totopotomoy Creek from a point on the Chickahominy River three miles south of an important cross-roads at Cold Harbor. The terrain was entirely new to Grant, but to *Lee* it was completely familiar, for it was the same battlefield where he had defeated the Army of the Potomac, then commanded by McClellan, in the fierce fighting during June 1862. The ground was equally familiar to many of Grant's subordinates, who must have had painful memories of their previous experiences there.

The Confederate position, although only hastily entrenched, had considerable natural strength, for its right flank was covered by the marshy valley of the Chickahominy, while its left rested on the Totopotomoy Creek. Neither flank could therefore be easily turned. The ground in front was fairly level, but difficult to move across owing to swamps, gullies and thickets. There were also the usual slashings of timber, forming a fairly continuous abatis. The right sector was held by *Anderson*'s i Corps; in the centre was *Hill*'s iii Corps, and on his left the ii Corps, now commanded by *Jubal Anderson Early*, as *Ewell* was again on the sick list. *Lee*'s army had now been reinforced by the divisions of *George E. Pickett* and *Robert F. Hoke* from *Beauregard*'s command on the James River, and by *Breckinridge*'s division from the Shenandoah Valley, which brought his strength up to nearly 60,000, against which Grant could muster 108,000 when reinforced by Smith's xviii Corps.

21   Union field battery in action at Cold Harbor, June 1864

22   Union siege battery before Petersburg, July 1864

23 *Lieutenant-General Grant in camp at City Point, 1864*

Sheridan's Cavalry Corps, as we have seen, had on 31 May seized the cross-roads at Cold Harbor after driving back *Fitzhugh Lee*'s cavalry division. *Hoke*'s newly arrived division counter-attacked strongly, and Sheridan was about to evacuate Cold Harbor when he received an order from Grant to hold it at all hazards until reinforcements could reach him. Grant ordered Wright's VI Corps, then north of Totopotomoy Creek, to make a forced march through the night to relieve Sheridan. *Lee* had already ordered *Anderson*'s I Corps to move forward and take Cold Harbor. *Anderson* attacked soon after dawn on 1 June, but Sheridan's troopers kept them at bay with the rapid fire of their magazine carbines until Wright's men arrived at 9 a.m., footsore and weary after their arduous night march of 15 miles over difficult country. The VI Corps then took over the Cold Harbor sector in relief of the cavalry, having the V Corps on its right near Bethesda Church, and the IX and II Corps still further to the north. It is difficult to understand why Grant relieved the cavalry with the VI Corps, which had much farther to march than the V; IX or II Corps.

On 24 May Grant had at last rationalized the command system in the Army of the Potomac by placing Burnside's IX Corps directly under Meade's orders. Eighteen months earlier, in the Fredericksburg campaign, Meade had been a divisional commander in the Army of the Potomac, then commanded by Burnside, who was far senior to Meade as a Major-General. Burnside had been demoted by Lincoln for incompetence but, being a genial and good-natured person, he made no difficulty now about serving under Meade, as he realized that the latter merely acted as a post-box for Grant.

On 27 May Grant had ordered Smith's XVIII Corps, then serving under Butler's command on the James River, to embark at City Point and disembark at White House on the Pamunkey to join the Army of the Potomac. Smith's corps, numbering 16,000 men, embarked on 28 May and during the 30th and 31st disembarked at White House, only 15 miles from Cold Harbor. There Smith received a written order signed by Brigadier-General Rawlins, Grant's Chief of Staff, to leave a garrison to protect his base at White House and at once to march the remainder of his corps to New Castle Ferry on the Pamunkey, four miles below Hanover Town. Owing to the shortage of river steamers, the XVIII Corps had landed without their regimental transport wagons, so that when they started their march on the afternoon of the 31st the men had to hump all their rations and ammunition. After a 12-mile march they arrived late that night within three miles of New Castle Ferry. The troops were very tired, as they were unaccustomed to long marches, having sat inactively on the banks of the James River for the last fortnight after their repulse at Drewry's Bluff on 16 May. On the road Smith received another order from Grant, dated the previous evening, giving him the position of the other corps of the army, and confirming his previous order 'to march up the south bank of the Pamunkey to New Castle, there to await further orders.' At daylight on 1 June Smith received from Grant's headquarters an urgent order 'to proceed at once to New Castle Ferry, and there to place his command between v and vi Corps.' Smith at once started off northward, even before his troops had time to prepare their breakfasts, but on reaching the bank of the Pamunkey at New Castle Ferry, he was mystified to find no sign of any other troops. A few hours later a staff officer from Grant's headquarters arrived to say that there had been an error in his last order – it should have read 'Cold Harbor' instead of 'New Castle Ferry'. This is the only mistake ever known to have been made by Rawlins, Grant's meticulous Chief of Staff; it had unfortunate consequences, for the xviii Corps then had to march eight miles in the opposite direction to reach Cold Harbor. The day was very hot and the dust was stifling, so that the ranks were much thinned by exhausted men falling out. On the road, Smith received his first order from Meade, to deploy his corps between Bethesda Church and Cold Harbor (three miles apart) on the right of vi Corps, and to attack the enemy immediately in conjunction with that corps. Smith complied with this order, but sent a message to Meade to say that his men had no ammunition except what they carried in their cartridge-boxes. However, the vi and xviii Corps attacked at about 5 p.m. and, in spite of heavy fire, carried the first line of enemy rifle-pits and captured 500 prisoners, but were held up by the Confederate main defensive position. The two corps suffered 2,200 casualties.

At 12.30 a.m. on 2 June Smith received from Meade the following order timed at 10.05 p.m. on the 1st:

> You will make your dispositions to attack tomorrow morning on General Wright's right, and in conjunction with that officer's attack. This attack should be made with your whole force and as vigorously as possible.

This was typical of the vague and unhelpful orders which Meade issued to the formations under his command. No zero hour was given, no objectives for the attack were indicated, nor was any boundary fixed between the two corps taking part. No arrangements were made for ammunition supply, a serious matter, as Smith's corps had arrived without its regimental transport; worst of all, no opportunity was given to the two corps commanders to reconnoitre the ground over which their tired troops were to assault an enemy whose dispositions were unknown. One can therefore sympathize with Smith's reply to his army commander, which was as follows:

> Your order for an attack is received. I have endeavored to represent to you my condition. In the present position of my line an attack by me would be simply preposterous – not only that, but an attack on the part of the enemy of any vigor would probably carry my lines more than half their length. I have called on General Wright for about 100,000 rounds of ammunition, and have asked it tonight.

This remonstrance apparently produced some effect on higher authority, for about 2.30 a.m. on 2 June Smith received a further order postponing the attack until 5 p.m. The day was therefore spent in entrenching the front line and in refilling the men's cartridge-boxes with ammunition borrowed from vi Corps. On Smith's right was a gap of two miles between him and v Corps, which made him anxious about his right flank.

Grant now appears to have realized that his attack orders had been unduly hurried. At 2.30 p.m. on 2 June Meade issued the following circular order to all corps:

> The attack ordered for 5 p.m. this day is postponed to 4.30 a.m. tomorrow. Corps commanders will employ the interim in making examinations of the ground on their front and perfecting the arrangements for the assault.

This meant that a general assault was to be made along the whole battle-front of seven miles. No reserve was retained to exploit any penetration made.

Meanwhile the right sector of Grant's line, held by Hancock (ii) and Burnside (ix), had been attacked on 1 June by *Early*'s ii Corps, but this was not pressed home, so during the night of the 1/2 June Grant moved Hancock (ii) round from the Totopotomoy Creek sector on the right flank and brought him in on the extreme left flank opposite *Anderson*'s i Corps. Hancock's corps, in consequence, had to make a night march of 12 to 15 miles across difficult country, and was deployed on the morning of 2 June to fill the two-mile gap between Cold Harbor and the Chickahominy River. Burnside's ix Corps was withdrawn to Bethesda Church, three miles north of Cold Harbor, while Warren's v Corps was extended to fill the three-mile gap between the right flank of Smith's xviii Corps and the Totopotomoy Creek. All this cross-shuffling of formations immediately previous to an operation must have had an unsettling effect on the troops and their commanders. It also interfered with unit supply arrangements and made it impossible for subordinate commanders to study the ground over which they would have to advance.

Grant, however, felt that he had only one last chance of crushing *Lee*'s army before it fell back behind the Richmond defences. He intended to deliver a powerful blow at the Confederate right flank south of Cold Harbor. His plan was to roll up that flank and drive a wedge between *Lee*'s troops and the Chickahominy River, behind which loomed the formidable redoubts of the Richmond fortified perimeter. This main thrust was to be made by the xviii, vi and ii Corps, while on the other flank the ix and v Corps would wheel in and complete the destruction of *Lee*'s army. The xviii, vi and ii Corps were to act as the hammer while the ix and the v formed the anvil.

Grant had intended that the main attack should be made at dawn on 2 June, but this unfortunately proved impracticable; ii Corps had received conflicting orders, had lost its way and was late in reaching its assembly area; xviii Corps was still short of ammunition; the attack was postponed until 4.30 a.m. on the 3rd. The delay was fatal. *Lee* quickly noticed that the Union ii Corps had been withdrawn from the Totopotomoy Creek sector, and guessed Grant's intentions. He pulled out *Hill*'s iii Corps and *Breckinridge*'s division from that sector and transferred them to reinforce his right flank south of Cold Harbor. His troops had shorter distances to go than Grant's, and were all in their new positions on the evening of the 2nd. *Lee* also ordered *Early's* II Corps to deliver an immediate attack on Warren's V Corps. This was carried out successfully on 2 June, and Warren was driven back almost to Bethesda Church, where Grant had just established his headquarters. Later in the day Grant moved his command post further to the left near Cold Harbor, where he could be in closer touch with the forthcoming battle.

At 4.30 a.m. on 3 June the three Union corps, XVIII, VI and II, sprang from their hastily constructed rifle-pits and advanced to assault the Confederate trenches. They were met with a murderous fire of musketry and artillery which caused heavy casualties. The regiments of XVIII Corps were worst off, as there was still a wide gap on their right, and they were subjected to intense enfilade fire from that flank. Three times they attempted to reach the Confederate breastworks, but on each occasion they were driven back. The corps commander has recorded the subsequent events as follows:

> Later in the day I received a verbal order from General Meade to make another assault, and that order I refused to obey.... An assault under such conditions I looked on as involving a wanton waste of life.[3]

Grant at once sent one of his aides, Lieutenant-Colonel Cyrus Ballou Comstock, to report on the situation at the front. Comstock was an experienced engineer officer; he returned to Grant's command post with the confirmation that further progress was impossible. The attacks of VI and II Corps were also halted with heavy casualties. On the extreme left, II Corps captured an advanced portion of the Confederate lines, taking several hundred prisoners and three guns, but nowhere else did the Union troops penetrate the enemy trenches. Grant soon realized that his attempt had failed; at 7 a.m. he issued the following directive to Meade:

> The moment it becomes certain that an assault cannot succeed, suspend the offensive; but when one does succeed, push it vigorously and if necessary pile in troops at the successful point from wherever they can be taken.[4]

But it was only too clear that no further progress could be made. By 7.30 a.m. the fighting died down, and at 11 a.m. Grant rode round the command posts of the corps commanders to ascertain their views. All except Burnside, who 'thought something could be done in his front', said that their troops could do no more. So at 12.30 p.m. Grant gave Meade the following instruction:

> The opinion of corps commanders not being sanguine of success in case an assault is ordered, you may direct a suspension of farther advance for the present. Hold our most advanced positions and strengthen them. Whilst on the defensive our line may be con-

3. *Battles and Leaders*, IV, 227.
4. *Grant*, II, 270.

tracted from the right if practicable. Reconnaissances should be made in front of every corps and advances made to advantageous positions by regular approaches. . . . It is necessary that we should detain all the army now with *Lee*. . . . To do this effectually it will be better to keep the enemy out of the entrenchments of Richmond than to have them go back there.

Wright and Hancock should be ready to assault in case the enemy should break through General Smith's lines, and all should be ready to resist an assault.[5]

The next four days were occupied with an exchange of letters, by no means friendly, between Grant and *Lee* regarding arrangements for the collection of the numerous dead and wounded lying out between the opposing lines.

The figures of the Union casualties incurred in the Cold Harbor fighting speak for themselves, and illustrate the sacrifice demanded of the three corps which delivered the main assault:

II	Corps	3,510
VI	,,	2,715
XVIII	,,	3,019
V	,,	1,340
IX	,,	1,701
		12,285[6]

Of these the killed numbered nearly 1,800.

Grant has been heavily blamed for the 'unnecessary' losses incurred in the Cold Harbor battle. The general war situation, however, quite apart from the political conditions on the home front, called for the maintenance of the offensive. Grant rightly felt that this was his last chance of catching *Lee*'s army outside the Richmond defences, and he was determined to exploit it. He had concentrated an army of 108,000 men on the battlefield, while the Confederates certainly could not muster more than 70,000. With such a superiority his chances of success in a pitched battle in the open were good. Grant was no ruthless butcher; he was essentially kind-hearted and humane. But he was a man of inflexible purpose and indomitable will; he could not be deflected from his objectives by difficulties or set-backs. He was caught up, however, in a wheel of tactical mishaps; his main object had been to concentrate superior numbers on the battlefield before *Lee* had time to entrench, but some of his units were delayed by faulty orders, and all of them were tired and worn out by long marches. The subordinate commanders were thus not given time to carry out reconnaissance or to coordinate their operational plans. Grant was at a great disadvantage in being unfamiliar with the ground, while *Lee* knew every yard of it; he certainly was guilty of grave miscalculations; he grossly under-

5. *Grant*, II, 272–3.
6. *Battles and Leaders*, IV, 187, but *Grant*, II, 290, gives a lower figure, 10,058, 'from a statement of losses compiled in the Adjutant-General's office'.

estimated the morale and stamina of the Confederate troops as well as the tactical skill of their commander. He never seemed to realize that all his attempts to outflank *Lee* involved arduous marches on exterior lines across difficult country, while his opponent, with shorter distances to go and in familiar terrain, was always there before him. And the Confederate infantrymen were adepts at hastily constructing bullet-proof cover of timber and earth.

Above all, Grant failed to appreciate the stopping power of the rifle against troops in the open, in spite of his experiences at Vicksburg and Spottsylvania. He was too confident that a determined effort, pushed relentlessly as at Chattanooga, would achieve victory. The First World War produced many instances of the same mistaken optimism.

The Union infantry at Cold Harbor were handicapped by a shortage of artillery support. In order to accelerate his progress through the difficult country of the Wilderness and on the poor roads of the region beyond, Grant had sent back to the base nearly half his number of guns. Had this additional fire-power been available, the Union artillery might have blasted a way through the Confederate defences. But, apart from this, the Union infantry arriving on the battlefield were suffering from the strain imposed by four weeks of continuous marching and fighting in hot weather; they no longer attacked with the same *élan* which they had displayed in the Wilderness and at Spottsylvania. They were beginning to feel that it was certain death to assault the enemy entrenchments over open ground, and this naturally depressed their morale. On the evening before the final Cold Harbor assault, one of Grant's aides, Horace Porter, when visiting the troops in the front line, noticed

> That the men were calmly writing their names and home addresses on slips of paper, and pinning them on the backs of their coats, so that their dead bodies might be recognized upon the field, and their fate made known to their families at home.... Such courage is more than heroic – it is sublime.[7]

It may have been heroic, but it showed rather a spirit of fatalistic resignation—'Their's but to do and die', or *morituri te salutant*.

7. *Porter*, 174–5.

XXI

The Crossing of the James and Assault on Petersburg
7–18 June 1864

The failure at Cold Harbor made it obvious that there would be no further chance of forcing *Lee* to fight in the open, so that Grant's objective must now be to shut him up in Richmond and capture that city. With Sherman moving relentlessly on Atlanta, the Confederates could hardly continue the war after losing their capital and their main field army. Grant's immediate problem, therefore, resembled to some extent the task which had confronted him twelve months earlier at Vicksburg. Just as he had found that the only entry to Vicksburg was by the back door, namely by crossing the Mississippi lower down, he now realized that the best way to approach Richmond was by crossing the James River and capturing Petersburg, 22 miles south of Richmond, the key to the capital's communications with the remaining resources of the South. Even before the battle of Cold Harbor Grant had foreseen that he would eventually have to cross the James to outflank *Lee*, for on 26 May he had asked Halleck to collect all the available pontoon-boats and have them brought up the James.

To ensure *Lee*'s final defeat, it was essential to cut as many as possible of his lines of communication with the west and south. These were:

(a) The Virginia Central Railroad, running north-west from Richmond to Gordonsville, where it joined the East Tennessee and Virginia Railroad.

(b) The James River Canal, running westward to Lynchburg and the Alleghenies.

(c) The Richmond and Danville Railroad, running south-west to the Carolinas.

(d) The Richmond, Petersburg and Weldon Railroad, running south to Petersburg and North Carolina.

The most vital of these links was the last one, through Petersburg, which was connected by railroad with both the south and the west. At the opening of the campaign in May Butler could easily have captured Petersburg by a *coup de main*, but that opportunity had been lost through his ineptitude. Petersburg was therefore Grant's first objective, but to seize it before *Lee* could get his army there presented a difficult problem, for Grant's army of 100,000 men would first have to cross the James River, which below Richmond was nearly a third of a mile wide. This was a hazardous operation, for it would have to be carried out in proximity to a hostile army, with which the Union army was still in close contact. Hitherto *Lee* had always succeeded in forestalling Grant when the latter had attempted to turn his flank. *Lee* held the advantage of being on the inner circle, and therefore always had shorter distances to march. He had the additional advantage of being more familiar with the country and, as he was operating in his own territory, was able to obtain quicker and more reliable intelligence about his enemy's movements than could Grant.

In order to cut the direct communications between Richmond and the west, Grant intended that David Hunter, with the Army of West Virginia, should advance up the Shenandoah Valley and capture Lynchburg, an important railway and canal centre on the upper James River. The capture of both Petersburg and Lynchburg would leave Richmond with only one link with the south-west, namely the Richmond and Danville Railroad.

After Sigel's repulse in the upper Shenandoah Valley in mid-May, he had been replaced in command of the Army of West Virginia by David Hunter, who received orders from Grant to advance up the Shenandoah Valley and cut the East Tennessee and Virginia Railroad at Lynchburg on the upper James River. Hunter began his forward move on 1 June with a force of 8,500 men, and on the following day drove a weaker Confederate force out of Harrisonburg. Hunter continued his advance and the Confederates were driven back beyond Staunton with the loss of 1,500 men and three guns. At Staunton Hunter was reinforced by a column under Crook and Averell which had advanced on his right flank through the Alleghenies. This brought Hunter's force up to 18,000 men and 30 guns, and he continued his advance on Lynchburg. Immediately after the battle of Cold Harbor, *Lee*, perturbed by Hunter's threat to his communications with the west, dispatched *Breckinridge*'s division to seize Rockfish Gap and cover Lynchburg. On 11 June Hunter reached Lexington, 36 miles north-west of Lynchburg, where he was confronted by *Breckinridge*'s division, only 4,000 strong. *Lee*, now thoroughly alarmed by Hunter's progress, on 12 June dispatched *Early*'s II Corps from Richmond to reinforce *Breckinridge*. *Early* started westward on the morning of the 13th and, after a forced march of 100 miles, partly by rail, reached Lynchburg on the afternoon of the 17th. Hunter had now missed his chance; on the 18th he made a half-hearted attack on Lynchburg, but did not press it vigorously. On the morning of the 19th *Early* launched a counter-attack but found to his surprise that Hunter had already retreated. *Early* then drove Hunter's force westward into the Alleghenies and continued to advance northward down the Shenandoah Valley unopposed. His subsequent invasion of Maryland and threat to Washington will be described in the next chapter.

In order to cooperate with Hunter's advance up the Shenandoah Valley against Lynchburg, on 7 June Grant despatched Sheridan with two of his cavalry divisions westward with orders to destroy as much as possible of the Virginia Central Railroad, and then to move on to Charlottesville and try and link up with Hunter. Sheridan managed to do some damage to the railway east of Gordonsville, but on 11 June he was overtaken by the cavalry divisions of *Wade Hampton* and *Fitzhugh Lee* which had been sent after him by *Lee*. As Sheridan was now cut off from his objective, and learnt from prisoners that Hunter was nowhere near Charlottesville, he withdrew on the following day and returned to his base at White House on 21 June.

Thus Grant was once more frustrated in his attempt to cut *Lee*'s communications with the west, and had now to concentrate on the reduction of Petersburg.

On 9 June Butler, who had been left at Bermuda Hundred on the right bank of the James, attempted an attack on Petersburg with 4,500 men of x Corps, but this was easily repulsed by the Confederate garrison of 2,500. For the second time Butler had missed a great opportunity, for the defences at Petersburg were then by no means complete.

Meanwhile Grant was maturing his bold plan of transferring the Army of the Potomac to the south bank of the James. On communicating his intention to Halleck, the latter protested that the move was a risky one and would endanger the safety of Washington. He suggested that it would be preferable to attack Richmond from the north-east, so as to keep the Army of the Potomac between *Lee*'s army and Washington. Grant's reply to this was:

> We can defend Washington best by keeping *Lee* so occupied that he cannot detach enough troops to capture it. If the safety of the city should really become imperilled, we have water communication, and can transport a sufficient number of troops to Washington at any time and hold it against attack.

This was sound strategic sense, and is of interest with regard to what actually happened when the capital was threatened by *Jubal Early*'s raid in the following month.

The first step in planning the crossing of the James was to select a bridging site sufficiently far down stream to enable the army to cross before *Lee* got wind of the operation and interfered with it. Grant entrusted this important task to two capable members of his own personal staff, Lieutenant-Colonels Comstock and Porter, the former an Engineer, the latter an Ordnance Officer. On the morning of 7 June Comstock and Porter rode over to White House and there took steamer down the Pamunkey and York Rivers and up the

James, reaching Butler's headquarters at Bermuda Hundred on the following day. On the 10th they started down the river, carefully reconnoitring the banks and the approaches on each side. Their final choice for the crossing site was at Fort Powhatan, 11 miles below City Point and 26 miles south-east of Richmond, where the estuary narrowed and there was a good approach road to each bank. They returned to Grant's headquarters with their report on 12 June. The site selected was the best available, but it presented a formidable technical task, for the river there had a width of 700 yards and a tidal rise and fall of four feet. The current was fairly strong, and the depth in mid-stream was 90 feet.

Grant and Meade meanwhile were carrying out the delicate operation of breaking contact with the enemy on the Cold Harbor position and moving their troops to the north bank of the James. Smith's XVIII Corps was re-embarked at White House, and returned to Bermuda Hundred by water, as it had come. In order to cover the withdrawal of the rest of the army, Wilson's cavalry division and Warren's V Corps side-slipped down the Chickahominy River and crossed it five miles farther down stream. They then took up a covering position near Malvern Hill, north of the James, as if to threaten Richmond from that direction. The II, VI and IX Corps moved south by separate roads for 20 or 30 miles through low-lying wooded country to the crossing point at Fort Powhatan.

The withdrawal from the Cold Harbor position started after dark on 12 June. Hancock's II Corps formed the advanced guard and reached the north bank of the James on the 14th. It was then ferried across the river to establish a bridgehead on the south bank, under cover of which an engineer battalion of 450 men started the construction of the pontoon bridge. Before the work started Grant had three schooners laden with stones sunk in the fairway above the bridge site to prevent interference by the Confederate gunboats patrolling the river near Richmond. The work of anchoring the pontoons began at 4 p.m. on 14 June and the bridge was completed seven hours later. The operation was directed by Brigadier-General Henry Washington Benham, who had considerable experience of pontoon bridging. In all, 101 pontoons were used and the roadway had a width of 13 feet. It was one of the great pontoon bridges of history, and may rank with those by which Xerxes crossed the Hellespont in 480 B.C. and Napoleon the Danube below Vienna in 1809.[1]

The Army of the Potomac completed its crossing by 7 p.m. on 18 June, and the bridge was then dismantled and the pontoons rafted to City Point.

On the morning of 13 June the Confederate troops on the Cold Harbor line discovered that the Union trenches in front of them were deserted. Deceived by the appearance of Warren and Wilson at Malvern Hill, *Lee* jumped to the conclusion that Grant had merely made another short side-slip southwards,

1. The width of the Hellespont was 1,500 yards; that of the Danube, between Kaiser-Ebersdorf and the island of Lobau about 750.

but had no idea that the bulk of his army was crossing the James. *Early* having been despatched to the Shenandoah Valley, *Lee*'s Army of Northern Virginia now consisted of only *Anderson*'s Corps and *Hill*'s III Corps for the defence of Richmond, and *Beauregard*, with two weak infantry brigades at his disposal, was responsible for the defence of Petersburg, for his two other divisions were facing Butler in his entrenched position at Bermuda Hundred. For the first time, Grant had turned the tables on *Lee* and had out-manœuvred him. He must now strike quickly at Petersburg, before *Lee* discovered his move to the south bank of the James.

The town of Petersburg, with 18,000 inhabitants, was a vital link in the Confederate communications. It lay on the right (south) bank of the Appomattox River, eight miles above the junction of that river with the James. The town was protected on the north by the Appomattox and on the south by a semi-circular perimeter of earthworks, situated at a distance of two to three miles from the town centre, and strengthened by a series of redans and lunettes containing medium artillery. By the middle of June, however, only about four miles of this line had been properly entrenched, namely the eastern sector between the river and the Petersburg–Norfolk Railroad.

Butler, with some 10,000 men of X Corps, all that remained of the Army of the James, still held his old lines west of Bermuda Hundred, some seven miles north of Petersburg, to which he had retired after his defeat at Drewry's Bluff in May. On the afternoon of 14 June Butler was rejoined by Smith's XVIII Corps, which disembarked at Bermuda Hundred after having been transported by river from White House. Grant had already sent orders to Butler that Smith's corps was to move off at once, cross the Appomattox by a pontoon bridge and attack the Petersburg entrenchments at dawn the following morning, in the hope that they could be rapidly captured by a surprise assault. In fact they were at that moment only held by *Beauregard*'s two weak infantry brigades, amounting in all to 3,000 men. Butler reinforced Smith's corps (10,000) with August Valentine Kautz's cavalry division (2,400) and Edward Ward Hinks's negro division (3,700), bringing his strength up to 16,000.

Smith's force started off at 4 a.m. on 15 June and cautiously approached the east front of the Petersburg defences. Smith had been informed that he would be supported later in the day by Hancock's II Corps, which had been the first to cross the great pontoon bridge and was now on its way up to Bermuda Hundred. It was unfortunate that the important task of carrying out the surprise assault on Petersburg had been assigned to William Farrar Smith. We have already seen how this officer had refused to obey Meade's order to attack at Cold Harbor. He was by nature insubordinate and prone to criticize his superiors. At Cold Harbor he had seen his corps decimated in attempting to storm hastily constructed entrenchments. Now at Petersburg he was confronted by permanent fortifications and medium artillery. Instead of attacking immediately, he spent the rest of the day in reconnoitring the enemy position.

He then issued orders for an attack to be made at 5 p.m., but found that his artillery commander could not get his guns into position as he had sent his horses back to be watered. Having waited in vain for Hancock's arrival, Smith eventually attacked at 7 p.m. Hinks's negro division successfully carried the Confederate trenches on a front of two miles, capturing 15 guns and 300 prisoners. The road to Petersburg was now open, but Smith merely consolidated his position in the captured trenches and waited for Hancock.

Grant had intended Hancock's corps to move up in support of Smith on arriving at Bermuda Hundred, but he sent the orders for Hancock to Meade's headquarters, which were then on the way up from the bridge. Consequently Hancock never received Grant's orders, nor did he receive his rations. The muddle was due to the fact that Smith belonged to Butler's army and Hancock to Meade's. As Grant himself admitted:

> I also informed General Meade that I had ordered rations from Bermuda Hundred for Hancock's corps, and desired him to issue them speedily, and to lose no more time than was absolutely necessary. The rations did not reach him, however, and Hancock, while he got all his corps over during the night, remained until half-past ten in the hope of receiving them. He then moved without them, and on the road received a note from General W. F. Smith, asking him to come on. This seems to be the first information that General Hancock had received of the fact that he was to go to Petersburg, or that anything particular was expected of him.[2]

Unfortunately, Grant's staff had omitted to send a copy of Hancock's instructions to Butler, so Hancock, with his corps of 20,000 men, was sent off in the wrong direction and did not join Smith until late that night, when Smith insisted on him relieving his own men in the front line. Thus Grant's hope of a rapid capture of Petersburg was once more frustrated; as Grant himself has recorded:

> I believed then, and still believe, that Petersburg could have been easily captured at that time. It only had about 2,500 men in the defences besides some irregular troops.

During the night *Beauregard* reinforced his tired troops in front of Petersburg with two weak divisions which he withdrew from the sector north of the Appomattox facing Butler. Thus on the morning of the 16th he had collected 14,000 men to defend the Petersburg sector. On the Union side, Burnside's IX Corps came up, and Grant also arrived to take a look at the battlefield. All three corps were now deployed facing the Petersburg defences, Smith (XVIII) on the right, Hancock (II) in the centre and Burnside (IX) on the left, in all, some 48,000 men. Warren's V Corps was also on the way and was due to arrive on the following day. Grant then took a step which had fatal consequences. At 10.15 a.m. he sent an order to Meade to come up and take command of the attack on Petersburg. He then went back to his headquarters at City Point, so

2. *Grant*, II, 294–5.

as to be able to keep control of both Meade's army and Butler's, as he feared that *Lee* might attack Butler's lines at Bermuda Hundred and push him back into the James. Grant's action was of course logical and in accordance with normal procedure, but Meade, as Grant should have known, was not fit to be entrusted with the conduct of a major battle. Ever since the beginning of the campaign Grant himself had directed all the operations, Meade being merely used as a post-box for transmitting orders to the corps commanders and to attend to their administrative requirements. In this critical battle Grant should certainly have continued to direct personally the operations at Petersburg.

On his way up to the front Meade met Grant, who gave him verbal orders to deliver a vigorous attack later in the day with the object of driving *Beauregard* across the Appomattox. After establishing his command post at 2 p.m., Meade issued orders for a frontal attack to be made by all three corps at 6 p.m. A little time spent in reconnaissance would have shown Meade that the trenches on the south side of the Petersburg perimeter were not manned, and that a turning movement round *Beauregard*'s right flank would have rolled up his whole line, cutting him off from the town. Instead of that, Meade made a frontal attack with all three of his corps against the east sector of the perimeter, the only one which was manned. Hancock's men in the centre overran the Confederate line and captured four redans, but suffered heavy casualties. It was Cold Harbor all over again.

At 7.45 a.m. on the 16th *Beauregard* had telegraphed to *Lee* that he had captured a prisoner of Hancock's corps, and asked for reinforcements, but *Lee* was convinced that the bulk of Grant's army still faced him on the Richmond front, and only sent him one brigade from north of the James.

At dawn on the 17th Burnside's ix Corps launched a surprise attack on *Beauregard*'s right sector and made a small penetration, but the Confederates counter-attacked and heavy fighting continued all day. *Beauregard* then ordered another and shorter line of trenches to be dug 2,000 yards in rear, but told his men in the front line 'to hold on at any cost'. In reply to his further appeals for more reinforcements, *Lee* replied at noon on the 17th:

> Until I can get more definite information of Grant's movements, I do not think it prudent to draw more troops to this side of the river.

In the course of the severe fighting on the 17th, however, *Beauregard* did obtain further intelligence regarding Meade's strength, and at 5 p.m. he wired to *Lee*:

> Prisoners just taken represent themselves as belonging to ii, ix and xviii Corps. They state that v and vi Corps are behind coming on.

At last *Lee* began to see daylight, and at once dispatched *Hill*'s iii Corps and two divisions of *Anderson*'s i Corps to reinforce *Beauregard* at Petersburg.

These troops kept arriving during the night, and had all reached him by noon on the following day. The struggle continued until 11 p.m. on the 17th. After midnight *Beauregard* quietly withdrew his troops to the second line of trenches which he had constructed in rear.

Meade had also been reinforced during the 17th by the arrival of Warren's v Corps, which brought his strength up to 95,000, and ordered the assault to be renewed at 4 a.m. on the 18th. When the Union troops advanced, however, they found the Confederate trenches empty, so patrols were pushed out to locate the enemy's new position, and Meade ordered a fresh attack to be made at noon by 11, 1x and v Corps. By this time *Beauregard*'s reinforcements had arrived from Richmond, and his reserve line was now manned by 38,000 men. *Lee* himself reached Petersburg at 11.30 a.m., being at last convinced that the whole of Grant's army was now south of the James. Meade's midday assault failed completely, all three corps being repulsed with heavy losses.

Grant now realized that his attempt to forestall *Lee* at Petersburg had been frustrated; he decided to give his sorely tried troops a much needed rest, and to resort to siege operations to reduce the town. As *Beauregard* wrote in his account of the struggle:

> The spade took the place of the musket, and the regular siege was begun. It was only raised April 2, 1865.

The unsuccessful battle for Petersburg, 14–18 June, was a costly one for the Union, their casualties being approximately 10,000, nearly as heavy as at Cold Harbor. The Confederate losses have not been accurately recorded but, as their men were fighting behind strong entrenchments, were probably not more than one-third of the Union casualties.

It is impossible to explain or excuse the crass ineptitude of the Union leadership at Petersburg. Grant himself must take some of the blame. Having deprived Meade of any operational responsibility from the very start of the campaign, he suddenly threw the onus of command on him when the battle had already begun, and then left him to his own devices without any further guidance. Meade himself possessed little initiative or energy. He had been content to assume a passive role under Grant's domination, and any faculty for command that he may have possessed had atrophied in consequence. Horace Porter, Grant's liaison officer at Meade's headquarters throughout the final day of the battle, described his nervous irascibility, perhaps in too flattering terms, as follows:

> He showed himself the personification of earnest, vigorous action in rousing his subordinate commanders to superior exertions. Even his fits of anger and his resort to intemperate language stood him at times in good stead in spurring on every one upon that active field. He sent ringing despatches to all points of the line, and paced up and down upon the field in his nervous, restless manner, as he watched the progress of the operations and made running comments on the actions of his subordinates.... He had

much to try him on this occasion, and if he was severe in his reprimands and showed faults of temper, he certainly displayed no faults as a commander.[3]

It was not the way in which the cool and collected Grant would have conducted the battle. The most blameworthy of the Union commanders, however, was William Farrar Smith, who was given the fleeting opportunity of seizing Petersburg before it was reinforced. There was no excuse for his dilatory and pusillanimous conduct. Butler had lent him Kautz's cavalry division to assist him in reconnaissance duties, but he made no use of it. He was evidently suffering from 'cold feet' after his experiences at Cold Harbor, and dallied all day in the hope that Hancock would arrive to carry out the assault. A month later Grant relieved him of his command. Smith was insubordinate and spiteful by nature; he described his Army Commander, Benjamin Butler, as 'helpless as a child on the field of battle'. At Chattanooga Grant had formed an exaggerated opinion of Smith's abilities and obtained for him accelerated promotion, which Smith repaid by spreading malicious slanders on Grant's conduct.

The hero of the Petersburg battle was undoubtedly the Confederate commander, *Gustave Toutant Beauregard*, who was the grandson of a French settler in Louisiana, named Toutant, and assumed the name of Beauregard from his family estate in the South. *Beauregard* was one of the ablest of the Confederate leaders, though never on the best of terms with either *Jefferson Davis* or *Lee*.

3. *Porter*, 209.

XXII

The Siege of Petersburg
June–July 1864

Grant's brilliant strategic conception of transferring the Army of the Potomac to the south bank of the James River had been nullified by the tactical errors of his subordinates. For this he had himself to blame. Having kept the tactical direction of every previous action in his own hands, on the eve of the Petersburg battle he delegated the conduct of the operations to Meade, who was not equal to the task now suddenly thrust upon him. It was not till noon on 18 June that *Lee* had sent *Hill*'s corps south to reinforce *Beauregard*, so on that morning Meade had 95,000 men under his command against 20,000 Confederates. Instead of using his superiority in numbers to work round *Beauregard*'s open right flank, Meade's only idea was to hurl three corps in futile frontal attacks against strong entrenchments manned by a resolute enemy. Grant might well have dismissed Meade and Smith, as well as Butler, for their failure to seize the tactical opportunities presented to them. He would indeed have been justified in placing on their shoulders the entire blame for the miscarriage of his plans, but he was by nature too magnanimous to off-load his responsibilities in this way. At 10 p.m. on the 18th he wrote to Meade:

> I am perfectly satisfied that all has been done that could be done, and that the assaults of today were called for by all the appearances and information that could be obtained. Now we will rest the men, and use the spade for their protection until a new vein can be struck.[1]

He even went so far as to recommend Meade for promotion to Major-General in the Regular Army.

In other ways too Grant must bear the blame for the failure of the Petersburg attack. His dynamic drive had overtaxed the physical endurance of his officers and men. In the course of the six weeks' campaign the Union losses had amounted to some 65,000, while the Confederates, who had been fighting

1. *Porter*, 210.

24   Grant and some of his staff at City Point, 1864. From left to right:
Brig.-Gen. Rawlins, Lt.-Col. Comstock, Janes, Gen. Grant, Capt. Dunn, Lt.-Col.
Morgan, Lt.-Col. Hudson, Lt.-Col. Parker, Lt.-Col. Babcock

25   Grant as Union Commander-in-Chief

from behind strong entrenchments, except in the Wilderness battle, could not have suffered more than 30,000 casualties. Throughout this period the Union troops had been marching and fighting without a rest and were physically worn out. Many of the most reliable veteran officers, as well as the cream of the private soldiers, had fallen in battle, and the ranks were now filled with inexperienced replacements. Discipline and morale had in consequence suffered. Grant realized this, and knew that his troops must be given a period of rest and recuperation, such as could only be afforded by the comparative inaction of trench warfare. But he never lost sight of his ultimate objective, the destruction of *Lee*'s army, which could now only be achieved by constant attrition and by cutting its communications with the south and west.

Grant had established his headquarters on a high bluff at City Point, overlooking the broad estuary of the James River, a mile below its confluence with the Appomattox. There he was centrally placed to control the armies of Butler and Meade, and had deep-water communication with his rear supply base at Fort Monroe and with the Government in Washington. The Petersburg and City Point Railroad was now repaired as far as the front, and a branch line from it was constructed by Grant's engineers, parallel to the front, to convey supplies and ammunition to each corps headquarters. Butler's army threw a pontoon bridge from Bermuda Hundred to Deep Bottom on the north bank of the James, only ten miles south-east of Richmond, so that *Lee* might be kept in uncertainty as to whether the next attack would be directed on Richmond or Petersburg.

On Tuesday 21 June a historic event occurred: President Lincoln arrived at City Point by steamer to pay his first visit to Grant's armies in the field. Lincoln disembarked feeling very unwell, having had a stormy passage across Chesapeake Bay. One of Grant's staff seized the occasion to suggest a glass of champagne as a certain cure for seasickness. 'No, my friend, I have seen too many fellows seasick ashore from drinking that very stuff', replied the President austerely. Lincoln then expressed a wish to visit the troops at the front, so Grant mounted him on his favourite bay charger 'Cincinnati', while he himself rode his black pony 'Jeff Davis'.[2] Lincoln must have looked an incongruous figure, dressed in black frock-coat and trousers, with a very tall silk hat. But he received an enthusiastic welcome from Butler's and Meade's troops, who hailed him affectionately as 'Uncle Abe'. Grant then took him to visit Hinks's negro division of xviii Corps, which had distinguished itself on the first day of the Petersburg battle. The President was greeted still more vociferously by the coloured troops, who, since his Emancipation Proclamation of 1 January 1863, had regarded him as their particular liberator. Lincoln himself had first proposed the recruitment of negro troops by voluntary enlistment in spite of

2. So named because he was captured on the plantation of President *Jefferson Davis*'s brother Joseph.

much prejudiced opposition. This was only the second occasion on which negro regiments, with white officers, had been used as combat troops.

Lincoln had just been nominated for re-election by the National Republican Convention, but political circles were protesting loudly against the heavy casualties being incurred in the course of Grant's campaign. Before returning to Washington, the President remarked significantly to Grant: 'I cannot pretend to advise, but I do sincerely hope that all may be accomplished with as little bloodshed as possible.'

Grant now set his troops to work on entrenching a continuous line of works for the investment of Petersburg. At the same time he organized a major raid to interrupt Lee's railway communications with the south. Meade's army held the front southwards from the Appomattox in the following order: ix (Burnside), v (Warren), ii (David B. Birney, who had replaced Hancock, sick), vi (Wright); Smith's xviii Corps had reverted to Butler's army at Bermuda Hundred. On 22 June Birney (ii) was ordered to advance westward and seize the Petersburg–Weldon Railroad, while Wright (vi) was to move parallel to him and push still farther west in order to cut the Southside Railroad from Petersburg to Lynchburg. Owing to the wooded nature of the country, however, the two corps got widely separated and lost contact with each other. Lee at once moved Hill's iii Corps southward to counter the Union advance. Hill found the gap between the two corps and struck hard at Birney's left flank. The Union troops lost 2,962 men and four guns; Wright's corps was forced to retire, so the operation ended in complete failure.

At the same time Grant sent Wilson's cavalry division (5,500) on a raid still farther west to Burkesville, the junction of the Southside Railroad with the Danville line. Wilson succeeded in tearing up 60 miles of track, but on his way back he was intercepted by a Confederate force, losing 1,500 men and 12 guns. Wilson's raid was a considerable blow to the Confederate communications, though they soon managed to repair the damaged track.

Meanwhile unexpected events were taking place in the Shenandoah Valley, which was an important source of food, forage and remounts for Lee's army. As mentioned in the previous chapter, after the battle of Cold Harbor Lee had dispatched first Breckinridge's division and then Early's ii Corps to check Hunter's advance up the Shenandoah Valley to Lynchburg. Having driven Hunter westward into the Alleghenies on 20 June, Early advanced northward down the Shenandoah Valley unopposed. His instructions from Lee were to dispose of Hunter, and then to make a raid across the Potomac and threaten Washington. Early's force consisted of 10,000 infantry, 4,000 cavalry and 48 guns. After resting his troops on 22 June, Early marched north on the following day, reaching Staunton on the 26th. On 2 July he entered Winchester, and on the next day attacked Martinsburg, which was held by Sigel with a Union division left there to guard the Potomac crossings. Sigel hastily retired, and on 5 July Early's column crossed the Potomac above Harper's Ferry and invaded

Maryland, holding the towns of Hagerstown and Boonesboro to ransom. On 9 July *Early* entered Frederick, but two miles to the south-east his advanced guard was held up on the line of the Monocacy River by a Union force, 6,000 strong, consisting of a division of Lew Wallace's VIII Corps and a division of Wright's VI Corps, hastily dispatched by water from Grant's army to defend Washington. Neither Grant nor Halleck knew anything of *Early*'s raid until 5 July, when Lincoln appealed to Grant to come himself to the rescue of the capital. Grant sensibly refused, saying: 'It would have a bad effect for me to leave here', but he sent Wright's VI Corps by water to defend the capital. Its leading division reached Baltimore on 8 July and was put at the disposal of Lew Wallace, commanding VIII Corps, who hastily occupied a line on the Monocacy River in order to halt *Early*'s advance. The XIX Corps under William Hemsley Emory had just arrived at Fort Monroe by sea from Louisiana, destined to join the Army of the Potomac at Petersburg, and this corps also was diverted by Grant to defend Washington.

After a brief fight on the Monocacy, *Early* drove Lew Wallace's force back to Baltimore with the loss of 1,880 men, the Confederate casualties being less than 700. The road to Washington was now open, and *Early* pushed on, although his men were very exhausted after their long marches in intense heat and stifling dust. On 11 July they came within range of Fort Stevens, the most northerly outwork of the Washington defences. The Union capital, after three years of war, had been very thoroughly fortified. On both sides of the Potomac, and including Alexandria, it had been surrounded by a circle of permanent works, mounting guns, with a radius of four to six miles from the Capitol. These forts were sited on every prominent point, at intervals of about half a mile, constituting a perimeter of 36 miles, and the intervals were closed by infantry parapets. It was a formidable defensive system, and might stand comparison with that with which Wellington checkmated Massena at Torres Vedras. The troops available to defend this vast perimeter, however, were by no means commensurate with its extent, for there were only 3,600 men holding the sector north of the Potomac, with 5,800 south of the river, besides a reserve of 8,000 elderly reservists in the city. *Early*, therefore, had a good chance of invading the capital, and his arrival before the outer defences caused a considerable panic in the city. It was fortunate that Grant had dispatched his reinforcements so speedily. The remainder of VI Corps, together with XIX Corps, reached Washington on 11 July, just in time to man the defences as the Confederates arrived.

Early's advanced guard came under fire from Fort Stevens and the adjacent works, and he could see beyond them clouds of dust which showed that the defences were being reinforced. That night *Early* received information that at least two corps of Grant's army had already arrived, so he wisely decided to withdraw to Virginia before he could be cut off. As Grant said:

If *Early* had been but one day earlier he might have entered the capital before the arrival of the reinforcements I had sent.[3]

Early commenced his retreat after dark on the 12th, without any interference on the part of the enemy. On the morning of the 14th the Confederates re-crossed the Potomac above Leesburg, carrying off the prisoners they had captured at the Monocacy, as well as a plentiful booty of beef cattle and horses. Wright's vi Corps (14,000) followed up slowly, but failed to catch them. *Early* withdrew up the Shenandoah Valley to Strasburg, which he reached on 22 July. On the following day Grant, thinking that *Early* was finished with, recalled vi Corps to Petersburg, leaving xix Corps to defend Washington.

We can now return to Petersburg, where both sides had settled down to trench warfare, the Confederates extending their entrenchments westward to cover the south side of the town, while Meade's army followed suit and dug itself in, the opposing lines being only 100–200 yards apart. Grant was busy getting siege artillery transported by sea from Washington.

After the failure of Meade's last attack on 18 June, an officer commanding a Pennsylvania regiment in Burnside's corps conceived the idea of running a mine-gallery under the enemy trenches and blowing up one of his redans. The breach thus created might be exploited by an infantry assault. This officer, Lieutenant-Colonel Henry Pleasants, was a mining engineer in civil life, and his regiment was recruited from miners of the upper Schuylkill coalfield in Pennsylvania. His proposal was put to Burnside, who warmly supported it, but Meade disapproved of the idea, which his Chief Engineer turned down as completely impracticable. Grant, however, gave his approval that the experiment should be tried, though he considered that the proposed site was unsuitable for tactical exploitation, as Burnside's corps held the centre sector of the front. Pleasants was told to go ahead with his scheme, but was given little material assistance. At the point he had selected the opposing front-line trenches were 130 yards apart. Pleasants started his men mining on 25 June and the work was completed on 23 July. The main gallery was 511 feet in length, terminating in two lateral galleries with a total length of 75 feet to act as mine chambers. A charge of 8,000 pounds of black powder was laid in the lateral galleries, and tamped with 38 feet of earth in the main gallery. Burnside's corps consisted of three white divisions and one negro division, the latter commanded by Edward Ferrero, a dancing master in civil life. This negro division had not yet been engaged in combat. During the Wilderness campaign it had been employed in guarding the lines of communication, but Burnside intended to use it to carry out the assault from the mine crater as it was the freshest and strongest of his divisions. The coloured troops, who were full of enthusiasm, were given a week's special training for the operation, and it was decided to explode the mine at dawn on 30 July.

3. *Grant,* ii, 306.

On the day before the appointed time, however, Meade told Burnside that, for political reasons, the coloured troops were not to be put in first, and Grant concurred. Burnside then summoned his three white divisional commanders and made them draw lots to decide which should lead the assault. The division thus selected was, unfortunately, the weakest in the corps, and its commander, James Hewitt Ledlie, the least competent. According to Burnside's original plan, the two leading brigades would sweep to the right and left of the mine crater in order to widen the breach, but at the last moment this plan was changed by Meade, who insisted that the troops should advance straight to their front and capture a further objective known as Cemetery Hill. Consequently there was no opportunity for preliminary rehearsal or reconnaissance by Ledlie's division.

The mine was exploded at 4.45 a.m. on 30 July. It was a technical success, but a tactical disaster. An enormous crater was blown in the enemy's front line, 170 feet wide, 60 feet across and 30 feet deep. Ledlie's division, followed closely by Ferrero's negro division, poured into the crater, which then became a death-trap, for as soon as the men tried to climb out of it they were mown down by rifle and mortar fire from the enemy's second-line and flanking trenches. The more troops that crowded into the crater, the worse a shambles it became. Grant himself, accompanied by one A.D.C., made his way up to the front line an hour later to see what was happening. He then went to Burnside's command post and told him:

> The entire opportunity has been lost. There is now no chance of success. These troops must be immediately withdrawn. It is slaughter to leave them here.[4]

The two Union divisions had suffered 4,400 casualties; the Confederate loss was about 1,000. Grant commented on the operation in his Memoirs:

> The effort was a stupendous failure. It cost us about four thousand men, mostly, however, captured; and all due to inefficiency on the part of the corps commander and the incompetency of the division commander who was sent to lead the assault.[5]

A Court of Inquiry was afterwards held on the conduct of the operation; blame was attributed to Burnside, Ledlie, Ferrero and two other commanders, and a fortnight later Burnside was relieved of command of IX Corps and was replaced by his Chief of Staff, John Grubb Parke. The corps commander was perhaps the least blameworthy; he had been enthusiastic about the enterprise from the start and had made sensible plans which had been countermanded by Meade at the last moment. There was certainly faulty leadership on the part of the two divisional commanders, who were reported to have remained throughout the operation in a dug-out behind their own lines, drinking hospital rum and leaving their brigadiers to direct the fighting.

4. *Porter*, 267.
5. *Grant*, II, 315.

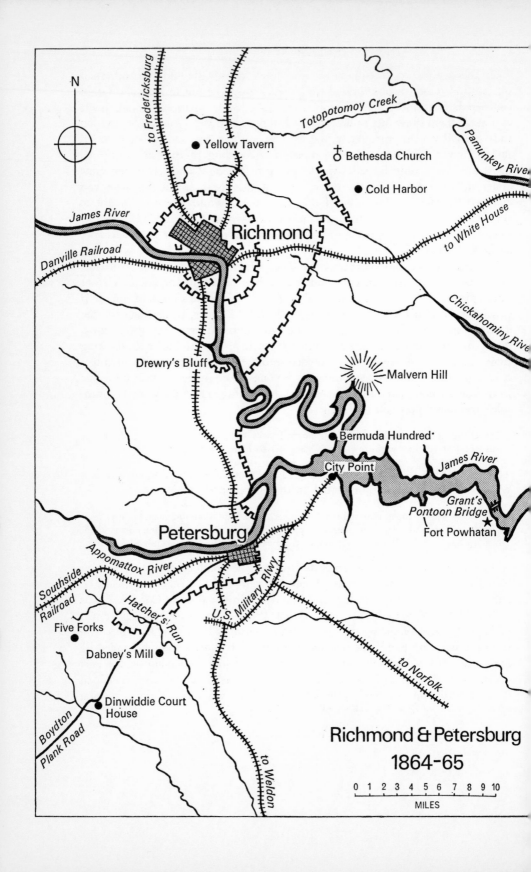

N

Totopotomoy Creek

to Fredericksburg

Pamunkey River

● Yellow Tavern

☨ Bethesda Church

● Cold Harbor

James River

Richmond

to White House

Danville Railroad

Chickahominy River

Drewry's Bluff

Malvern Hill

Bermuda Hundred ·

City Point

James River

Grant's Pontoon Bridge

★ Fort Powhatan

Petersburg

Appomattox River

Southside Railroad

Hatcher's Run

U.S. Military Rlwy.

Five Forks ●

Dabney's Mill ●

to Norfolk

Boydton Plank Road

Dinwiddie Court House ●

to Weldon

Richmond & Petersburg
1864-65

0 1 2 3 4 5 6 7 8 9 10

MILES

XXIII

Sheridan's Shenandoah Campaign
August–December 1864

In the preceding chapter we have followed *Jubal Early*'s bold advance to the gates of Washington during the first half of July and his subsequent withdrawal to Strasburg in the Shenandoah Valley. He had thus successfully carried out the task given him by *Lee,* namely to force Grant to disperse his troops and to disrupt the Union plans by threatening Washington. Grant had indeed saved the capital by his immediate dispatch of VI and XIX Corps, but he then temporarily lost control of the situation owing to a break-down in the telegraphic communication between his headquarters and Washington. Thus VI and XIX Corps were left without orders, *Early* was allowed to withdraw unmolested, and Halleck as usual was incapable of taking action. On 12 July, when *Early* decided to withdraw, Charles Anderson Dana, Assistant Secretary of War, wrote from Washington to Grant:

> General Halleck will not give orders except as he receive them; the President will give none, and until you direct positively and explicitly what is to be done, everything will go on in the deplorable and fatal way in which it has gone on for the past week.

Grant was paying the penalty for having tied his headquarters too closely to Butler's and Meade's armies, and had thus lost his grip on the general direction of the war. Thinking that *Early* had rejoined *Lee* at Richmond, he now ordered VI Corps back to the Army of the Potomac, leaving XIX to defend Washington.

As soon as *Early* found that VI Corps had been withdrawn, he again seized the initiative and on 24 July attacked Crook's VIII Corps which was holding Winchester. Crook hurriedly retreated north-east to Harper's Ferry, after losing 1,000 men. *Early* then made another bold dash for the Potomac, crossed it at Williamsport on the 26th, and on the 30th sent a cavalry division 25 miles to the north to raid and burn Chambersburg (Pa). Panic and confusion once more reigned in Washington, and Grant now had to take firm measures to prevent a *débâcle*. He decided to organize a separate command in the Shenandoah Valley in order to remove once and for all the constant menace to Washington. This task must be entrusted to some leader on whom he could rely, for he had already been let down by Sigel and Hunter. His choice fell on the 33-year-old Philip Sheridan. On 1 August he countermanded the return of VI Corps and wrote to Halleck:

> I am sending General Sheridan for temporary duty whilst the enemy is being expelled from the border. Unless General Hunter is in the field in person, I want Sheridan put in command of all the troops in the field, with instructions to put himself south of the enemy and follow him to the death. Once started up the valley they ought to be followed until we get possession of the Virginia Central Railroad.[1]

Halleck and Stanton demurred at this appointment of the youthful Sheridan, but when Lincoln heard of it he gave his hearty approval and wrote to Grant on 3 August:

> I have seen your despatch.... This, I think, is exactly right, as to how our forces should move.... I repeat to you it will neither be done nor attempted unless you watch it every day and hour, and force it.

Lincoln's advice was wise, but unfortunately Grant did not follow it. He held such a high opinion of Sheridan's qualities as a leader that he merely gave him a clear, general directive and ample troops to carry it out, after which he returned to City Point and resumed his preoccupation with Richmond and Petersburg, now of secondary strategic significance, leaving Sheridan to act independently, as he had done with Sherman. Sheridan, unfortunately, was no Sherman, as we shall see; Grant would have done better to have taken charge himself of the Shenandoah operations, as he had done with the Army of the Potomac. With the forces available for the Army of the Shenandoah, he would have been able to drive *Early* back beyond Lynchburg, and thus cut *Lee*'s vital line of supply. That would have brought Confederate resistance to an end before the close of the year.

On receiving Lincoln's approval of his plans, Grant at once left for the Monocacy (Md), where on 5 August he met Hunter, who generously agreed to relinquish his command, as 'he was so embarrassed with orders from Washington moving him first to the right and then to the left that he had lost all trace of the enemy'. Grant then telegraphed to Sheridan to come to Harper's Ferry and take over command of the newly created Army of the Shenandoah. This formation numbered rather more than 50,000 men with 108 guns. It consisted of:

> VI Corps (Wright)
> VIII Corps (Crook)
> XIX Corps (Emory)
> Cavalry Corps (Torbert) of three cavalry divisions.

1. *Grant*, II, 317–18.

To face this formidable force *Early* could only muster some 13,000 men, but ten days later *Lee* reinforced him with another infantry division and a cavalry division, bringing his strength up to 18,000 with 92 guns.

On 10 August Sheridan advanced cautiously from Harper's Ferry to Winchester, *Early* falling back to Strasburg. On hearing from Grant, however, that *Early* had received reinforcements, Sheridan withdrew down the valley to Berryville. When *Early*, with only half Sheridan's strength, followed him up, Sheridan retreated further to Harper's Ferry. *Early* left one division to hold Sheridan and on the 25th made a dash for Williamsport on the upper Potomac, 20 miles to the north-west. This presented Sheridan with a splendid opportunity of attacking *Early* from the rear and cutting him off, but he remained inactive, guarding the important crossing at Harper's Ferry.

Sheridan's timidity may have been due to the message which he received from Grant that *Lee* had dispatched two divisions to reinforce *Early*. Actually, these were weak divisions, numbering in all not more than 7,000 men, so that *Early*'s force was never stronger than 20,000, against Sheridan's 50,000. *Early* has recorded his impressions of Sheridan's abilities as follows:

> The events of the last month had satisfied me that the commander opposed to me was without enterprise, and possessed an excessive caution which amounted to timidity.[2]

Sheridan wrote to Halleck explaining his conduct: 'I have thought it best to be prudent, everything considered.' He was not exactly the dashing leader that Grant had expected to see.

Early realized that he was not strong enough to invade Maryland again, so on 26 August, after effectively destroying the Baltimore and Ohio Railroad as well as the Chesapeake and Ohio Canal, both of which were vital to the Union communications, he withdrew unmolested up the Opequon Creek towards Winchester. His bold advance to the Potomac had enabled the Confederates to harvest the crops in the Shenandoah Valley, which were essential for the maintenance of *Lee*'s army at Richmond and Petersburg. Sheridan slowly followed up *Early*'s withdrawal, and by 3 September he was facing *Early* at Berryville, 10 miles east of Winchester.

Meanwhile Grant was keeping up a steady pressure on *Lee*'s lines at Petersburg. After making a feint against Richmond by moving troops to the north side of the James River, on 18 August he dispatched Warren's v Corps, supported by ix Corps, to make a raid westward to capture the Petersburg–Weldon Railroad, which his troops had failed to seize on 22 June. In spite of very heavy casualties, Warren succeeded in getting across the railway and established the left flank of the Union line to the west of it. Severe fighting continued until 24 August, the Union losses being 7,020. *Lee*'s lines of communication were thus reduced to the Virginia Central Railroad and the Richmond–Danville Railroad.

2. *Battles and Leaders*, IV, 522.

Sheridan's continued inaction was now causing considerable anxiety in Washington, so on 15 September Grant went by train to Charlestown, eight miles west of Harper's Ferry, to have a personal discussion. As a result it was decided that Sheridan would at once advance with a view to clearing the lower Shenandoah Valley. He had indeed already planned to do so, having learnt that the reinforcements previously sent to *Early* had been recalled to Richmond, and that *Early*, after sending two divisions to raid the Baltimore and Ohio Railroad, had only two with him covering Winchester. This small Confederate force held a strong position on a ridge just east of Winchester, with an outpost line five miles farther east along the Opequon Creek.

The Opequon Creek is a right-bank tributary of the Potomac, rising in the Alleghenies some miles south of Winchester and flowing northward, parallel to and west of the Shenandoah. It has steep banks and forms a considerable military obstacle.

Leaving a strong detachment to guard the Potomac Valley, Sheridan advanced westward from Berryville before dawn on 19 September to attack the Confederate position at Winchester. Five miles east of Winchester the Berryville road passes through a narrow defile at the point where it bridges the Opequon. The river line was only held by weak Confederate cavalry pickets, but the passage of this bottle-neck by the three corps of Sheridan's army caused a considerable delay, so that *Early* had time to recall his other two divisions from the north, and by the afternoon had concentrated his whole force at Winchester. Even then, of course, he was greatly outnumbered by Sheridan. A severe engagement took place on the ridge just east of Winchester, the Confederates contesting stubbornly every yard of ground. Their position was, however, gradually outflanked by the advance of Sheridan's cavalry divisions both north and south of the town, and as darkness fell they were forced to evacuate Winchester and retreat southwards, leaving five of their guns behind.

The battle of Winchester, or Opequon Creek, involved both sides in considerable loss, 5,000 for the Union troops and 4,000 for the Confederates. It was a definite victory for Sheridan, as the lower Shenandoah Valley was now firmly in Union hands, and all danger of an invasion of the North was finally averted. On the following day Sheridan received a letter of congratulation from Lincoln. It was not, however, a brilliant tactical success. Had the Union troops crossed the Opequon on a broader front and with less delay, they would have caught *Early*'s divisions separated, and could have destroyed them in detail. *Early*'s comment on the result was:

> When I look back to this battle, I can but attribute my escape from utter annihilation to the incapacity of my opponent.[3]

During the night the Confederates retreated southward for 20 miles and took

3. *Battles and Leaders*, IV, 524.

up a strong position at Fisher's Hill, their right flank covered by the North Fork of the Shenandoah and the steep Massanutten Mountain, and their left protected by the main ridge of the Alleghenies. Sheridan pursued them on 20 September, and spent the 21st in carefully reconnoitring the strong Confederate position. There was a thick belt of forest between the Confederate left flank and the mountain range to the west. Deploying VI and XIX Corps to face the three miles of ridge held by the enemy, during the night he quietly moved VIII Corps through this wooded belt round the Confederate left flank, and sent two of his cavalry divisions through the Luray Valley round the other flank to intercept the enemy's retreat. On the evening of the 22nd the VI and XIX Corps attacked the Confederate position frontally, while VIII Corps delivered a surprise attack on their left flank and rear, causing them to retreat in confusion. During the night *Early* withdrew rapidly to Woodstock, 15 miles farther south, followed closely by Sheridan's army. The Confederate withdrawal continued through New Market and Harrisonburg to Port Republic, where *Early* was rejoined on the 26th by the two divisions which *Lee* had previously recalled to Richmond.

Sheridan was now in a position to pursue the main objective assigned to him by Grant, namely to push on southward and destroy *Lee*'s railway communications with the west and south, which meant the occupation of Charlottesville, Gordonsville and Lynchburg. But the Union leader was growing anxious about his own ever-lengthening line of communications through a hostile country infested by guerrillas. He therefore decided to destroy methodically all the crops and provisions in the Valley, so as to deny them to the enemy, and then withdrew northward to a strong position three miles north-east of Strasburg. This position, which his army occupied on 10 October, was protected by the North Fork of the Shenandoah and its left-bank tributary, Cedar Creek.

Sheridan now came under increasing pressure, both from Halleck at Washington and Grant at City Point, to push on southward and attain his main objective. As he expressed reluctance to do so, on 15 October he was summoned to Washington for consultation, leaving Wright in temporary command of the army. Meanwhile the indomitable *Early* had followed up Sheridan's withdrawal, and from a commanding observation post at the north end of Massanutten Mountain could reconnoitre every detail of the Union position. He observed that the Union cavalry divisions were posted away on the west flank, while VIII and XIX Corps were encamped behind the cover of Cedar Creek, but not protected by outlying pickets. *Early*'s topographical engineer also discovered a ford by which Cedar Creek could be crossed on the east flank of the Union position.

Early decided to strike at once. During the night of 18 October the Confederate divisions, aided by a dense fog, moved stealthily up and crossed the Cedar Creek without being detected. Before dawn on the 19th they rushed and overran the VIII Corps camp, taking the Union troops completely by surprise, thus reversing the battle of Fisher's Hill a month earlier. It was, indeed, a repetition of the battle of Shiloh. The men of VIII and XIX Corps fled in panic, but those of VI Corps, who were encamped farther back, stood firm, and Wright made preparations to deliver a counter-attack. At 11 a.m. Sheridan himself arrived from his Washington conference. He had spent the previous night at Winchester but, on hearing heavy gun-fire, had ridden hard to the battlefield, encountering on the way hundreds of panic-stricken fugitives. Sheridan's inspiring presence rallied the troops; with the cavalry divisions and VI Corps he restored the situation and at 4 p.m. delivered a decisive counter-attack. The Confederate troops were exhausted by the day's fighting, following on a long night march, and many of them had scattered to plunder the Union camp. After an obstinate struggle they were forced to relinquish their gains, and at nightfall *Early* withdrew to the south, abandoning 24 guns. Cedar Creek was no bloodless victory for the Union troops, who suffered 5,764 casualties, while the Confederates lost over 4,000.

Even after his victory at Cedar Creek, Sheridan declined to pursue *Early*, in spite of further pressure from Grant. Having already thoroughly devastated the upper Shenandoah Valley, he would have found neither food nor forage to maintain his army. He did, however, receive a further letter of congratulations from the President.

Apart from a few cavalry raids during November and December, no other major operations took place in the Shenandoah Valley for the rest of the year, mainly owing to difficulties of supply. Sheridan withdrew to the neighbour-hood of Winchester, and *Early* to New Market, and eventually to Staunton. On 19 December Torbert was sent with two cavalry divisions to attack the Virginia Central Railroad at Gordonsville and Staunton, but the attempt failed owing to vigorous action by the Confederate cavalry.

The total Union casualties incurred in Sheridan's Valley campaign were 16,952, while *Early*'s were about 10,000. It cannot be said to have enhanced Sheridan's reputation, and Grant appears to have grossly over-estimated his abilities as an army commander.

XXIV

Sherman's Campaign in Georgia and Hood's Invasion of Tennessee
August–December 1864

Sherman's original directive from Grant (see Chapter XVII, p. 138) was:

> To move against *Johnston*'s army, to break it up and to get into the interior of the enemy's country as far as you can, inflicting all the damage you can against their war resources.

Although Atlanta was not specifically mentioned in this directive, it was obviously a primary objective for Sherman's operations, as it was one of the main remaining centres of the Confederate war resources. In Chapter XIX we followed Sherman's advance southward during May and June, until he had driven *Johnston*'s army to within a few miles of Atlanta. On 17 July *Johnston* was removed from his command and replaced by *John Bell Hood*, one of his corps commanders and 24 years his junior.

Hood, then aged 33, was one of the more remarkable leaders produced by the Civil War. He was a fair-haired, six-foot-two giant, but not particularly gifted with brains. From the Military Academy at West Point he had passed out 44th in a class of 52, in which McPherson took the first place, Schofield the 7th and Sheridan the 34th. He had lost an arm at Gettysburg and his right leg at Chickamauga, but, strapped to his saddle, he continued to lead his men with dash and energy. He was inspiring as a brigadier and divisional commander, but his reputation for recklessness hardly fitted him for higher command.

When *Hood* took over command, his army had been pressed back beyond the Chattahoochee River to its tributary, Peach Tree Creek, only four miles north of Atlanta. Sherman now closed in on the city from both north and east. He moved McPherson's army round to the left flank in order to move down the Georgia Railroad from Decatur[1] and turn *Hood*'s right flank. Severe fighting took place on 20 July. Schofield's army was now in the centre, with Thomas's

---

1. Not to be confused with the Decatur in the neighbouring State of Alabama.

on the right. The latter secured a shallow bridgehead across Peach Tree Creek, but a gap of two miles developed between the flanks of these two armies, and *Hood* struck hard at Thomas's left with the corps of *Stewart*[2] and *Hardee*. The Confederate attack started at 3 p.m. and lasted fiercely for three hours. The Union troops at first gave way, but Thomas managed to restore the situation. The Union casualties were 1,600, those of the Confederates 2,300. Meanwhile McPherson had reached the Georgia Railroad at Decatur, and broke it up to sever *Hood*'s direct link with Richmond.

On 21 July *Hood* withdrew into the Atlanta defences, having *Stewart*'s corps facing north to confront Thomas, and *Hardee* facing east to withstand Schofield and McPherson. The latter continued his advance down the railway and occupied a hill only two miles east of Atlanta, dominating the town. *Hood* moved *Hardee*'s corps eastward to check his advance, but without success. On 22 July Sherman, wrongly thinking that the enemy was evacuating Atlanta, ordered McPherson to launch an attack. *Hardee*'s corps, however, assisted by *Joseph Wheeler*'s cavalry division, had now succeeded in outflanking McPherson south of the railway, and a fierce battle took place, in the course of which McPherson was killed, much to Grant's sorrow. Sherman filled his place with Oliver Otis Howard,[3] the commander of IV Corps in Thomas's army. At first *Hardee*'s attack met with great success, 13 Union guns and a number of prisoners being captured. Sherman himself, however, now intervened in the battle; massing Schofield's batteries on a commanding position, he raked the Confederate ranks at close range, forcing *Hardee* to give up the ground he had won. Sherman failed to press the attack with Thomas's army on the right flank, and *Hood* managed to hold on to his defensive position covering Atlanta. In this battle Sherman's loss was 3,521, while *Hood*, who had attacked continuously, lost about 9,000.

Having failed to envelop Atlanta from the east, on 27 July Sherman switched the Army of the Tennessee (now commanded by Howard) from his left flank to the right at Ezra Church, 2½ miles west of the town, and on the following day *Hood* attacked him there, but the Confederate attack failed. *Hood* still hung on grimly to Atlanta, and extended its entrenched perimeter southward for four miles to cover East Point, the junction of the Macon Railroad with the Montgomery and Atlanta Railroad, *Hood*'s only remaining supply links with the south. Sherman now decided to manœuvre round Atlanta and sever these lines of communication. Leaving a small force with some heavy artillery to bombard the town, on 25 August he moved the bulk of his troops to the southwest. On 28 August the armies of Howard and Thomas cut the Montgomery line and then swung eastwards, reaching the Macon line at Jonesboro on the

---

2. *Alexander Peter Stewart* had replaced *Leonidas Polk*, killed on 14 June by an artillery projectile at Pine Mountain.

3. After the war he founded the Howard University for Negroes in Washington.

30th. Sherman then proceeded methodically to break up both railway lines. *Hood*'s position was now untenable, so he slipped away after destroying the military stores and concentrated his army to the south of Jonesboro. On 2 September Henry Warner Slocum's xx Corps entered Atlanta without opposition.

The capture of Atlanta was a distinct triumph for Sherman. It is true that he had not accomplished his first objective, the destruction of *Hood*'s army, but he had broken the back of Confederate resistance in the western theatre and greatly damaged their war potential. His Atlanta campaign had been won at the cost of 31,687 Union casualties, compared with the Confederate loss of 34,979. Politically too the capture of Atlanta was of great advantage to the cause of the Union, and ensured Lincoln's victory at the polls two months later over his opponent, the ex-Commander-in-Chief, George Brinton McClellan. Four days before Atlanta fell the Democratic National Convention in Washington had adopted a resolution declaring the war a failure and demanding the cessation of hostilities.

The news of the fall of Atlanta reached Grant in his tent at City Point on the evening of 4 September. Needless to say, he was delighted, for it confirmed his trust in the abilities of Sherman as an independent army commander. He at once wrote his congratulations, adding:

> In honor of your great victory I have ordered a salute to be fired with shotted guns from every battery bearing upon the enemy. The salute will be fired within an hour, amid great rejoicing.

It is of interest to record Grant's general comment on the Confederate strategy throughout the Atlanta campaign:

> My own judgment is that *Johnston* acted very wisely: he husbanded his men and saved as much of his territory as he could, without fighting decisive battles in which all might be lost.... *Hood* was unquestionably a brave, gallant soldier and not destitute of ability; but unfortunately his policy was to fight the enemy wherever he saw him, without thinking much of the consequences of defeat.[4]

Grant and Sherman had, separately, given much thought to what the next move should be after the capture of Atlanta. They both came to the same conclusion, that Sherman should continue his advance by the shortest route to the Atlantic, destroying on the way all the sources of supply for *Lee*'s army in the Richmond–Petersburg box. The risk involved by such a manœuvre was obvious. At Atlanta Sherman had already advanced 125 miles from his base at Chattanooga on the Tennessee River. From Atlanta to Savannah, the nearest point on the sea-coast, was a march of at least double that distance, and *Hood*'s army of 40,000 men, which had retired to the south-west from Atlanta, was still at large and capable of cutting Sherman's long and tenuous line of communication at

4. *Grant*, II, 344–5.

any point. Also, the cavalry divisions of those enterprising leaders, *Wheeler* and *Forrest*, numbering 10,000 troopers, were raiding far into Tennessee. Sherman's problem was a vaster and far more hazardous one than Sheridan's in the Shenandoah Valley, from which the latter had recoiled. It meant in fact that Sherman would have to cut loose from his supply line and live entirely on the country, a logistic risk which Grant had taken in the Vicksburg campaign, though on a smaller scale.

On 12 September Grant dispatched his most trusted aide, Lieutenant-Colonel Horace Porter, to Sherman's headquarters at Atlanta in order to concert their views on the subject of the next move. In the letter which Porter took with him Grant wrote:

> My object now in sending a staff-officer is not so much to suggest operations for you as to get your views and have plans matured by the time everything can be got ready. It will probably be the 5th of October before any of the plans herein indicated will be executed.[5]

During Porter's visit to Atlanta the pros and cons of Sherman's proposed operation were fully discussed; Sherman and Grant were agreed that a march to the sea was the best strategic course open to them; it was a well-calculated risk, provided that adequate measures were taken to deal with a possible counter-stroke by *Hood*'s army. When Grant was dealing with a subordinate on whom he could rely implicitly, as he felt he could with Sherman, this method of consultation through the medium of a liaison officer worked admirably, and was in direct contrast with Napoleon's system of dictating imperious orders to distant Marshals, which proved so disastrous in the Peninsular, Leipzig and Waterloo campaigns.

On 10 October Sherman telegraphed to Grant that *Hood* was heading for the west:

> If he passes over to the Mobile and Ohio Railroad, had I not better execute the plan of my letter sent by Colonel Porter, and leave General Thomas with the troops now in Tennessee to defend the State?

Grant replied on the following day that '*Hood* would probably strike for Nashville', but he left the decision to Sherman's judgment. Sherman then wired to say that he would prefer to start on his march to the sea. Grant replied on 12 October:

> If you are satisfied the trip to the sea-coast can be made, holding the line of the Tennessee firmly, you may make it.

Sherman never received this message owing to the telegraph wires being interrupted, but he did receive a further message from Grant on 2 November:

5. *Porter*, 289.

With the force, however, you have left with General Thomas, he must be able to take care of *Hood* and destroy him. I really do not see that you can withdraw from where you are to follow *Hood* without giving up all we have gained in territory. I say, then, go as you propose.

On 7 November Grant sent Sherman a final message:

Great good fortune attend you. I believe you will be eminently successful, and at worst can only make a march less fruitful of results than is hoped for.

After that the wires were definitely cut, and Sherman was left to his own devices.

In order to protect the State of Tennessee from invasion by *Hood*, Sherman left behind two of his army commanders, Thomas and Schofield, with a total strength of 60,000 men, under the over-all command of Thomas, with orders to defend the vital points of Chattanooga and Nashville. After destroying the railways north and south of Atlanta and all the military stores there, Sherman issued three weeks' rations to his own army and set off on his expedition on 15 November. Sherman's army numbered 62,000, consisting of 57,000 infantry and gunners, 5,000 cavalry and 64 guns. The cavalry division was commanded by Hugh Judson Kilpatrick, a swashbuckling and somewhat irresponsible leader, about whom Sherman is reputed to have said:

I know Kilpatrick is a hell of a damned fool, but I want just that sort of man to command my cavalry on this expedition.

It was in some ways an unfortunate selection.

Sherman organized his army in two wings: the right wing was formed by the Army of the Tennessee, under Howard, consisting of xv and xvii Corps; the left wing, under Henry Warner Slocum, was called the Army of Georgia, made up of xiv and xx Corps. In order to keep the enemy guessing, he moved his two wings in diverging directions, the right wing to the south down the Macon railway, and the left wing eastwards along the Augusta line. He met with only slight and sporadic opposition, the fighting being mainly confined to cavalry encounters. As he advanced, he systematically destroyed railway tracks, rolling stock, factories and all material resources of any military value. Finally, on 21 December, his army entered Savannah, which was evacuated without a fight by *Hardee*, who then withdrew northward to Charleston (s.c.). Grant had already arranged to replenish Sherman's stores by sea at Savannah.

Sherman's march through Georgia has been much criticized on account of the undue hardships which he inflicted on the civilian population. General Fuller has commented:

That his march had a decisive strategical and political influence on the war is beyond question, but because of Sherman's ruthlessness and wasteful destruction it had a bad influence on the peace which followed the war.[6]

6. *The Generalship of Ulysses S. Grant*, 323.

There is no doubt that much wanton destruction was perpetrated, particularly by Kilpatrick's troopers, who were ill-disciplined. Other Union commanders did their best to check such abuses; on 22 November Howard issued an order to his troops that:

> Any officer or man discovered in pillaging a house or burning a building without proper authority, will, upon sufficient proof thereof, be shot.

Southern writers have recorded numerous instances of wanton brutality. Grant, himself a humane individual, dismisses them rather cursorily in his Memoirs:

> Notwithstanding these anecdotes, and the necessary hardship they would seem to imply, I do not believe there was much unwarrantable pillaging considering that we were in the enemy's territory and without any supplies except such as the country afforded.[7]

Meanwhile, the audacious *Hood* had conceived the ambitious plan of invading Tennessee behind Sherman's back and re-conquering that State for the Confederacy, after which he would push on into Kentucky. Moving swiftly across northern Alabama, *Hood* reached the neighbourhood of Decatur at the end of October. On 15 November, the day that Sherman started for the sea, *Hood* crossed the Tennessee River and occupied Florence, where he concentrated an army of 40,000 infantry and 7,000 cavalry. On Thomas's orders, Schofield with 34,000 men retired northward to Columbia (Tenn) in order to dispute the passage of the Duck River. On 29 November, however, *Forrest*'s cavalry crossed the river higher up and turned this position, whereupon Schofield withdrew to Franklin, 15 miles south of Nashville, where Thomas had collected 26,000 men. At Franklin Schofield organized a strong defensive bridgehead south of the Harpeth River. Against the advice of his subordinate commanders, *Hood* insisted on launching a frontal assault on the Union position, which was repulsed with heavy loss, the Confederate casualties being 6,252, while the Union troops lost only 2,326. Thomas made no effort to support Schofield, but ordered him to continue his retreat to Nashville, which he had now fortified strongly to cover the crossing of the Cumberland River.

The authorities in Washington were now thoroughly alarmed by *Hood*'s unexpected invasion of Tennessee, and Grant at City Point could not understand why Thomas, with such a considerable numerical advantage over his opponent, could not pass to the offensive. On 2 December he telegraphed to Thomas:

> If *Hood* is permitted to remain quietly about Nashville, you will lose all the [rail]road back to Chattanooga and possibly have to abandon the line of the Tennessee. Should he attack you it is all well, but if he does not you should attack him before he fortifies.

Grant had had bitter experience of the difficulty of turning the Confederates out of entrenched positions at Spottsylvania, Cold Harbor and Petersburg.

7. *Grant*, 11, 365.

Thomas, however, being a slow and deliberate fighter, was in no hurry to attack. He knew that he could beat *Hood* in the long run, but he had seen too many Union victories thrown away by not being followed up with a vigorous pursuit. His cavalry commander, Wilson, was still short of several thousand horses to complete his establishment, and Thomas intended to wait until Wilson was ready to play his part in the pursuit. But Grant was getting increasingly impatient. On 6 December he wired again to Thomas:

> Attack *Hood* at once and wait no longer for a remnant of your cavalry. There is great danger of delay resulting in a campaign back to the Ohio River.

On the evening of the 8th Grant sent a further exhortation:

> Why not attack at once?... Now is one of the finest opportunities ever presented of destroying one of the three armies of the enemy. If destroyed he never can replace it. Use the means at your command, and you can do this and cause a rejoicing that will resound from one end of the land to the other.

To this Thomas replied on the 9th:

> I had nearly completed my preparations to attack the enemy tomorrow morning, but a terrible storm of freezing rain has come on today, which will make it impossible for our men to fight to any advantage. I am therefore compelled to wait for the storm to break, and make the attack immediately after.... Major-General Halleck informs me that you are very dissatisfied with my delay in attacking. I can only say I have done all in my power to prepare, and if you deem it necessary to relieve me I shall submit without a murmur.

The storm, however, still continued, delaying the attack. Grant at last lost patience and directed the Secretary of War to relieve Thomas by Schofield, but on Halleck's advice, he suspended this order 'until it is seen whether he will do anything'. On the 11th Grant wired once more to Thomas:

> If you delay attack longer the mortifying spectacle will be witnessed of a rebel army moving for the Ohio River, and you will be forced to act, accepting such weather as you find. Let there be no further delay.... I am in hopes of receiving a dispatch from you today announcing that you have moved. Delay no longer for weather or reinforcements.

On 13 December there was still no news of Thomas moving. On that day the former commander of xv Corps, John Alexander Logan, happened to visit Grant at City Point. Logan was not a Regular Army officer, but he had impressed Grant by his powers of leadership as a divisional commander in the Vicksburg campaign. Logan had actually been appointed to command the Army of the Tennessee after the death of McPherson in the battle of Atlanta, but Sherman had removed him after a few days for administrative incompetence and replaced him by Schofield. Grant now ordered Logan to proceed to Nashville and take over from Thomas if the latter had not yet launched his attack.

On reconsidering the situation the next day, the 14th, Grant decided to go himself to Nashville and take command of the operations, feeling that this would be a lesser blow to Thomas on being superseded. The Commander-in-Chief left City Point that evening by steamer, reaching Washington on the evening of 15 December. On landing, he was handed two telegrams, one from Thomas to Halleck saying that he was attacking that morning, and another from Van Duzer, the director of telegraphs, reporting that the attack was progressing successfully. Grant was immensely relieved, and at once telegraphed to Thomas:

> I was just on my way to Nashville, but receiving a dispatch from Van Duzer detailing your splendid success of today, I shall go no further. Push the enemy now and give him no rest until he is entirely destroyed. Your army will cheerfully suffer many privations to break up *Hood*'s army and render it useless for future operations. Do not stop for trains or supplies, but take them from the country as the enemy have done. Much is now expected.

On reaching his hotel, Grant received a telegram from Thomas:

> I attacked the enemy's left this morning and drove it from the river, below the city, very nearly to the Franklin Pike, distance about eight miles.

Thomas had indeed gained a striking victory, one of the most decisive of the Civil War. The town of Nashville lay on the left (south) bank of the Cumberland River, which formed the last really defensible line south of the Ohio. Thomas had constructed a strongly entrenched perimeter extending for six or seven miles on the south side of the town, with both flanks resting on the river, which was patrolled by Union gunboats. He had concentrated an army of 50,000 men, while *Hood* could muster only half that number, for he had weakened his force by sending off *Forrest* with two cavalry divisions and three infantry brigades to break up the Nashville and Chattanooga Railroad near Murfreesboro. The three Confederate corps were extended on a front of five miles at a distance of one to two miles from the Union trenches. Having insufficient troops to embrace the Union defensive perimeter, both of *Hood*'s flanks were in the air, particularly his left one, which was separated from the river by a gap of four miles. This gap was weakly held by his only remaining cavalry division, dismounted.

Thomas's trained eye detected the weakness of *Hood*'s position. The weather having turned warmer, he decided to attack at dawn on 15 December. His plan was to swing forward his right wing, consisting of xvi and iv Corps, in order to drive back the Confederate cavalry division and envelop *Hood*'s exposed left flank. The right flank of this wheel would be screened by Wilson's cavalry division, while a subsidiary attack by a division on the left flank would divert *Hood*'s attention from the main thrust. Schofield's xxiii Corps was retained as a general reserve.

Thomas's tactical plan succeeded admirably. After stiff fighting throughout the day, the Confederates were driven back to a ridge of broken hills two miles in rear, where they could only man a line three miles in extent. Thomas now moved up Schofield's corps and Wilson's dismounted cavalry division to envelop *Hood*'s left wing. The battle continued throughout the 16th and was fiercely contested, but Thomas's turning movement on the right proved decisive. At 4 p.m. the XVI and XXIII Corps with Wilson's dismounted cavalry made a concerted assault and rolled up *Hood*'s left wing. The Confederate troops saw that the day was lost and took to flight, leaving 53 guns and more than 4,000 prisoners in Union hands. The Union casualties were 3,061. Wilson now sent for his horses, but darkness and the waterlogged state of the country prevented a very close pursuit. *Hood*'s army was no longer capable of offensive action and retired to Tupelo (Miss); his audacious invasion of Tennessee had been a gamble from the start, and the gamble failed. One might say of him, as Napoleon said of Field-Marshal Suvórov, '*Il avait l'âme d'un grand général, mais il n'en avait pas la tête.*'

By the end of 1864 Grant's objectives in the western theatre had thus been attained. Sherman's march across Georgia to the sea had effectively crippled the Confederate war resources, while Thomas had virtually destroyed their western army. It now only remained for Grant to crush *Lee*'s Army of Northern Virginia, beleaguered in Richmond and Petersburg, and retaining only a tenuous link with a restricted area of supply.

XXV

Grant's Final Victory
January–April 1865

The winter of 1864–65 was a grim one for the Confederate cause. The time factor, which earlier had seemed to favour the Southerners, had now turned against them. Lincoln, the enemy of compromise, had won the election; the European Powers, France, Britain and Austria, were less likely than ever to intervene on behalf of the South; only one seaport, Wilmington (N.C.), remained as a precarious haven for blockade runners[1]; *Lee*'s army, its resources dwindling daily, was boxed up in Richmond and Petersburg; *Hood*'s army had indeed escaped destruction by Sherman and was still at large in north-eastern Mississippi, but it had been badly hammered at Nashville by Thomas; a few scattered detachments, under *Beauregard, Bragg, Hardee* and *Johnston*, still held the field in the Carolinas, but the morale of the troops had sunk to a low level, and hundreds deserted the ranks daily.

Despite this hopeless outlook, the Confederate leaders were determined to continue the struggle. On 9 February President *Jefferson Davis* at last placed *Lee* in command of all the Confederate armies, which ensured in some measure unity of command. There was little that *Lee*, besieged in Richmond, could do to restore the situation, but he brought back *Joseph Johnston*, relieved by *Davis* in favour of *Hood*, to command all the forces in South Carolina, with *Beauregard* as his second-in-command.

Grant's aim now was to bring the struggle to an end as soon as possible, and with the minimum number of casualties. That meant tightening the noose round *Lee*'s army. The first step was to stop supplies reaching him through the port of Wilmington, a measure which Grant, strange to say, had hitherto entirely neglected. Wilmington is situated on Cape Fear River, about 200 miles south of Petersburg, with which it was connected by the Weldon Railroad. Although Grant's troops were astride this railway south of Petersburg, supplies

1. Charleston (S.C.) was finally evacuated by the Confederates on 18 February 1865, as a result of Sherman's advance.

could still be moved from the railway by road round the flank of the Union investing lines.

The entrance to the Cape Fear River was defended by a powerful coast fortress, Fort Fisher, mounting 44 heavy guns and three mortars. At the beginning of December Grant had ordered an attack to be made on Fort Fisher by a landing force of 6,500 men from Butler's army, supported by a naval squadron of 50 vessels under Rear-Admiral David Dixon Porter, his old associate at Vicksburg. Against Grant's orders, Butler insisted on commanding the operation in person. The attack took place between 25 and 27 December, but, owing to Butler's incompetence, was a complete failure. Now that the Presidential election was over, Grant at last obtained Lincoln's consent to remove Butler from command of the Army of the James, and replaced him on 31 January by Edward Ord, the commander of xxiv Corps.

In January Grant repeated the attempt on Fort Fisher. This time he organized a provisional corps of 8,000 men under Alfred Howe Terry, the new commander of xxiv Corps, who had had previous experience of landing operations. His force embarked at Bermuda Hundred on 4 January, escorted by a powerful fleet of 60 vessels under Porter, mounting 627 guns. The expedition arrived off Fort Fisher on 12 January and captured the fortress on the 15th after a stern struggle. The Union army and navy suffered 1,000 casualties, and 2,000 prisoners were taken.

The Confederates being now deprived of their last seaports on the Atlantic coast, Grant turned to the severing of *Lee*'s remaining railway communications. The last attempt to cut the Southside Railroad, running south-west from Petersburg, had been made on 27 October, when II, V and IX Corps, numbering 32,000 men, made an advance westward, but failed to achieve their objective owing to a fierce Confederate counter-attack. Grant called off the operation to avoid excessive casualties. After that attempt the heavy winter rains brought operations in Virginia to a standstill. Grant's next idea was to close the ring round *Lee* by bringing Sherman's army of 60,000 to the James River by sea from Savannah, but Sherman himself proposed that he should march overland on Richmond through the Carolinas. Grant accepted this proposal, as it would effectively deprive *Lee* of these two States as a source of supply. Simultaneously with Sherman's march northward, he intended that Sheridan should advance southward up the Shenandoah Valley to Staunton and Lynchburg to cut the Danville Railroad. At the same time Grant ordered Thomas to send Schofield's xxiii Corps from Tennessee to Alexandria by rail, from where it would proceed by sea transport to Wilmington, and then march inland to Goldsboro to link up with Sherman. Thomas, with the remainder of his troops, was to cross the Alleghenies and invade South Carolina. This, in outline, was the grand concentric manœuvre by which Grant planned to encircle and crush *Lee*'s army.

Sherman's great march through the Carolinas started on 1 February. He pushed steadily northward through South Carolina, in spite of some opposition by *Hardee* and other Confederate forces, and reached Columbia on the 16th. Although delayed by bad roads and heavy rains, he pushed on to Fayetteville in North Carolina, which he reached on 12 March. Continuing his march, he was confronted at Bentonville by *Johnston*, who had at last managed to concentrate a force of 21,000 men. A severe engagement took place here on 19 March, *Johnston* being forced to withdraw after suffering 2,606 casualties, while the Union troops lost 1,646. On 22 March Schofield's leading troops, having landed at Wilmington, joined Sherman at Goldsboro, 80 miles north of Wilmington, which increased his numbers to 80,000. Sherman's march of 425 miles in 50 days through the Carolinas made a notable contribution to Grant's campaign.

Meanwhile, north of the upper James River, Sheridan with his force of 10,000 cavalry was intended to act as the other claw of Grant's pincer operation against *Lee*'s communications with the south-west. In accordance with his orders, Sheridan left Winchester on 27 February and advanced up the Shenandoah Valley to Staunton, which he reached on 2 March. There he learnt that a brigade of *Early*'s force was at Waynesboro, to the east of him, covering the Rockfish Gap through the Blue Ridge. Sheridan at once turned eastward and without difficulty crushed this small detachment, capturing 1,600 prisoners and 11 guns. He should then, in fulfilment of his task, have pushed on southward to Lynchburg. The country, however, was so waterlogged that his supply trains failed to reach him, so he decided to move eastward and reached Charlottesville on 4 March. After breaking up the railway south of that junction, he headed south-east, reaching Columbia on the upper James River on the 10th. Finding that all the bridges across the James had been destroyed, 'little Phil' repeated his performance of the previous autumn and abandoned the task assigned to him. Instead of moving on Lynchburg and Danville, as ordered, he made his way round the north of Richmond to the mouth of the Pamunkey, reaching White House on 19 March, and then rejoined Grant's army. Grant, who was always lenient in his dealings with Sherman and Sheridan, took it all in good part.

At the end of November 1864 the Confederate entrenchments east and south of Petersburg stretched from the right bank of the Appomattox, a mile east of the town, for a distance of ten miles in a south-westerly direction, the right flank resting on the Hatcher's Run stream. During the winter months *Lee* had extended these lines three or four miles farther west in order to afford better protection to the Southside Railroad, three miles in rear. As March wore on, *Lee*'s situation was becoming increasingly perilous, for the jaws of Grant's pincers were steadily closing on him. He agreed with President *Davis* that some action must be undertaken to relieve the pressure on Richmond and enable him to sally out and unite with *Johnston* in order to crush Sherman before he joined Grant. With the object of diverting Grant's attention, *Lee* planned a surprise attack on Fort Stedman, a strong redoubt near the right flank of the Union lines. Fort Stedman was 1½ miles south of the Appomattox and only 150 yards distant from the Confederate trenches. The attack was to be carried out by *John Brown Gordon*, who was temporarily in command of *Early*'s II Corps. *Gordon*'s attack was launched at 4 a.m. on 25 March and took the Union troops completely by surprise. Fort Stedman and the adjoining trenches were captured. Three hours later, however, a division of IX Corps counter-attacked, and the Confederates were driven back to their own lines after suffering 5,000 casualties; the Union loss was 2,080. *Lee*'s diversion was thus frustrated.

Sheridan having returned to the fold, Grant decided that the time was now ripe to set his armies in motion to complete the encirclement of *Lee*'s army, without waiting for Sherman's arrival. His plan was to hold his entrenched line with a nucleus force, while the bulk of the Armies of the Potomac and the James would side-slip to their left and turn *Lee*'s right flank; Sheridan's cavalry would then make a wide sweep to the left and finally sever *Lee*'s remaining two railways. On 24 March he issued the following directive to Meade, Ord and Sheridan:

> On the 29th instant the armies operating against Richmond will be moved by our left, for the double purpose of turning the enemy out of his present position at Petersburg, and to insure the success of the cavalry under General Sheridan, which will start at the same time, in its efforts to reach and destroy the South Side and Danville Railroads. Two corps of the Army of the Potomac will be moved first in two columns, taking the two roads crossing Hatcher's Run. . . .
> General Sheridan will then move independently, under other instructions which will be given him. . . .
> Major-General Parke will be left in command of all the army left for holding the lines about Petersburg and City Point. . . .
> The 9th army corps will be left intact, to hold the present line of works. . . .
> The movement of troops from the Army of the James will commence on the night of the 27th instant. . . .
> All the troops will move with four days' rations in haversacks and eight days' in wagons. . . . Sixty rounds of ammunition per man will be taken in wagons. . . . The densely wooded country in which the army has to operate making the use of much artillery impracticable, the amount taken with the army will be reduced to six or eight guns to each division, at the option of the army commanders. . . .
> I would have it particularly enjoined upon corps commanders that, in case of an attack from the enemy, those not attacked are not to wait for orders from the commanding officer of the army to which they belong, but that they will move promptly, and notify the commander of their action. I would also enjoin the same action on the part of division commanders when other parts of their corps are engaged. In like manner, I would urge the importance of following up a repulse of the enemy.[2]

This masterly directive shows Grant at the top of his form as a military commander. It was a product of his broad strategic vision, his acute tactical sense and his logistic foresight. These in turn were the fruit of four years' experience of active combat in every rank from command of an infantry regiment to that of a group of armies.

2. *Grant*, II, 616–18.

Four days later, on the eve of the battle, Grant issued his final instruction to Sheridan:

It is not the intention to attack the enemy in his intrenched position, but to force him out, if possible. Should he come out and attack us, or get himself where he can be attacked, move in with your entire force in your own way, and with the full reliance that the army will engage or follow, as circumstances will dictate. I shall be on the field, and will probably be able to communicate with you. Should I not do so, and you find that the enemy keeps within his main intrenched line, you may cut loose and push for the Danville [Rail]Road. If you find it practicable, I would like you to cross the South Side [Rail]Road, between Petersburg and Burkesville, and destroy it to some extent. I would not advise much detention, however, until you reach the Danville [Rail]Road, which I would like you to strike as near to the Appomattox as possible. Make your destruction on that [rail]road as complete as possible. You can then pass on to the South Side Road, west of Burkesville, and destroy that in like manner.

After having accomplished the destruction of the two railroads, which are now the only avenues of supply to *Lee*'s army, you may return to this army, selecting your road further south, or you may go on into North Carolina and join General Sherman.

Here again, the Commander-in-Chief's intentions were fully and lucidly expressed to his subordinate.

At Grant's invitation, President Lincoln himself arrived at City Point on 24 March, for they both felt that the climax of the struggle was approaching. Lincoln arrived on the eve of the Confederate sortie against Fort Stedman; after the repulse of this attack, Grant escorted the President to the front, where he inspected the troops, both north and south of the James. Grant also introduced him to both Sheridan and Sherman, the latter having reached City Point by water on the 27th from Wilmington for a conference with Grant. It was arranged that Sherman's army would advance on 10 April from Goldsboro (N.C.) and head for Weldon on the Roanoke River so as to support Grant's operations against *Lee*'s army.

During the nights of 27 and 28 March the Union troops moved westward behind the screen of their entrenchments in accordance with Grant's orders, only one corps of the Army of the James being left north of that river, facing the Richmond defences. At dawn on the 29th Meade's and Ord's armies continued their westward move; Ord's army only consisted of xxiv Corps, now commanded by John Gibbon, and one other division. Humphreys's II Corps[3] and Warren's v Corps crossed Hatcher's Run and then swung northward to turn the Confederate right flank. Their right wheel was followed by Wright (vi) and Gibbon (xxiv), who came up on their right. On the extreme Union left flank, Sheridan's force of 9,000 cavalry made a wide détour further south and by nightfall reached Dinwiddie Court House, on the Boydton Plank Road, 14 miles south-west of Petersburg.

3. Andrew Atkinson Humphreys, previously Meade's Chief of Staff, had assumed command in November of II Corps from Hancock, incapacitated by his Gettysburg wound.

From Dinwiddie Court House a road ran north for five miles to a road junction known as Five Forks, which was within three miles of the vital Southside Railroad from Petersburg.

Lee was quick to observe the westward shift of the Union troops. He at once hurried reinforcements to his right flank from north of the James and occupied the entrenchments constructed during the winter to the west of Hatcher's Run. He also sent to hold the important road junction at Five Forks a force under *George Edward Pickett*,[4] consisting of that officer's division of *Longstreet*'s corps and a cavalry corps under his nephew, *Fitzhugh Lee*,[5] some 19,000 in all. This force hastily entrenched a line, a mile and a half in length facing south, to cover Five Forks. Between the left of this line and the right flank of the main Confederate position astride Hatcher's Run was a gap of three miles.

So far Grant's great turning movement had progressed satisfactorily, and he thought that he had at last cornered *Lee*, so he decided, instead of sending Sheridan off to cut the railway at Lynchburg and Danville, to swing him round in order to complete the encirclement of *Lee*'s army. On the afternoon of the 29th, therefore, he sent fresh orders to Sheridan:

> Our line is now unbroken from the Appomattox to Dinwiddie. . . . I now feel like ending the matter, if it is possible to do so, before going back. I do not want you, therefore, to cut loose and go after the enemy's [rail]roads at present. In the morning push around the enemy, if you can, and get on to his right rear. The movements of the enemy's cavalry may, of course, modify your action. We will act all together as one army here, until it is seen what can be done with the enemy. The signal-officer at Cobb's Hill reported at half-past eleven a.m., that a cavalry division had passed that point from Richmond towards Petersburg, taking forty minutes to pass.[6]

But Grant's operation then received a set-back. Torrential rain began to fall on the evening of the 29th and continued for 36 hours; the country became a sea of mud, the creeks were flooded, and wheeled transport was unable to move except on the few corduroy roads. Men shouted to their officers: 'When are the gunboats coming up?'

Grant and his headquarter staff had left City Point on the morning of the 29th by train, on the military railway which ran west for 13 miles. At the terminus they mounted their horses and rode five miles to the south-west to Dabney's Sawmill, south of the Hatcher's Run valley, where Grant's headquarter camp was established. Lincoln saw them off at City Point and then returned to his steamer to await the outcome of the battle. On the 30th it rained so hard that Grant's staff urged him to postpone the operation, but Sheridan

---

4. A gallant fighter, though he 'wore his dark hair in long, perfumed ringlets that fell to his shoulders'.

5. Cousin of *William Henry Fitzhugh Lee*, *Lee*'s second son, who commanded a division under him.

6. *Grant*, II, 621.

rode over from Dinwiddie Court House, seven miles to the south-west, and persuaded the Commander-in-Chief to carry on. 'I can drive in the whole cavalry force of the enemy with ease', he said, 'and if an infantry force is added to my command, I can strike out for *Lee*'s right, and either crush it or force him to so weaken his intrenched lines that our troops in front of them can break through and march into Petersburg.' Grant was always ready to listen to Sheridan's advice, and decided to put an infantry corps under his command to execute the enveloping manœuvre on *Lee*'s right flank.

On the morning of the 31st the rain had ceased but the weather was still cloudy and dismal. The troops were busy corduroying the roads to enable the guns to be moved forward. Sheridan advanced a few miles northward on the road to Five Forks, but was held up by the Confederate cavalry. He reported to Grant that the enemy were entrenching at Five Forks. There was now a dangerous gap of three miles between Sheridan and the left flank of Warren's v Corps, which was endeavouring to turn the right flank of the Confederate lines. *Pickett*'s force delivered a strong counter-attack, driving back both Sheridan's cavalry and the head of Warren's corps. Sheridan again appealed to Grant for infantry support, and asked if he might be given Wright's vi Corps, which had been under his command the previous autumn in the Shenandoah Valley. This was out of the question, as vi Corps was miles away near the right flank of the army; the only solution was to give Sheridan Warren's v Corps, which was nearest to him, but Grant did this with some reluctance, as he considered Warren a slow mover and unlikely to get on with Sheridan. The night of the 31st saw a scene of some confusion at Grant's and Meade's headquarters; Horace Porter describes it as follows:

> Generals were writing dispatches and telegraphing from dark to daylight. Staff-officers were rushing from one headquarters to another, wading through swamps, penetrating forests, and galloping over corduroy roads, carrying instructions, getting information, and making extraordinary efforts to hurry up the movement of the troops.[7]

As the result of several orders and counter-orders, Warren managed to get one of his divisions moving over to reinforce Sheridan that night, but his troops were delayed by crossing swollen streams, and it was not until 8 a.m. on 1 April that his first two divisions reached Dinwiddie; Warren himself with the third division reported to Sheridan at 11 a.m. 'Little Phil', chafing at the delay and anxious to launch his attack, was not best pleased. Matters were not improved by the arrival at noon of a staff officer from Grant with a verbal message that if Sheridan felt that v Corps would do better under one of the divisional commanders, he was authorized to relieve Warren and order him to report to Grant's headquarters.

At 1 p.m. Sheridan received a message from Merritt, his cavalry commander, that the enemy appeared to be retiring to their entrenched position at Five

7. *Porter*, 432–3.

Forks, which *Pickett* was holding with about 12,000 men. Sheridan had now been reinforced with another cavalry division, so that he disposed of 12,000 cavalry and the 16,000 infantry of Warren's corps. He ordered an immediate attack by Warren's corps advancing north-west to turn *Pickett*'s left flank, while the Union cavalry made a holding attack on his front. Warren appeared reluctant to attack so soon; his men had been marching all night through the mud. The Union attack was eventually launched at 4 p.m. and Sheridan insisted on leading it in person. Riding his 17-hand, black charger 'Rienzi', which had carried him on his 20-mile ride from Winchester to Cedar Creek the previous October, Sheridan roused the energies of his tired troops and led them in a sweep round the left flank of the enemy position, while Merritt's cavalry attacked it frontally. The whole Confederate line collapsed, and *Pickett*'s force melted away, leaving behind 4,500 prisoners. At 7 p.m. Sheridan removed the unfortunate Warren from command of V Corps and replaced him by Charles Griffin, the senior divisional commander, a bluff and bellicose gunner who was more to 'little Phil's' liking. Sheridan reported to Grant that:

General Warren did not exert himself to get up his corps as rapidly as he might have done, and his manner gave me the impression that he wished the sun to go down before dispositions for the attack could be completed.

Fourteen years later a Court of Inquiry exonerated Warren of these charges.

Grant learnt of Sheridan's victory at Five Forks at 9 p.m. and at once ordered a general assault to be made on the Confederate lines by the remaining corps at dawn the following morning. A heavy bombardment by the artillery was kept up all night, and at 4.45 a.m. on the 2nd the IX, VI, XXIV and II Corps carried the enemy works after severe fighting. Wright's attack was particularly successful; on carrying the first line of trenches, he swung to the left and rolled up the whole Confederate line as far as Hatcher's Run, taking 3,000 prisoners. The two corps on his left then swept forward to the inner line of the Petersburg defences, and Sheridan on the extreme left advanced from Five Forks to cut the Southside Railroad. At 4.40 p.m. Grant sent a telegram to City Point:

We are now up and have a continuous line of troops, and in a few hours will be intrenched from the Appomattox below Petersburg to the river above.... The whole captures since the army started out gunning will amount to not less than twelve thousand men, and probably fifty pieces of artillery.... I think the President might come out and pay us a visit tomorrow.[8]

To which Lincoln at once replied:

Allow me to tender you, and all with you, the nation's grateful thanks for the additional and magnificent success. At your kind suggestion, I think I will meet you tomorrow.

8. *Grant*, II, 452.

That night *Jefferson Davis* and *Lee*, seeing that their position was no longer tenable, decided to abandon Petersburg and Richmond. Before dawn on 3 April Petersburg surrendered, and the Confederate army streamed westward up the Appomattox Valley. Sheridan had already started off on a parallel route with the Cavalry, v, vi and ii Corps; on 4 April he was across the Danville Railroad, thus depriving *Lee* of his last chance of joining forces with *Johnston*'s army.

Grant had now won his war. All that remained to be done was to gather in the fruits of victory. On 5 April *Lee* managed to collect the shattered corps of *Longstreet*, *Ewell*, *Anderson* and *Gordon* at Amelia Court House, on the Danville Railroad 34 miles west of Petersburg, where he had ordered rations for the army to be collected. Unfortunately these never turned up, for on the previous day Sheridan had cut that escape route and was astride the Danville Railroad at Jetersville, ten miles to the south-west. *Lee*'s only hope now was to continue his westward march to Farmville on the upper Appomattox, where supplies awaited him, and then to push on through Lynchburg on the upper James, and unite with *Johnston* in North Carolina. But this too was a vain hope, for *Johnston* was 170 miles away, with Sherman on his heels. On that day Grant telegraphed to Sherman:

> All indications now are that *Lee* will attempt to reach Danville with the remnant of his force.... If you can possibly do so, push on.... Rebel armies now are the only strategic points to strike at.[9]

On the following day he ordered him to 'Push *Johnston* at the same time, and let us finish this job all at once.' Grant was in complete control of the strategic situation; he had seen too many Union tactical victories spoilt by the failure to carry out a vigorous pursuit, and he was now driving Sherman and Sheridan to the limit of their powers.

Grant's own forces were now marching westward in two parallel columns, some five to ten miles apart, parallel to and south of the line of *Lee*'s retreating army. The northern column, headed by Sheridan's cavalry and comprising vi, v and ii Corps, was nominally commanded by Meade, but Meade was sick and was travelling in an ambulance wagon, and Sheridan actually took charge. Grant and his staff rode with the southern column, commanded by Ord and consisting of xxiv and ix Corps, which followed the line of the South-side Railroad. Grant's order to Sheridan on 3 April had been: 'The first object of present movement will be to intercept *Lee*'s army.' Sheridan felt that the best way to execute this task was to push on and capture High Bridge on the Appomattox, east of Farmville, but Meade wished him to turn aside and attack *Lee*'s column. Sheridan sent a message to Grant explaining the trouble, adding: 'I wish you were here yourself.' Grant received this message when

9. *Grant*, ii, 624.

ten miles east of Burkesville on the evening of 5 April. Telling Ord to continue the advance to Burkesville and Farmville, Grant at once rode northward across country, reaching Sheridan's bivouac at 10 p.m. after a ride of 16 miles. Meade's orders were modified on Grant's instructions and the westward pursuit was continued.

On 6 April Grant put Wright's vi Corps directly under Sheridan's orders to back the cavalry in the pursuit. Together they caught up with *Ewell*'s corps, which formed *Lee*'s rearguard, and outflanked it while crossing Sailor's Creek, a tributary of the Appomattox. A stiff combat took place, the bulk of *Ewell*'s and *Anderson*'s corps being cut off, and 8,000 prisoners were captured, including *Ewell* himself. On 7 April ii Corps succeeded in capturing and crossing High Bridge over the Appomattox before *Lee*'s rearguard could destroy it, and another action was fought. His army was in a desperate condition. The troops had left Petersburg with only one day's ration in their haversacks, and since then they had been living on the country. Grant felt that *Lee* must now be convinced of the futility of continuing the struggle. At 5 p.m. on the 7th he wrote to him from Farmville:

> The results of the last week must convince you of the hopelessness of further resistance on the part of the Army of Northern Virginia in this struggle. I feel that it is so, and regard it as my duty to shift from myself the responsibility of any further effusion of blood, by asking of you the surrender of that portion of the Confederate States army known as the Army of Northern Virginia.[10]

Lee replied the same evening, asking what terms Grant would offer. The answer sent on the following day was as follows:

> In reply I would say that, *peace* being my greatest desire, there is but one condition I would insist on, namely: that the men and officers surrendered shall be disqualified for taking up arms again against the Government of the United States until properly exchanged. I will meet you, or will designate officers to meet any officers you may name for the same purpose, at any point agreeable to you, for the purpose of arranging definitely the terms upon which the surrender of the Army of Northern Virginia will be received.[11]

It was the same formula which he had laid down at Vicksburg, and more kindly in tone than the brusque 'unconditional surrender' demanded at Fort Donelson.

All that afternoon and night Grant suffered from a splitting headache, the cumulative effect of the mental and physical strain and lack of sleep during the last ten days. But this passed off on the following morning, Sunday, 9 April, when he rode over to the village surrounding Appomattox Court House to meet his veteran opponent. It was just three years since the Sunday of Shiloh.

Their historic meeting was dignified, but the two great protagonists of the

10. *Grant*, ii, 625–6.
11. *ibid.*

epic struggle presented a curious contrast as they cordially shook hands. They had met briefly only once before, during the Mexican War, when *Lee* was a Colonel and Chief of Staff to Winfield Scott, and Grant was a subaltern in the 4th Infantry. On the present occasion Grant was somewhat casually attired in an unbuttoned, mud-splashed, dark-blue tunic, wearing riding-boots, but without belt, sword or spurs. The Confederate Commander-in-Chief, older than Grant by 16 years and taller by five inches, looked the beau ideal of an aristocratic officer. He was immaculately dressed in his parade double-breasted frock-coat, with sword-sash and a handsome sword with jewel-studded hilt, presented to him by a group of sympathetic English ladies. *Lee* was accompanied by his Military Secretary, Colonel *Charles Marshall*. Grant had with him four of his personal staff, together with Sheridan and two of his cavalry commanders. One of Grant's attendants was his Military Secretary, Colonel Ely S. Parker, the full-blooded Indian; *Lee* looked at him with some astonishment, thinking that Grant had a negro on his staff.

At *Lee*'s request, Grant wrote out on a triplicate message form his final conditions for the surrender. They were generous; besides the paroling of all officers and men not to take up arms again, they required:

> The arms, artillery and public property to be parked and stacked, and turned over to the officers appointed by me to receive them. This will not embrace the side-arms of the officers, nor their private horses or baggage. This done, each officer and man will be allowed to return to his home, not to be disturbed by the United States authority so long as they observe their paroles and the laws in force where they may reside.[12]

When *Lee* read these terms he was greatly touched by Grant's generous permission for his officers to retain their swords, and remarked: 'This will have a very happy effect on my army.'

On Grant asking him if he had any suggestions to make, *Lee* observed that in the Confederate army the cavalry troopers and gunners rode their own horses; could they be allowed to retain them? Grant had not been aware of that but, having a fellow feeling for horsemen, he conceded the request, saying that, without altering the written terms, he would instruct the officers receiving the paroles to let any man who claimed to own a horse or mule to take it home to work his farm. Grant was a generous victor.

The Union Commander-in-Chief then signed the articles of surrender, which *Lee* formally accepted in a written letter. The total number of Confederate officers and men who surrendered at Appomattox was 28,356, all that remained of *Lee*'s army of 54,000 at the opening of the campaign.

Joseph Johnston signed an armistice with Sherman at Greensboro (N.C.) on 18 April, and his army surrendered a week later.

12. *Grant*, II, 628.

XXVI

Summing up

The record of Ulysses Grant's career affords ample testimony to his stature as a Great Captain. He certainly stood head and shoulders above any of his contemporaries and compatriots, including such able commanders as *Robert E. Lee*, William T. Sherman and *Stonewall Jackson*. Grant may not have been gifted with any intuitive genius for warfare; there were no lightning strokes, no brilliant flashes, few daring gambles. His success as a commander rested on more solid qualities: fixity of purpose, balanced judgment, imperturbable courage and, above all, sturdy common sense. As Wellington once said, 'When one is strongly intent on an object, common sense will usually direct one to the right means.'

Grant's military achievements were largely the product of his innate human qualities, his *persona*, influenced by his experience of life and environmental conditions. There is abundant evidence from which to draw a character sketch, his biographers having left no stone unturned in recording anecdotes of his career. One is at once struck by the stark simplicity, even naïvety, of his nature, a trait apparent in his early life which persisted to the end; indeed disastrously so, for his child-like trust in the integrity of others brought about financial ruin in his declining years. One might hardly consider this simplicity of outlook to be an asset to a leader in a ruthless war and in a competitive environment, but in fact it did inspire affection and loyalty, and gave rise to the intense mutual trust and esteem which linked him with Sherman, and the confidence which he inspired in Lincoln, a shrewd judge of character.

Intrigue was completely foreign to Grant's nature, though he had to climb the ladder through a crowd of competitors tainted with envy and malice. His humility of character may have put him at an initial disadvantage when dealing with intriguers like McClernand, Rosecrans and William Farrar Smith, or even with the sneering Halleck or the jealous Buell, but it triumphed in the long run. One aspect of it was his dislike of anything in the way of bombast or pompous display; on the first occasion when he visited Meade's headquarters, he noticed a large purple flag with a gold and silver eagle floating over the army commander's tent; 'What's this? Is Imperial Caesar anywhere about?' he remarked to one of his staff. He certainly paid little attention to his own appearance; when he met *Lee* at Appomattox to discuss the final terms of surrender, he apologized to his vanquished opponent for having left his sword miles behind with his personal baggage.

In his dealings with his favourite subordinates, Sherman and Sheridan, Grant perhaps carried trustfulness too far. He had such complete confidence in Sherman, for instance, that he never attempted to dictate an operation order to him, only giving him a general outline of his intention. Sherman, though a good enough soldier, was guilty of many failures, both strategic and tactical. After the battle of Atlanta he spent so much time in tearing up railway tracks, which were quickly repaired, that he neglected to envelop and destroy *Hood*'s army, which was the principal objective given him by Grant. His confidence in Sheridan's ability as an independent commander was even more misplaced; Sheridan certainly won three important tactical victories in the Shenandoah Valley over *Early*'s much weaker army, but he completely failed to carry out the main task assigned to him, namely the cutting of *Lee*'s remaining railway arteries, which could have shortened the war by six months. Grant's refraining from a closer control of Sheridan's Shenandoah campaign sprang from an exaggerated feeling of delicacy, which he himself described as follows:

> I also decided not to remain with him [Sheridan] during the movement ... for fear it might be thought that I was trying to share in a success which I wished to belong solely to him.

This was carrying deference to a subordinate too far. It may have been the same spirit of self-effacement which caused him to hand over to Meade the sole leadership in the main assault at Petersburg on 16 June, 1864; if so, it was equally misplaced. On all other occasions Grant exercised tight control of Meade's army during vital operations, an unorthodox method, but justified by Meade's limitations as an independent commander.

On the whole, Grant was poorly served by his subordinate Generals, just as in the Leipzig and Waterloo campaigns Napoleon was let down by the ineptitude of his Marshals. But Napoleon had himself selected and trained his Marshals, so the blame was his own, whereas Grant's lieutenants, with the exception of Sherman, Sheridan and William Farrar Smith, were thrust upon him for political reasons or by force of circumstances. Grant's initial strategic plan for operations in the Shenandoah Valley was completely frustrated by the incapacity, first of Sigel and then of Hunter, both forced on him for political reasons. Butler, another political appointment, could have walked into Petersburg in May 1864, when it was practically undefended, but the opportunity was missed, involving an enormous sacrifice of life during the next twelve months.

The June operation against Petersburg was bungled, first by Smith and then by Meade. Smith's promotion to command troops was one of the few bad mistakes that Grant made; he was a capable engineer officer, and had been largely responsible for organizing the 'cracker line' which solved the Union army's supply problem at Chattanooga. Grant was so impressed with his efficiency that he got him promoted, first to command a division and then a corps, but Smith's failure in leadership at Petersburg was so palpable that Grant had to remove him from command of his corps.

The case of Meade was slightly different, as he was not one of Grant's selections. Meade, like Smith, was a competent engineer officer and a specialist in topographical survey, but prior to the war had no experience of handling troops. During the first six months of the war, indeed, he was employed on a hydrological survey of Lake Superior. A few days before the battle of Gettysburg he had, somewhat fortuitously, been appointed to command the Army of the Potomac, and had that victory to his credit, though he had made little contribution to it. On assuming supreme command, Grant had had no opportunity of judging Meade's fitness for command; he soon realized, however, that he must control Meade's operations very closely.

The only subordinate who seems to have been unfairly treated by Grant was George Henry Thomas, the stolid Virginian whose steadfastness at Chickamauga had saved the Union army from disaster. In November 1864, when *Hood* invaded Tennessee and Thomas retreated to Nashville, and then delayed his counter-attack for understandable reasons, Grant was so infuriated that he ordered Thomas's immediate dismissal, which was only averted by Halleck's intervention. Grant appears to have conceived a prejudice against 'slow-trot Thomas', whose sterling qualities he failed to appreciate.

Perhaps Grant's greatest qualities as a commander were his wide strategic vision and his fixity of purpose. Few of the other leaders of the Civil War could see beyond the range of their immediate battle-front. Grant's perspective embraced the whole scope of the twin theatres of war, and he was never deflected by purely geographical objectives from his main purpose of destroying the Confederate armies. He had the sense to exploit fully the facilities, first of river transport to further his operations in the western theatre, and later of the Virginian estuaries to keep advancing his supply base to the latitude of Richmond. His original strategic plan for the encirclement of the Southern armies was masterly, although delayed and partially frustrated by the mistakes of his subordinates, and also by the skill of his major opponent in conducting defensive operations on interior lines. Grant's three major strategic achievements were the Vicksburg campaign, the outflanking of *Lee* by crossing the James, and the final tenacious pursuit to Appomattox. None of these could have succeeded without his inflexible determination. As Sherman said of him, 'He has all the tenacity of a Scottish terrier.'

Grant has been charged with a callous disregard for human life in pursuing his objectives, with particular reference to the battle of Cold Harbor. This is hardly a fair criticism, for he was by nature an essentially humane man, and few were more averse from bloodshed than he was. At Spottsylvania and Cold Harbor he undoubtedly incurred disproportionate casualties, but he was then under considerable political pressure to end the war quickly before the autumn Presidential election. He felt that by launching all-out attacks on *Lee*'s army before it could retire within the fixed defences of Richmond he could terminate the struggle within weeks and save an enormous effusion of blood and treasure. That was a gamble that failed. But a gamble that succeeded was the launching of his army across the Mississippi in the Vicksburg campaign, when he cut loose from his base and ordered his troops to live on the country.

In his earlier battles, for example at Belmont and Shiloh, Grant was guilty of serious tactical faults, such as neglect of reconnaissance and security measures, and also failure to exploit success. But he profited by experience and these errors were not repeated in his later operations. Perhaps the most valid criticism of Grant's generalship has been made by General Fuller:

> What he did not understand, and what no general of his day understood, and few since have understood, was that the art of war had been revolutionized by the rifle, and to apply old tactics to new weapons, was tantamount to applying a whip to a locomotive.[1]

Harsh words have been written and spoken about Grant's alleged addiction to strong liquor. The evidence points to his having given way to this weakness at an earlier period of his life, but none exists to show that it affected his efficiency in the Civil War, with the one exception of the incident recorded on pages 119–120, footnote. The legend of his intemperance was fostered by military rivals and political opponents; it has been perpetuated in a humorous but cruel skit by James Thurber, entitled 'If Grant had been drinking at Appomattox.'[2] A greater American humorist than Thurber, Mark Twain, has left us a kinder and truer picture of Ulysses Grant as a man and has paid tribute to:

> His patience; his indestructible equability of temper; his exceeding gentleness, kindness, forbearance, lovingness, charity; his *loyalty* to friends, to convictions, to promises . . . his aggravatingly trustful nature; his genuineness, simplicity, modesty, diffidence, self-depreciation . . . he *was* the most lovable great child in the world.[3]

1. *The Generalship of Ulysses S. Grant*, 359.
2. Originally published in *Scribner's Magazine*; reprinted in *The Thurber Carnival* by Harper & Brothers, New York, 1931.
3. *Mark Twain's Letters* (2 vols., Harper & Brothers, N.Y., 1917), II, 460.

APPENDIX I

The flags they fought under

UNION

The Union forces fought, naturally, under the traditional 'Stars and Stripes' of the United States. When the Civil War broke out, 34 States had been admitted to the Union, the last being Kansas on 29 January 1861. The Union flag consisted of a field of 13 horizontal stripes, alternately red and white,

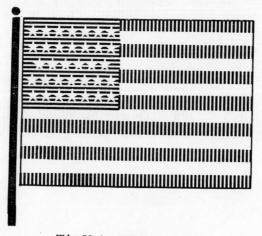

The Union Flag (34 stars)

representing the 13 original States which declared their independence in 1776, with a blue canton charged with 34 stars[1] for the existing States of the Union. On the outbreak of war, no stars were removed for the seceding States, as Lincoln's whole policy was based on maintaining the integrity of the Union.

1. All the 'stars' mentioned were five-pointed; they are more accurately described in heraldic terminology as 'mullets'.

On 4 July 1863 an extra star was added to the existing 34 in order to include the new State of West Virginia, which had broken away from secessionist Virginia in August 1862 and had been officially admitted into the Union on 20 June 1863. Most of the Union troops, however, continued to fight under the 34-star flag until the end of the war.

CONFEDERACY

At Montgomery (Ala) on 4 March 1861 the Convention of the seven Southern States which had then seceded from the Union adopted the 'Stars and Bars' as the national flag of the Confederacy. It had been designed in the previous month by Professor Nicola Marschall. The field of this flag consisted of three equal horizontal bars, red, white and red, with a blue canton charged with a circle of seven white stars, representing the seven original seceding States: South Carolina, Mississippi, Florida, Alabama, Georgia, Louisiana and Texas.

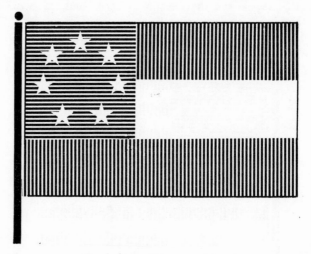

Confederate 'Stars and Bars'

After the first battle of Bull Run or Manassas (21 July 1861), the Confederate troops found their 'Stars and Bars' to be too similar to the 'Stars and Stripes' of the Union, especially on a windless day. A committee, presided over by General *Pierre Gustave Beauregard*, then adopted an entirely new national flag, popularly known as the 'Southern Cross'. This had a red field charged with blue saltire, or St. Andrew's cross, edged with white. The blue diagonal cross was charged with 13 white stars, 11 representing the Secession States, including Virginia, Arkansas, North Carolina and Tennessee, with two additional stars for Kentucky and Missouri, in the hope that those two borderland States would be won over to the Confederacy. The 'Southern Cross' remained the battle flag of the South throughout the war, in spite of two later attempts by the Congress at Richmond in 1863 and 1865 to alter it.

Confederate battle flags captured by the Union troops during the war were returned to the South in 1905, during the Presidency of Theodore Roosevelt.

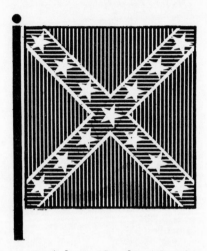

Confederate 'Southern Cross'

APPENDIX II

Casualties incurred under Grant's command

			Union	Confed.
7 Nov.	1861	Belmont	485	641
6 Feb.	,,	Fort Henry	0	90
16 Feb.	,,	Fort Donelson	2,886	16,623 (a)
6–7 April	1862	Shiloh	13,047	10,694
19 Sep.	,,	Iuka	790	700
3–4 Oct.	,,	Corinth	3,090	4,838
29 Dec.	,,	Chickasaw Bluffs	1,776	207
11 Jan.	1863	Arkansas Post	1,061	4,931 (b)
May–July	,,	Vicksburg campaign	9,362	39,490 (c)
23–25 Nov.	,,	Chattanooga	5,815	8,683 (d)
4–7 May	1864	The Wilderness	17,666	11,400
9–20 May	,,	Spottsylvania	18,399	10,000
12–16 May	,,	Drewry's Bluff	6,245	3,499
23–26 May	,,	North Anna and Totopotomoy	3,986	2,000 (?)
3 June	,,	Cold Harbor	12,737	1,500 (?)
15–18 June	,,	Petersburg	9,964	3,000 (?)
22 June	,,	Weldon Railroad	2,962	1,000 (?)
9 July	,,	The Monocacy	1,880	700
30 July	,,	Petersburg crater	4,400	3,000 (?)
18–24 Aug.	,,	Weldon Railroad	7,020	3,720 (?)
Aug.–Oct.	,,	Sheridan in Shenandoah	16,952	10,000 (?)
May–Dec.	,,	Sherman in Georgia	31,687	34,979
30 Nov.	,,	Franklin (Tenn)	2,326	6,252
15–16 Dec.	,,	Nashville (Tenn)	3,061	6,462 (e)
13–15 Jan.	1865	Fort Fisher (N.C.)	1,059	2,783
19 March	,,	Bentonville (N.C.)	1,646	2,606
March–Apr.	,,	Petersburg to Appomattox	10,515	54,000 (f)
			190,817	243,798

(a) including 14,623 prisoners of war.
(b)   ,,   4,791   ,,   ,,   ,,
(c)   ,,   31,600   ,,   ,,   ,,   who surrendered at Vicksburg.
(d)   ,,   6,142   ,,   ,,   ,,
(e)   ,,   4,462   ,,   ,,   ,,
(f)   ,,   28,356   ,,   ,,   ,,   who surrendered at Appomattox.

Note: Authorities differ considerably in their estimates of casualties in the Civil War. For the later stages of the war the Confederate records are particularly scanty and incomplete; during the final retreat from Petersburg to Appomattox in April 1865 the regimental returns were all destroyed.

Chronological Table

1807	19 January	*Robert Edward Lee* born (Virginia)
1808	3 June	*Jefferson Davis* born (Kentucky)
1809	12 February	Abraham Lincoln born (Kentucky)
1822	27 April	Hiram Ulysses Grant born (Ohio)
1829	July	*Robert E. Lee* commissioned in U.S. Corps of Engineers
1839	14 June	Ulysses Simpson Grant entered West Point as cadet
1843	July	Grant from West Point commissioned in 4th Infantry
1846	March	U.S. declares war on Mexico
1847	13 September	Grant promoted Brevet Captain for gallantry at Chapultepec
1848	2 February	Peace Treaty of Guadalupe Hidalgo ends war with Mexico
	22 August	Grant's marriage to Julia Dent of St. Louis (Mo)
1852	March	Grant's regiment ordered to California
1854	31 July	Captain U. S. Grant resigns his army commission
1859	16 October	John Brown's raid on Harper's Ferry arsenal (W.Va)
	2 December	Execution of John Brown
1860	6 November	Abraham Lincoln elected President, U.S.A.
	20 December	South Carolina secedes from the Union
1861	9 January	Mississippi secedes from the Union
	10 January	Florida secedes from the Union
	11 January	Alabama secedes from the Union
	18 January	Georgia secedes from the Union
	26 January	Louisiana secedes from the Union
	1 February	Texas secedes from the Union
	4 February	Confederacy formed by seven seceding States
	18 February	*Jefferson Davis* inaugurated President of Confederacy
	4 March	Lincoln inaugurated as 16th President, U.S.A.
	12 April	Confederates open fire on Fort Sumter (S.C.) Civil War begins

1861	14 April	Fort Sumter surrenders to Confederates
	15 April	Lincoln calls up 75,000 Militiamen for three months
	17 April	Virginia secedes from the Union
	23 April	Grant rejoins U.S. Army as a Volunteer at Springfield (Ill)
	3 May	Lincoln calls for 42,000 Volunteers
	6 May	Arkansas secedes from the Union
	8 May	Confederate capital transferred from Montgomery (Ala) to Richmond (Va)
	20 May	North Carolina secedes from the Union
		Kentucky declares itself neutral
	17 June	Grant promoted Colonel commanding 21st Illinois Regiment
	24 June	Tennessee secedes from the Union
	2 July	Frémont appointed to command Department of Missouri
	21 July	First battle of Bull Run or Manassas; *Beauregard* and *Johnston* defeat Union Army under McDowell
	22 July	Union Congress calls for 500,000 Volunteers
	29 July	Grant given command of S.E. District of Missouri
	7 August	Grant promoted Brigadier-General (antedated to 17 May)
	3 September	*Polk* invades Kentucky and occupies Columbus
	4 September	Grant appointed District Commander at Cairo (Ill)
	6 September	Grant occupies Paducah (Ky)
	12 September	Kentucky, previously neutral, joins the Union
	1 November	McClellan replaces Scott as Union Commander-in-Chief
	2 November	Hunter takes over Department of Missouri from Frémont
	7 November	Grant captures Belmont (Mo) but withdraws
	19 November	Halleck takes over Department of Missouri from Hunter
1862	19 January	Thomas defeats *Zollicoffer* at Mill Springs (Ky)
	6 February	Grant captures Fort Henry (Tenn)
	16 February	Grant captures Fort Donelson (Tenn)
		Grant promoted Major-General of Volunteers
	9 March	Naval engagement in Hampton Roads between 'Monitor' and '*Merrimac*' (indecisive)
	11 March	Lincoln takes over war direction from McClellan
	23 March	Battle of Kernstown: *Jackson* attacks Shields
	6–7 April	Battle of Shiloh: Grant and Buell defeat *Johnston* and *Beauregard*
		Pope captures Confederate stronghold at Island No. 10 (Miss)
	11 April	Halleck appoints Grant as his Second-in-Command
	29 April	Farragut captures New Orleans (La)
	8 May	*Jackson* defeats Milroy and Schenck at McDowell
	23 May	*Jackson* defeats Banks at Front Royal

1862

30 May	Halleck occupies Corinth (Miss)
31 May	Battle of Fair Oaks or Seven Pines (indecisive)
1 June	*Lee* appointed to command the Army of Northern Virginia
5 June	Confederates evacuate Fort Pillow (Tenn)
6 June	Union gunboats capture Memphis (Tenn)
8 June	*Jackson* defeats Frémont at Cross Keys
9 June	*Jackson* defeats Shields at Port Republic
26 June	Battle of Mechanicsville: Porter repulses *A. P. Hill*
	Pope appointed to command Army of Virginia
27 June	Battle of Gaines's Mill: *Lee* defeats Porter
	Bragg succeeds *Beauregard* in command of western theatre
	Farragut attacks Vicksburg (Miss)
30 June	Battle of Frayser's Farm (indecisive)
1 July	Battle of Malvern Hill: McClellan repulses *Lee*
11 July	Lincoln appoints Halleck Commander-in-Chief Union Army
	Grant appointed to command Armies of the Tennessee and the Mississippi
9 August	*Jackson* defeats Banks at Cedar Mountain
20 August	West Virginia secedes from Virginia
29–30 August	Second Battle of Bull Run or Manassas: *Lee* defeats Pope
4–7 September	*Lee* crosses the Potomac and invades Maryland
14 September	Burnside defeats *Longstreet* at South Mountain (Md)
15 September	*Jackson* captures Harper's Ferry
16–17 September	Battle of Antietam or Sharpsburg (Md): *Lee* repulses McClellan but withdraws to Virginia
19 September	*Price* repulses Rosecrans at Iuka (Miss)
3–4 October	Grant defeats *Van Dorn* at Corinth (Miss)
8 October	*Bragg* retreats after drawn battle at Perryville (Ky)
16 October	Grant appointed to command the Department of the Tennessee
7 November	Burnside replaces McClellan in command of the Army of the Potomac
24 November	*J. E. Johnston* appointed Commander-in-Chief in western theatre
13 December	Battle of Fredericksburg: *Lee* repulses Burnside
20 December	*Van Dorn* destroys Grant's advanced base at Holly Springs (Miss)
29 December	*Pemberton* repulses Sherman at Chickasaw Bluffs, north of Vicksburg (Miss)
31 December	*Bragg* defeats Rosecrans at Murfreesboro or Stones River (Tenn), but retreats

1863

1 January	Lincoln emancipates all slaves in the Southern States
11 January	McClernand captures Arkansas Post (Ark)
25 January	Hooker replaces Burnside in command of Army of the Potomac

1863	30 January	Grant assumes command of operations against Vicksburg (Miss)
	30 April	Grant crosses the Mississippi below Vicksburg
		Hooker crosses the Rapidan
	1 May	Grant occupies Port Gibson (Miss)
	2–4 May	Battle of Chancellorsville: *Lee* defeats Hooker: *Stonewall Jackson* mortally wounded
	6 May	Hooker retires behind the Rappahannock
	14 May	Grant defeats *J. E. Johnston* at Jackson (Miss)
	16 May	Grant defeats *Pemberton* at Champion's Hill (east of Vicksburg)
	18 May	*Pemberton* retreats to Vicksburg
	19 & 22 May	Grant's unsuccessful attacks on Vicksburg
	17 June	*Lee* invades Maryland and Pennsylvania
	20 June	West Virginia admitted to the Union as a separate State
	28 June	Meade replaces Hooker in command of Army of the Potomac
	1–4 July	Battle of Gettysburg (Pa); Meade repulses *Lee*
	4 July	*Pemberton* surrenders Vicksburg to Grant
		Grant promoted Major-General in Regular Army
		Bragg retires before Rosecrans to Chattanooga (Tenn)
	9 July	Banks occupies Port Hudson (La)
	14 July	*Lee* retires to Virginia and behind the Rappahannock
	4 September	Rosecrans drives *Bragg* from Chattanooga (Tenn)
	18–20 September	*Bragg* defeats Rosecrans at Chickamauga Creek (Ga)
	16 October	Grant appointed Commander-in-Chief in western theatre
	24–25 November	Battle of Chattanooga (Tenn): Grant defeats *Bragg*
	28 Nov.–1 Dec.	Meade fails to turn *Lee*'s flank at Mine Run Creek
1864	3 March	Grant summoned by Lincoln to Washington to command all Union land forces
	9 March	Grant promoted Lieutenant-General, U.S. Army
		Halleck appointed Chief of Staff at Washington
	26 March	Grant establishes his headquarters at Culpeper Court House
	8 April	Banks defeated by Confederates in Louisiana
	4 May	Grant crosses the Rapidan to outflank *Lee*
	4–6 May	Indecisive Wilderness battle between Grant and *Lee*
	5 May	Butler's Army of the James lands at City Point
	7 May	Sherman starts to invade Georgia
	9–19 May	*Lee* repulses Grant at Spottsylvania
	9–24 May	Sheridan's Richmond raid
	15 May	*Breckinridge* defeats Sigel at New Market
	16 May	*Beauregard* repulses Butler at Drewry's Bluff
	23–26 May	*Lee* repulses Grant on the North Anna
	1–3 June	*Lee* repulses Grant at Cold Harbor
	14–16 June	Grant's army crosses the James River

1864
15–18 June	*Beauregard* repulses Meade at Petersburg
19–20 June	*Early* defeats Hunter at Lynchburg
21 June	Lincoln visits Grant's headquarters at City Point
27 June	*Johnston* repulses Sherman at Kenesaw Mountain (Ga)
	Early starts on his raid into Maryland
9 July	*Early* defeats Lew Wallace on the Monocacy (Md)
11 July	*Early* attacks Washington defences and withdraws
17 July	*Johnston* replaced by Hood
20 July	*Hood* attacks Sherman unsuccessfully at Peach Tree Creek (Ga)
22 July	Sherman defeats *Hood* at Atlanta (Ga)
30 July	Failure of the Petersburg mine crater attack
5 August	Battle of Mobile Bay (Ala): Farragut defeats Confederate naval squadron
18–21 August	Action on the Weldon–Petersburg Railroad
2 September	Sherman captures Atlanta (Ga)
19 September	Sheridan defeats *Early* at Opequon Creek (Winchester)
22 September	Sheridan defeats *Early* at Fisher's Hill (Strasburg)
29 September	Grant captures Fort Harrison on the James
19 October	Sheridan defeats *Early* at Cedar Creek (Strasburg)
8 November	Lincoln re-elected President, U.S.A.
15 November	Sherman begins his march through Georgia from Atlanta
30 November	Thomas repulses *Hood* at Franklin (Tenn)
15–16 December	Thomas defeats *Hood* at Nashville (Tenn)
21 December	Sherman enters Savannah (Ga)
25–27 December	Butler's failure to capture Fort Fisher, Wilmington (N.C.)

1865
15 January	Union troops capture Fort Fisher, Wilmington (N.C.)
1 February	Sherman begins his march through the Carolinas
9 February	*Lee* appointed Commander-in-Chief of all Confederate armies
17 February	Sherman reaches Columbia (S.C.)
18 February	Union troops occupy Charleston (S.C.)
22 February	Union troops occupy Wilmington (N.C.)
4 March	Lincoln inaugurated as U.S. President for second term
19 March	Sherman defeats *Johnston* at Bentonville (N.C.)
25 March	Repulse of Confederate attack on Fort Stedman (Petersburg)
29 March	Grant opens his final offensive at Petersburg
1 April	Sheridan defeats *Pickett* at Five Forks
2 April	*Lee* abandons Petersburg and Richmond
6 April	Confederate rearguard defeated at Sailor's Creek
9 April	*Lee* surrenders to Grant at Appomattox Court House
11 April	Union troops occupy Mobile (Ala)
14 April	Assassination of Lincoln; succeeded by Andrew Johnson

1865	18 April	*Johnston* signs armistice with Sherman at Greensboro (N.C.)
	26 April	*Johnston*'s army surrenders to Sherman
	10 May	President *Jefferson Davis* captured at Irwinsville (Ga)
1866	July	Grant promoted General (retired list)
1867	August	Grant appointed Secretary of War
1868	4 November	Grant elected U.S. President
1869	4 March	Grant inaugurated as 18th President
1870	12 October	Death of *Lee*
1873	4 November	Grant re-elected U.S. President
1885	23 July	Death of Grant
1889	6 December	Death of *Jefferson Davis*

Authorities Consulted

Adams, J. T., *Atlas of American History* (Charles Scribner's Sons, N.Y., 1943)

Battles and Leaders of the Civil War, 4 vols. (Century Press, N.Y., 1884-88)
Boatner, Lieut.-Col. Mark M., *The Civil War Dictionary* (David McKay Co. Inc., N.Y., 1959)
Burne, Lieut.-Col. Alfred H., *Lee, Grant and Sherman* (Gale & Polden, 1938)

Conger, A. L., *The Rise of U. S. Grant* (The Century Co., N.Y.); *Donelson Campaign Sources* (Fort Leavenworth, Kansas, 1912)

Esposito, Col. Vincent J., *The West Point Atlas of American Wars*, Vol. 1 (Frederick A. Praeger, N.Y., 1959)

Fiske, John, *The Mississippi Valley in the Civil War* (Houghton, Mifflin & Co., Boston, 1901)
Foster, J. W., *The Mississippi Valley: Its Physical Geography* (Griggs, Chicago, 1869)
Fuller, Col. J. F. C., *The Generalship of Ulysses S. Grant* (John Murray, 1929); *Grant & Lee* (Eyre & Spottiswoode, 1933)

Grant, U. S., *Personal Memoirs*, 2 vols. (Sampson, Low, Marston, 1885-86)

King, Gen. Charles, *The True Ulysses S. Grant* (J. B. Lippincott, Philadelphia, 1914)

Meredith, Roy, *Mr. Lincoln's General* (E. P. Dutton & Co., N.Y., 1959)

Porter, Gen. H., *Campaigning with Grant* (The Century Co., N.Y., 1897)

Ropes, J. C., *The Story of the Civil War*, 4 vols. (G. P. Putnam's Sons, N.Y., 1894-98, completed by Col. William Roscoe Livermore)

Sheppard, Major E. W., *The American Civil War, 1864–65* (Gale & Polden, 1938)

Sherman, Gen. William T., *Memoirs*, 2 vols. (C. L. Webster & Co., N.Y.)

Trollope, Anthony, *North America*, 2 vols. (Chapman & Hall, 1862)

Warner, Ezra J., *Generals in Blue* (Louisiana State Univ. Press, 1964); *Generals in Gray* (Louisiana State Univ. Press, 1959)

Weigley, Russell F., *History of the United States Army* (Batsford, 1968)

Williams, T. Harry, *Lincoln and his Generals* (Alfred A. Knopf, N.Y., 1952)

Wood, W. B. and Edmonds, J. E., *The Civil War in the United States* (Methuen, 1937)

Woodward, W. E., *Meet General Grant* (Horace Liveright, N.Y., 1928)

Index

The numerals in **heavy type** refer to the figure numbers of the illustrations

Map 17

WEST VIRGINIA

Missouri R.

ST. LOUIS

ILLINOIS

INDIANA

Ohio R.

Ohio R.

Frankfort

Louisville

Lexington

URI

KENTUCKY

Cape
Girardeau

Cairo

Bowling
Green

MOUNTAINS

Cumberland R.

Blue Ridge

MOUNTAINS

Paducah
Columbus

Belmont

Cumberland
Gap

Danville

New Madrid

Clarksville

ALLEGHENY

Greensboro

SAS

R.

Fort Donelson

NASHVILLE

Humboldt

Franklin

Knoxville

VIRGINIA

NORTH CAROLINA

Fort
Pillow

Jackson

Columbia

Murfreesboro

CUMBERLAND

AS

TENNESSEE

Charlotte

MEMPHIS

Shiloh

CHATTANOOGA

Greenville

Corinth

Florence

Stevenson

SOUTH

Decatur

Dalton

Tupelo

Rome

CAROLINA

Columbia

Grenada

Marietta
ATLANTA

Mississippi R.

Birmingham

Augusta

MISSISSIPPI

Tuscaloosa

GEORGIA

Macon

ALABAMA

CHARLESTON

VICKSBURG

Meridian

Columbus

Jackson

MONTGOMERY

Port
Gibson

SAVANNAH

Natchez

ATLANTIC

OCEAN

Port Hudson

IANA

MOBILE

Baton
Rouge

Pensacola

FLORIDA

NEW ORLEANS

Jacksonville

GULF OF MEXICO

WESTERN THEATRE OF WAR

0   50   100   150   200

Miles